(ex•ploring)

1. Investigating in a systematic way: examining. 2. Searching
into or ranging over for the purpose of discovery.

Getting Started with
VBA for Microsoft®
Office 2010

Robert T. Grauer

Keith Mulbery | Keith Mast | Mary Anne Poatsy

Prentice Hall
Upper Saddle River   London   Singapore
Toronto   Tokyo   Sydney   Hong Kong   Mexico City

Editor in Chief: Michael Payne
Acquisitions Editor: Samantha McAfee
Editorial Project Manager: Meghan Bisi
Editorial Assistant: Erin Clark
Director of Digital Development: Zara Wanlass
Executive Editor-Digital Learning & Assessment: Paul Gentile
Director-Media Development: Cathi Profitko
Senior Media Project Manager-Editorial: Alana Coles
Production Media Project Manager: John Cassar
Director of Marketing: Kate Valentine
Marketing Manager: Tori Olson Alves
Marketing Coordinator: Susan Osterlitz
Marketing Assistant: Darshika Vyas
Senior Managing Editor: Cynthia Zonneveld
Associate Managing Editor: Camille Trentacoste
Senior Operations Specialist: Natacha Moore
Senior Art Director: Jonathan Boylan
Cover Design: Jonathan Boylan
Cover Illustration/Photo: Courtesy of Shutterstock® Images
Composition: PreMediaGlobal
Full-Service Project Management: PreMediaGlobal
Typeface: 10.5/12.5 Minion

Credits and acknowledgments borrowed from other sources and reproduced, with permission, in this textbook appear on appropriate page within text.

Microsoft® and Windows® are registered trademarks of the Microsoft Corporation in the U.S.A. and other countries. Screen shots and icons reprinted with permission from the Microsoft Corporation. This book is not sponsored or endorsed by or affiliated with the Microsoft Corporation.

Copyright © 2012 by Pearson Education, Inc., Upper Saddle River, New Jersey, 07458.
All rights reserved. Manufactured in the United States of America. This publication is protected by Copyright and permission should be obtained from the publisher prior to any prohibited reproduction, storage in a retrieval system, or transmission in any form or by any means, electronic, mechanical, photocopying, recording, or likewise. To obtain permission(s) to use material from this work, please submit a written request to Pearson Education, Inc., Permissions Department.

Pearson Prentice Hall™ is a trademark of Pearson Education, Inc.
Pearson® is a registered trademark of Pearson plc
Prentice Hall® is a registered trademark of Pearson Education, Inc.

Pearson Education Ltd., London
Pearson Education Singapore, Pte. Ltd.
Pearson Education, Canada, Ltd.
Pearson Education–Japan
Pearson Education Australia PTY, Limited

Pearson Education North Asia Ltd., Hong Kong
Pearson Educación de Mexico, S.A. de C.V.
Pearson Education Malaysia, Pte. Ltd.
Pearson Education, Upper Saddle River, New Jersey

Many of the designations by manufacturers and seller to distinguish their products are claimed as trademarks. Where those designations appear in this book, and the publisher was aware of a trademark claim, the designations have been printed in initial caps or all caps.

10

www.pearsonhighered.com

ISBN-13: 978-0-13-214013-3
ISBN-10: 0-13-214013-6

DEDICATIONS

I dedicate this book in loving memory to Grandma Ida Lu Etta (Billie) Hort, who was a positive role model for me through her patience, caring personality, and perseverance through challenging situations. I treasure her support and encouragement throughout my personal and professional endeavors, including years of textbook writing.

Keith Mulbery

I would like to dedicate this book to my parents, John and Millie, who have given me all the love and support that a son could ever ask for.

Keith Mast

For my husband Ted, who unselfishly continues to take on more than his fair share to support me throughout this process; and for my children, Laura, Carolyn, and Teddy, whose encouragement and love have been inspiring.

Mary Anne Poatsy

ABOUT THE AUTHORS

Dr. Keith Mulbery, Excel Author

Dr. Keith Mulbery is the Department Chair and a Professor in the Information Systems and Technology Department at Utah Valley University (UVU), where he teaches computer applications, C# programming, systems analysis and design, and MIS classes. Keith also served as Interim Associate Dean, School of Computing, in the College of Technology and Computing at UVU.

Keith received the Utah Valley State College Board of Trustees Award of Excellence in 2001, School of Technology and Computing Scholar Award in 2007, and School of Technology and Computing Teaching Award in 2008. He has authored more than 15 textbooks, served as Series Editor for the Exploring Office 2007 series, and served as developmental editor on two textbooks.

Keith received his B.S. and M.Ed. in Business Education from Southwestern Oklahoma State University and earned his Ph.D. in Education with an emphasis in Business Information Systems at Utah State University. His dissertation topic was computer-assisted instruction using Prentice Hall's Train and Assess IT program to supplement traditional instruction in basic computer proficiency courses.

Keith Mast, Access Author

Keith A. Mast develops a wide range of Access applications that solve challenging business problems and improve efficiency. His solutions help businesses and organizations in manufacturing, pharmaceutical, financial services, and agriculture, among other industries. Clients include Visible Filing Concepts, Inc.; Moyer's Chicks, Inc.; Marcho Farms, Inc.; LANsultants, Inc.; Spector, Roseman, Kodroff, & Willis, PC; Sunshine Therapy Club, Inc..; DuPont; and Sony Entertainment. He is an adjunct faculty member at Montgomery County Community College, Blue Bell, Pennsylvania, continuing his long standing love of teaching and exemplified by his prior experience as a high school teacher, business school instructor, and as an Access seminar leader. Keith promotes the ethical standards of the consulting profession both in how Mast Consulting, LLC deals with its clients and as an active volunteer leader of the Independent Computer Consultants Association of the Delaware Valley. Keith resides in Norristown, Pennsylvania, a suburb of Philadelphia. In his free time, he enjoys biking, running, kayaking, ballroom dancing, and being in nature. For more information, visit him on Facebook, LinkedIn, or at www.keithmast.com.

Mary Anne Poatsy, Series Editor

Mary Anne is a senior faculty member at Montgomery County Community College, teaching various computer application and concepts courses in face-to-face and online environments. She holds a B.A. in psychology and education from Mount Holyoke College and an M.B.A. in finance from Northwestern University's Kellogg Graduate School of Management.

Mary Anne has more than 11 years of educational experience, ranging from elementary and secondary education to Montgomery County Community College, Muhlenberg College, and Bucks County Community College, as well as training in the professional environment. Before teaching, she was vice president at Shearson Lehman Hutton in the Municipal Bond Investment Banking Department.

Dr. Robert T. Grauer, Creator of the Exploring Series

Bob Grauer is an Associate Professor in the Department of Computer Information Systems at the University of Miami, where he is a multiple winner of the Outstanding Teaching Award in the School of Business, most recently in 2009. He has written numerous COBOL texts and is the vision behind the Exploring Office series, with more than three million books in print. His work has been translated into three foreign languages and is used in all aspects of higher education at both national and international levels. Bob Grauer has consulted for several major corporations including IBM and American Express. He received his Ph.D. in operations research in 1972 from the Polytechnic Institute of Brooklyn.

CONTENTS

ACKNOWLEDGMENTS

The Exploring team would like to acknowledge and thank all the reviewers who helped us prepare for the Exploring Office 2010 revision by providing us with their invaluable comments, suggestions, and constructive criticism:

Allen Alexander
Delaware Technical & Community College

Andrea Marchese
Maritime College, State University of New York

Andrew Blitz
Broward College, Edison State College

Angela Clark
University of South Alabama

Astrid Todd
Guilford Technical Community College

Audrey Gillant
Maritime College, State University of New York

Barbara Stover
Marion Technical College

Barbara Tollinger
Sinclair Community College

Ben Brahim Taha
Auburn University

Beverly Amer
Northern Arizona University

Beverly Fite
Amarillo College

Bonnie Homan
San Francisco State University

Brad West
Sinclair Community College

Brian Powell
West Virginia University

Carol Buser
Owens Community College

Carol Roberts
University of Maine

Cathy Poyner
Truman State University

Charles Hodgson
Delgado Community College

Cheryl Hinds
Norfolk State University

Cindy Herbert
Metropolitan Community College–Longview

Dana Hooper
University of Alabama

Dana Johnson
North Dakota State University

Daniela Marghitu
Auburn University

David Noel
University of Central Oklahoma

David Pulis
Maritime College, State University of New York

David Thornton
Jacksonville State University

Dawn Medlin
Appalachian State University

Debby Keen
University of Kentucky

Debra Chapman
University of South Alabama

Derrick Huang
Florida Atlantic University

Diana Baran
Henry Ford Community College

Diane Cassidy
The University of North Carolina at Charlotte

Diane Smith
Henry Ford Community College

Don Danner
San Francisco State University

Don Hoggan
Solano College

Elaine Crable
Xavier University

Erhan Uskup
Houston Community College–Northwest

Erika Nadas
Wilbur Wright College

Floyd Winters
Manatee Community College

Frank Lucente
Westmoreland County Community College

G. Jan Wilms
Union University

Gail Cope
Sinclair Community College

Gary DeLorenzo
California University of Pennsylvania

Gary Garrison
Belmont University

Gerald Braun
Xavier University

Gladys Swindler
Fort Hays State University

Heith Hennel
Valencia Community College

Irene Joos
La Roche College

Iwona Rusin
Baker College; Davenport University

J. Roberto Guzman
San Diego Mesa College

Jan Wilms
Union University

Janet Bringhurst
Utah State University

Jim Chaffee
The University of Iowa Tippie College of Business

Joanne Lazirko
University of Wisconsin–Milwaukee

Jodi Milliner
Kansas State University

John Hollenbeck
Blue Ridge Community College

John Seydel
Arkansas State University

Judith A. Scheeren
Westmoreland County Community College

Judith Brown
The University of Memphis

Karen Priestly
Northern Virginia Community College

Karen Ravan
Spartanburg Community College

Kathleen Brenan
Ashland University

Ken Busbee
Houston Community College

Kent Foster
Winthrop University

Kevin Anderson
Solano Community College

Kim Wright
The University of Alabama

Kristen Hockman
University of Missouri–Columbia

Kristi Smith
Allegany College of Maryland

Laura McManamon
University of Dayton

Leanne Chun
Leeward Community College

Lee McClain
Western Washington University

Linda D. Collins
Mesa Community College

Linda Johnsonius
Murray State University

Linda Lau
Longwood University

Linda Theus
Jackson State Community College

Lisa Miller
University of Central Oklahoma

Lister Horn
Pensacola Junior College

Lixin Tao
Pace University

Loraine Miller
Cayuga Community College

Lori Kielty
Central Florida Community College

Lorna Wells
Salt Lake Community College

Lucy Parakhovnik (Parker)
California State University, Northridge

Marcia Welch
Highline Community College

Margaret McManus
Northwest Florida State College

Margaret Warrick
Allan Hancock College

Marilyn Hibbert
Salt Lake Community College

Mark Choman
Luzerne County Community College

Mary Duncan
University of Missouri – St. Louis

Melissa Nemeth
Indiana University Purdue University
Indianapolis

Melody Alexander
Ball State University

Michael Douglas
University of Arkansas at Little Rock

Michael Dunklebarger
Alamance Community College

Michael G. Skaff
College of the Sequoias

Michele Budnovitch
Pennsylvania College of Technology

Mike Jochen
East Stroudsburg University

Mike Scroggins
Missouri State University

Nanette Lareau
University of Arkansas Community College–
Morrilton

Pam Uhlenkamp
Iowa Central Community College

Patrick Smith
Marshall Community and Technical College

Paula Ruby
Arkansas State University

Peggy Burrus
Red Rocks Community College

Peter Ross
SUNY Albany

Philip H Nielson
Salt Lake Community College

Ralph Hooper
University of Alabama

Ranette Halverson
Midwestern State University

Richard Cacace
Pensacola Junior College

Robert Dušek
Northern Virginia Community College

Robert Sindt
Johnson County Community College

Rocky Belcher
Sinclair Community College

Roger Pick
University of Missouri at Kansas City

Ronnie Creel
Troy University

Rosalie Westerberg
Clover Park Technical College

Ruth Neal
Navarro College

Sandra Thomas
Troy University

Sophie Lee
California State University, Long Beach

Steven Schwarz
Raritan Valley Community College

Sue McCrory
Missouri State University

Susan Fuschetto
Cerritos College

Susan Medlin
UNC Charlotte

Suzan Spitzberg
Oakton Community College

Sven Aelterman
Troy University

Terri Holly
Indian River State College

Thomas Rienzo
Western Michigan University

Tina Johnson
Midwestern State University

Tommy Lu
Delaware Technical and Community College

Troy S. Cash
NorthWest Arkansas Community College

Vicki Robertson
Southwest Tennessee Community College

Weifeng Chen
California University of Pennsylvania

Wes Anthony
Houston Community College

William Ayen
University of Colorado at Colorado Springs

Wilma Andrews
Virginia Commonwealth University

Yvonne Galusha
University of Iowa

We'd also like to acknowledge the reviewers of previous editions of Exploring:

Aaron Schorr
Fashion Institute of Technology

Alan Moltz
Naugatuck Valley Technical Community College

Alicia Stonesifer
La Salle University

Allen Alexander
Delaware Tech & Community College

Alok Charturvedi
Purdue University

Amy Williams
Abraham Baldwin Agriculture College

Andrea Compton
St. Charles Community College

Annette Duvall
Central New Mexico Community College

Annie Brown
Hawaii Community College

Antonio Vargas
El Paso Community College

Barbara Cierny
Harper College

Barbara Hearn
Community College of Philadelphia

Barbara Meguro
University of Hawaii at Hilo

Barbara Sherman
Buffalo State College

Barbara Stover
Marion Technical College

Bette Pitts
South Plains College

Beverly Fite
Amarillo College

Bill Daley
University of Oregon

Bill Morse
DeVry Institute of Technology

Bill Wagner
Villanova

Bob McCloud
Sacred Heart University

Bonnie Homan
San Francisco State University

Brandi N. Guidry
University of Louisiana at Lafayette

Brian Powell
West Virginia University–Morgantown Campus

Carl Farrell
Hawaii Pacific University

Carl M. Briggs
Indiana University School of Business

Carl Penzuil
Ithaca College

Carlotta Eaton
Radford University

Carole Bagley
University of St. Thomas

Carolyn DiLeo
Westchester Community College

Cassie Georgetti
Florida Technical College

Catherine Hain
Central New Mexico Community College

Charles Edwards
University of Texas of the Permian Basin

Cheryl Slavik
Computer Learning Services

Christine L. Moore
College of Charleston

Cody Copeland
Johnson County Community College

Connie Wells
Georgia State University

Dana Johnson
North Dakota State University

Dan Combellick
Scottsdale Community College

Daniela Marghitu
Auburn University

David B. Meinert
Southwest Missouri State University

David Barnes
Penn State Altoona

David Childress
Ashland Community College

David Douglas
University of Arkansas

David Langley
University of Oregon

David Law
Alfred State College

David Rinehard
Lansing Community College

David Weiner
University of San Francisco

Delores Pusins
Hillsborough Community College

Dennis Chalupa
Houston Baptist

Diane Stark
Phoenix College

Dianna Patterson
Texarkana College

Dianne Ross
University of Louisiana at Lafayette

Don Belle
Central Piedmont Community College

Douglas Cross
Clackamas Community College

Dr. Behrooz Saghafi
Chicago State University

Dr. Gladys Swindler
Fort Hays State University

Dr. Joe Teng
Barry University

Dr. Karen Nantz
Eastern Illinois University

Duane D. Lintner
Amarillo College

Elizabeth Edmiston
North Carolina Central University

Erhan Uskup
Houston Community College

Ernie Ivey
Polk Community College

Fred Hills
McClellan Community College

Freda Leonard
Delgado Community College

Gale E. Rand
College Misericordia

Gary R. Armstrong
Shippensburg University of Pennsylvania

Glenna Vanderhoof
Missouri State

Gregg Asher
Minnesota State University, Mankato

Hank Imus
San Diego Mesa College

Heidi Gentry-Kolen
Northwest Florida State College

Helen Stoloff
Hudson Valley Community College

Herach Safarian
College of the Canyons

Hong K. Sung
University of Central Oklahoma

Hyekyung Clark
Central New Mexico Community College

J Patrick Fenton
West Valley College

Jack Zeller
Kirkwood Community College

James Franck
College of St. Scholastica

James Gips
Boston College

Jana Carver
Amarillo College

Jane Cheng
Bloomfield College

Jane King
Everett Community College

Janis Cox
Tri-County Technical College

Janos T. Fustos
Metropolitan State College of Denver

Jean Kotsiovos
Kaplan University

Jeffrey A Hassett
University of Utah

Jennifer Pickle
Amarillo College

Jerry Chin
Southwest Missouri State University

Jerry Kolata
New England Institute of Technology

Jesse Day
South Plains College

Jill Chapnick
Florida International University

Jim Pepe
Bentley College

Jim Pruitt
Central Washington University

John Arehart
Longwood University

John Lee Reardon
University of Hawaii, Manoa

John Lesson
University of Central Florida

John Shepherd
Duquesne University

Joshua Mindel
San Francisco State University

Judith M. Fitspatrick
Gulf Coast Community College

Judith Rice
Santa Fe Community College

Judy Brown
The University of Memphis

Judy Dolan
Palomar College

Karen Tracey
Central Connecticut State University

Karen Wisniewski
County College of Morris

Karl Smart
Central Michigan University

Kathleen Brenan
Ashland University

Kathryn L. Hatch
University of Arizona

Kevin Pauli
University of Nebraska

Kim Montney
Kellogg Community College

Kimberly Chambers
Scottsdale Community College

Krista Lawrence
Delgado Community College

Krista Terry
Radford University

Lancie Anthony Affonso
College of Charleston

Larry S. Corman
Fort Lewis College

Laura McManamon
University of Dayton

Laura Reid
University of Western Ontario

Linda Johnsonius
Murray State University

Lisa Prince
Missouri State University

Lori Kelley
Madison Area Technical College

Lucy Parker
California State University, Northridge

Lynda Henrie
LDS Business College

Lynn Band
Middlesex Community College

Lynn Bowen
Valdosta Technical College

Malia Young
Utah State University

Margaret Thomas
Ohio University

Margie Martyn
Baldwin Wallace

Marguerite Nedreberg
Youngstown State University

Marianne Trudgeon
Fanshawe College

Marilyn Hibbert
Salt Lake Community College

Marilyn Salas
Scottsdale Community College

Marjean Lake
LDS Business College

Mark Olaveson
Brigham Young University

Martin Crossland
Southwest Missouri State University

Mary McKenry Percival
University of Miami

Meg McManus
Northwest Florida State College

Michael Hassett
Fort Hayes State University

Michael Stewardson
San Jacinto College–North

Midge Gerber
Southwestern Oklahoma State University

Mike Hearn
Community College of Philadelphia

Mike Kelly
Community College of Rhode Island

Mike Thomas
Indiana University School of Business

Mimi Duncan
University of Missouri–St. Louis

Minnie Proctor
Indian River Community College

Nancy Sardone
Seton Hall University

Pam Chapman
Waubonsee Community College

Patricia Joseph
Slippery Rock University

Patrick Hogan
Cape Fear Community College

Paul E. Daurelle
Western Piedmont Community
College

Paula F. Bell
Lock Haven University of Pennsylvania

Paulette Comet
Community College of Baltimore County,
Catonsville

Pratap Kotala
North Dakota State University

Ranette Halverson
Midwestern State University

Raymond Frost
Central Connecticut State University

Richard Albright
Goldey-Beacom College

Richard Blamer
John Carroll University

Richard Herschel
St. Joseph's University

Richard Hewer
Ferris State University

Robert Gordon
Hofstra University

Robert Marmelstein
East Stroudsburg University

Robert Spear
Prince George's Community College

Robert Stumbur
Northern Alberta Institute of Technology

Roberta I. Hollen
University of Central Oklahoma

Roland Moreira
South Plains College

Ron Murch
University of Calgary

Rory J. de Simone
University of Florida

Rose M. Laird
Northern Virginia Community College

Ruth Neal
Navarro College

Sally Visci
Lorain County Community College

Sandra M. Brown
Finger Lakes Community College

Sharon Mulroney
Mount Royal College

Shawna DePlonty
Sault College of Applied Arts and Technology

Stephen E. Lunce
Midwestern State University

Steve Schwarz
Raritan Valley Community College

Steven Choy
University of Calgary

Stuart P. Brian
Holy Family College

Susan Byrne
St. Clair College

Susan Fry
Boise State University

Suzan Spitzberg
Oakton Community College

Suzanne Tomlinson
Iowa State University

Thomas Setaro
Brookdale Community College

Todd McLeod
Fresno City College

Vernon Griffin
Austin Community College

Vickie Pickett
Midland College

Vipul Gupta
St. Joseph's University

Vivek Shah
Texas State University–San Marcos

Wei-Lun Chuang
Utah State University

William Dorin
Indiana University Northwest

Additionally, we'd like to extend our thanks to the Exploring 2010 technical editors:

Chad Kirsch

Cheryl Slavik

Elizabeth Lockley

Janet Pickard

Janice Synder

Joyce Nielsen

Julie Boyles

Lisa Bucki

Lori Damanti

Sandra Swinney

Sean Portnoy

PREFACE

The Exploring Series and You

Exploring is Pearson's Office Application series which requires students like you to think "beyond the point and click." With Office 2010, Exploring has embraced today's student learning styles to support extended learning beyond the classroom.

The goal of Exploring is, as it has always been, to go further than teaching just the steps to accomplish a task—the series provides the theoretical foundation for you to understand when and why to apply a skill. As a result, you achieve a deeper understanding of each application and can apply this critical thinking beyond Office and the classroom.

You are plugged in constantly, and Exploring has evolved to meet you half-way to work within your changing learning styles. Pearson has paid attention to the habits of students today, how you get information, how you are motivated to do well in class, and what your future goals look like. We asked you and your peers for acceptance of new tools we designed to address these points, and you responded with a resounding "YES!"

Here Is What We Learned About You

You go to college now with a different set of skills than students did five years ago. The new edition of Exploring moves you beyond the basics of the software at a faster pace, without sacrificing coverage of the fundamental skills that you need to know. This ensures that you will be engaged from page 1 to the end of the book.

You and your peers have diverse learning styles. With this in mind, we broadened our definition of "student resources" to include Compass, an online skill database; movable Visual Reference cards; relevant Set-Up Videos filmed in a familiar, commercial style; and the most powerful online homework and assessment tool around, myitlab. Exploring will be accessible to all students, regardless of learning style.

You read, prepare, and study differently than students used to. You use textbooks like a tool—you want to easily identify what you need to know and learn it efficiently. We have added key features that make the content accessible to you and make the text easy to use.

You are goal-oriented. You want a good grade and you want to be successful in your future career. With this in mind, we used motivating case studies and Set-Up Videos to aid in the learning now and to show the relevance of the skills to your future careers.

Moving Beyond the Point and Click and Extending Your Learning Beyond the Classroom

All of these additions will keep you more engaged, helping you to achieve a higher level of understanding and to complete this course and go on to be successful in your career. In addition to the vision and experience of the series creator, Robert T. Grauer, we have assembled a tremendously talented team of Office Applications authors who have devoted themselves to teaching you the ins and outs of Microsoft Word, Excel, Access, and PowerPoint. Led in this edition by series editor Mary Anne Poatsy, the whole team is equally dedicated to the Exploring mission of **moving you beyond the point and click, and extending your learning beyond the classroom.**

Key Features of Exploring Office 2010

- **White Pages/Yellow Pages** clearly distinguish the theory (white pages) from the skills covered in the Hands-On Exercises (yellow pages) so students always know what they are supposed to be doing.

- **Objective Mapping** enables students to skip the skills and concepts they know and quickly find those they do not know by scanning the chapter opener pages for the page numbers of the material they need.

- **Pull Quotes** entice students into the theory by highlighting the most interesting points.

- **Case Study** presents a scenario for the chapter, creating a story that ties the Hands-On Exercises together.

- **Key Terms** are defined in the margins to ensure student comprehension.

- **End-of-Chapter Exercises** offer instructors several options for assessment. Each chapter has approximately 12–15 exercises ranging from multiple choice questions to open-ended projects.

DISCOVER

- **Enhanced Mid-Level Exercises** include **Discover Steps**, which encourage students to use Help or to problem-solve to accomplish a task.

Instructor Resources

The Instructor's Resource Center, available at www.pearsonhighered.com includes the following:

- **Data and Solution Files**

- **Capstone Production Tests** allow instructors to assess all of the skills covered in a chapter with a single project.

- **Rubrics** for Beyond the Classroom Cases in Microsoft® Word format enable instructors to customize the assignments for their classes.

- **PowerPoint® Presentations** with notes for each chapter are included for out-of-class study or review.

- **Lesson Plans** provide a detailed blueprint to achieve chapter learning objectives and outcomes.

- **Objectives List** maps chapter objectives to Hands-On Exercises and end-of-chapter exercises.

- **Multiple Choice Answer Key**

- **Complete Test Bank**

- **Instructor Reference Cards**, available electronically that include a:
  - **Concept Summary** outlines the KEY objectives to cover in class with tips on where students get stuck as well as how to get them unstuck. This helps bridge the gap between the instructor and student when discussing more difficult topics.
  - **Scripted Lecture** provides instructors with a lecture outline that mirrors the Hands-On Exercises in the chapter.

Online Course Cartridges

Flexible, robust, and customizable content is available for all major online course platforms that include everything instructors need in one place. Please contact your Sales Representative for information on accessing course cartridges for WebCT, Blackboard, or CourseCompass.

Student Resources

Prentice Hall's Companion Web Site

www.pearsonhighered.com/exploring offers expanded IT resources and downloadable supplements. Students can find the following self-study tools for each chapter:

- Online Study Guide

- Chapter Objectives

- Glossary

- Chapter Objectives Review

- Web Resources

- Student Data Files

Senior Vice President, Editorial and Marketing: Patrick F. Boles
Editor: David Maltby
Development Editor: Christina Martin
Operations Manager: Eric M. Kenney
Production Manager: Jennifer Berry
Art Director: Renée Sartell
Cover Designers: Blair Brown and Kristen Kiley

Cover Art: Jerry Driendl/Getty Images, Inc.; Steve Bloom/Getty Images, Inc.; "Cheetah" courtesy of Marvin Mattelson/Getty Images; "Tabs" courtesy of Andrey Prokhorov/iStockphoto; "Open Doors" courtesy of Spectral-Design/iStockphoto; "Compass" courtesy of Laurent Hamels/Getty Images; "Fortune Teller" courtesy of Ingvald Kaldhussaeter/iStockphoto; "Ladder of Success" courtesy of iStockphoto; "Global Communication in Blue" courtesy of iStockphoto.

Copyright © 2012 by Pearson Learning Solutions
All rights reserved.

Permission in writing must be obtained from the publisher before any part of this work may be reproduced or transmitted in any form or by any means, electronic or mechanical, including photocopying and recording, or by any information storage or retrieval system.

Additional copyright information is included, where applicable, as a footnote at the beginning of each chapter.

The information, illustration, and/or software contained in this book, and regarding the above mentioned programs, are provided "as is," without warranty of any kind, express or implied, including without limitation any warranty concerning the accuracy, adequacy, or completeness of such information. Neither the publisher, the authors, nor the copyright holders shall be responsible for any claims attributable to errors, omissions, or other inaccuracies contained in this book. Nor shall they be liable for direct, indirect, special, incidental, or consequential damages arising out of the use of such information or material.

This special edition published in cooperation with Pearson Learning Solutions.

Printed in the United States of America.

Please visit our web site at *www.pearsoncustom.com/custom-library/custom-phit.*

Attention bookstores: For permission to return any unsold stock, contact us at *pe-uscustomreturns@pearson.com*.

Pearson Learning Solutions, 501 Boylston Street, Suite 900, Boston, MA 02116
A Pearson Education Company
www.pearsoned.com

ISBN 10: 1-256-18405-5
ISBN 13: 978-1-256-18405-8

Contents

VBA

GETTING STARTED WITH VBA

Extending Microsoft Office

CASE STUDY | ACME Consulting

ACME has four offices, which are located in different geographical regions of the United States: the East, Midwest, Rocky Mountain, and West. ACME consultants are located in cities throughout the regions, and each employee reports to the closest regional office. ACME stores a lot of important company data in Excel workbooks and Access databases. In particular, the head financial officer, McKynlee McAfee, stores customer loan information in Excel workbooks, and her assistant, Anthony Trujilo, stores employee payroll in an Access database.

During the past six months, you helped other ACME managers automate tasks with macros in Excel and Access. Because of this experience, McKynlee and Anthony have asked you to help them automate additional files using Visual Basic for Applications. Although you have limited programming experience, you have studied macro syntax (rules that you must follow for constructing code).

OBJECTIVES AFTER YOU READ THIS CHAPTER, YOU WILL BE ABLE TO:

1. Use the VBA interface
2. Identify code in the Code window
3. Create procedures
4. Create a message box
5. Get Help and debug errors
6. Declare and use variables and constants
7. Create an input box

8. Perform calculations
9. Use decision structures
10. Perform data validation
11. Use logical operators
12. Use the For...Next loop statement
13. Use the Do...Loop statement

From Chapter 1 of *Exploring Getting Started with VBA for Microsoft® Office 2010*, First Edition, Robert T. Grauer, Keith Mulbery, Keith Mast, Mary Anne Poatsy. Copyright © 2012 by Pearson Education, Inc. Published by Pearson Prentice Hall. All rights reserved.

Introduction to VBA

Visual Basic for Applications (VBA) is a programming language to enhance the functionality of Office applications.

Visual Basic for Applications (*VBA*) is a programming language that you can use to create and customize Office applications to enhance their functionality. VBA—which is included with Microsoft Office 2010—is a subset of Visual Basic, a stand-alone robust programming language that is part of Visual Studio. Programmers use Visual Basic to create Windows and Web-based applications. Unlike Visual Basic, VBA requires a host application (such as Word, Excel, Access, Outlook, or PowerPoint) that contains programming code to add functionality to your Office applications. Because VBA has a consistent user interface and utilizes the same technology in all Office applications, some procedures you write in one application can be exported to another. This way, your programming efforts are more efficient, because you can re-use some of the procedures you create.

You can use VBA to customize Excel workbooks or to enhance Access database objects. For example, you might want to modify a command button for exiting an Access database so that the user has an opportunity to cancel the procedure if he or she clicks the button by mistake. You can use VBA to create data entry forms, add custom menus, and hide or display interface elements depending upon user access. Office developers also use VBA to create custom functions, perform calculations using variables and constants, and process database records.

... use VBA to customize Excel workbooks or to enhance Access database objects.

In this section, you will use the VBA interface and identify types of code in the Code window. Finally, you will learn how to create procedures and display message boxes.

Using the VBA Interface

When you record a macro in Excel, Excel generates VBA code for the actions you take, such as changing margins and clearing cell contents. When you use a wizard to create an Access control, such as a command button, Access creates the VBA code to provide functionality for actions, such as clicking the button. If you have created macros in a Microsoft Office program, you might have had to edit the macro code to add functionality to the macro or correct an error. To modify macros, you use Microsoft Visual Basic for Applications (VBA).

Table 1 lists the different ways you can launch VBA in Excel and Access.

TABLE 1 Launch VBA	
Excel	**Access**
Click the Developer tab*, and then click Visual Basic in the Code group.	Click the Database Tools tab, and then click Visual Basic in the Macro group.
Click the Developer tab*, click Macros in the Code group, click a macro name in the Macro dialog box, and then click Edit.	Open a form or report in Design view, display the Property Sheet, click a specific control (such as a button) on the form or click the form itself, click the Event tab in the Property Sheet, click an event such as On Click, and then click Build. You may be prompted to select the Builder you want to use.
Click the View tab, click the Macros arrow in the Macros group, select View Macros, click a macro name in the Macro dialog box, and then click Edit.	
Press Alt+F11.	Press Alt+F11.

*If the Developer tab is not displayed, click the File tab, click Options, click Customize Ribbon, click the Developer check box in the Main Tabs list, and then click OK.

The Microsoft Visual Basic for Applications window is called the VB Editor. Figure 1 shows the VB Editor for an Excel workbook, and Figure 2 shows the VB Editor for an Access database. Notice the similarities between the windows: a menu bar, a toolbar, Project Explorer, Properties window, and the Code window.

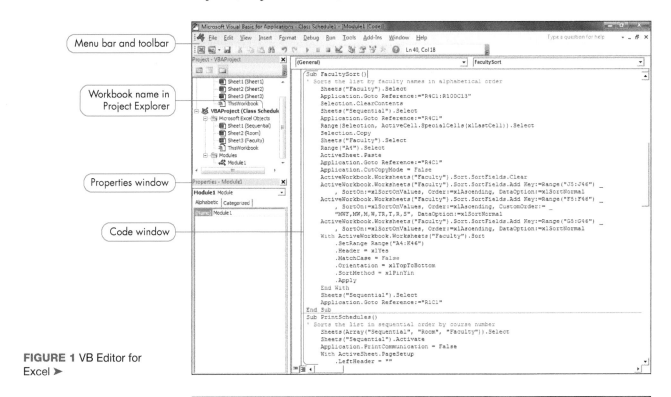

FIGURE 1 VB Editor for Excel ➤

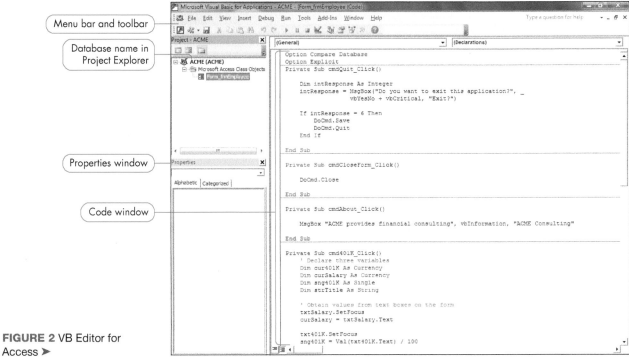

FIGURE 2 VB Editor for Access ➤

Menu Bar and Toolbar. The menu bar and toolbar provide access to commands similar to how the Ribbon organizes commands to perform in the respective Office programs. The toolbar also indicates the location of the insertion point, such as Ln 2, Col 1.

A **project** is a collection of modules and objects in an Office file, such as an Excel workbook or an Access database.

A **module** is a container to organize programming procedures within a project.

A **property** is an attribute or characteristic of an object for which you can set or change values.

The **Code window** is a text editor for writing and editing VBA statements.

A **procedure** is a named sequence of programming statements that perform a set of actions.

Design time is the mode for designing, writing, and editing programming statements.

Run time is the mode for executing a program.

Project Explorer. The left side of the VB Editor contains the Project Explorer, which is similar to the Windows Explorer. A *project* is a collection of modules and objects needed to run an application. In VBA, a project is a particular Microsoft Office file, such as a particular Excel workbook or an Access database, and its associated modules and macros. The Project Explorer lists all open projects. If you have three Excel workbooks open, Project Explorer lists three projects. The project or file includes objects within that file (such as Sheet1) and *modules*, which are containers to organize programming code. Click an object or module to display existing code or to write code for that particular object or module.

Properties Window. The Properties pane displays the *properties* or attributes for the currently selected object in the Project Explorer. The Properties window is similar to the Property Sheet you use to set properties for database objects in Access. For example, in Access, you can display the Property Sheet to set properties such as the number of decimal points for a calculated field in a query. In Figure 1, Module1 contains the FacultySort procedure, which is also the name of the macro created in Excel. If the Properties window is not displayed, select View from the menu, and then select Properties Window.

Code Window. Most of the VB Editor displays the *Code window*, a workspace text editor for writing and editing VBA programming statements. Programming statements include procedures, variable and constant declarations, mathematical expressions, etc. A module consists of one or more *procedures*, named sequences of statements that perform a series of actions for a defined task. When you create several macros in a workbook, Excel stores each macro as a procedure in one module. The name you enter when you record a macro becomes the name of an individual procedure in VBA.

When you create a VBA procedure using the VB Editor, you enter your code statements in *design time*, the mode for designing or creating programming code. When you run your procedure, VBA executes the procedure in *run time*, the mode during which a program is being executed.

> **TIP** Macro-Enabled Excel Workbook
>
> When you create macros or write VBA procedures for an Excel workbook, you must save it in the Macro-Enabled Workbook file format (.xlsm). Regular Excel workbooks (.xlsx) cannot store VBA code.

Identifying Code in the Code Window

Before you edit existing code or attempt to create your own code, you should learn about programming statements so that you can identify different elements in the Code window. At a first glance, the code may seem cryptic, but the more you study VBA statements generated by creating macros, the more you will be able to identify the code and start editing it or writing code from scratch. Programming code must follow proper syntax or rules. Programming syntax is similar to grammar and punctuation rules you follow when writing a paper for an English class; if you do not follow proper programming syntax, the program will fail to execute fully. Figure 3 identifies code elements.

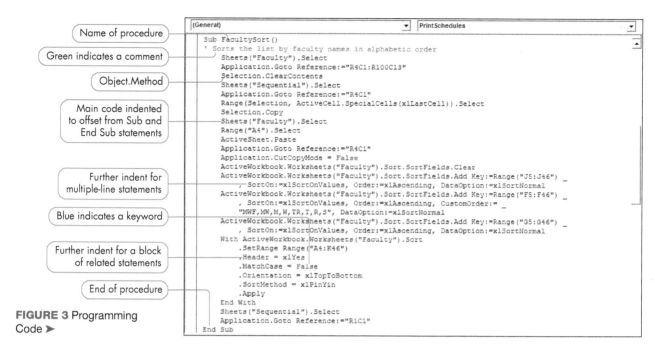

Name of procedure

Green indicates a comment

Object.Method

Main code indented to offset from Sub and End Sub statements

Further indent for multiple-line statements

Blue indicates a keyword

Further indent for a block of related statements

End of procedure

```
(General)                                                    PrintSchedules

Sub FacultySort()
' Sorts the list by faculty names in alphabetic order
    Sheets("Faculty").Select
    Application.Goto Reference:="R4C1:R100C13"
    Selection.ClearContents
    Sheets("Sequential").Select
    Application.Goto Reference:="R4C1"
    Range(Selection, ActiveCell.SpecialCells(xlLastCell)).Select
    Selection.Copy
    Sheets("Faculty").Select
    Range("A4").Select
    ActiveSheet.Paste
    Application.Goto Reference:="R4C1"
    Application.CutCopyMode = False
    ActiveWorkbook.Worksheets("Faculty").Sort.SortFields.Clear
    ActiveWorkbook.Worksheets("Faculty").Sort.SortFields.Add Key:=Range("J5:J46") _
        , SortOn:=xlSortOnValues, Order:=xlAscending, DataOption:=xlSortNormal
    ActiveWorkbook.Worksheets("Faculty").Sort.SortFields.Add Key:=Range("F5:F46") _
        , SortOn:=xlSortOnValues, Order:=xlAscending, CustomOrder:= _
        "MWF,MW,M,W,TR,T,R,S", DataOption:=xlSortNormal
    ActiveWorkbook.Worksheets("Faculty").Sort.SortFields.Add Key:=Range("G5:G46") _
        , SortOn:=xlSortOnValues, Order:=xlAscending, DataOption:=xlSortNormal
    With ActiveWorkbook.Worksheets("Faculty").Sort
        .SetRange Range("A4:K46")
        .Header = xlYes
        .MatchCase = False
        .Orientation = xlTopToBottom
        .SortMethod = xlPinYin
        .Apply
    End With
    Sheets("Sequential").Select
    Application.Goto Reference:="R1C1"
End Sub
```

FIGURE 3 Programming Code ▶

A procedure always begins with the *Sub* statement, and it always ends with the *End Sub* statement. The Sub statement contains the name of the procedure, such as Sub FacultySort(). The End Sub statement is the last statement and indicates the end of the procedure. Statements between these two lines of code define the tasks that will be executed when you run the procedure. You must define each procedure separately. You cannot nest one procedure within another procedure.

Typically, you indent the statements within a procedure to offset them from the Sub and End Sub statements for readability. In addition, if a statement takes up more than one line, you should indent the carryover lines so that other programmers know at a glance that the carryover lines are part of the same statement. You should further indent additional, related blocks of code to indicate coding hierarchy. Figure 3 illustrates these programming conventions or standards.

The Code window color-codes words in black, blue, green, and red. Black indicates properly written programming statements that are free from syntax errors. In addition, the Code window supports automatic completion of certain statements you enter or adjusts capitalization if needed.

Understand Keywords

A **keyword** is text or a symbol used for a specific purpose in a programming language.

Blue words, such as *Sub* and *End Sub*, are keywords. *Keywords* are words or symbols particular to a programming language and have specific purposes. Some general keywords include the following:

- With
- End With
- True
- False
- Do
- Loop

A **syntax error** occurs when code contains a misspelled or misused keyword, incorrect punctuation, or undefined elements.

Keywords are grouped into different categories. For example, procedural keywords include Call, Function, Property Get, Sub, etc. Decision-control structures use keywords such as Choose, If…Then…Else, Select Case, and Switch. Use Help to learn about the keywords specific to VBA. A *syntax error* occurs when you misuse or misspell a keyword, use incorrect punctuation, have not defined a procedure, or violated any other programming rules specific to the language.

 Errors in Keywords

If you enter code incorrectly, the Visual Basic Editor displays the syntax error in red.

Document Code with Comments

Documenting programs is important. As you write programming code, you know what it should do. However, after a few months you might not remember what the code does. Or, if you take over a project from another programmer or are working on a program with multiple programmers, you could spend a considerable amount of time deciphering the code others have written. Therefore, a good programming practice is to include comments within the code. Often programmers in an organization follow a set of coding conventions, such as comments, indenting, and naming techniques so that all programmers on a development team will create consistent programming code.

A comment is a textual description that explains a section of programming code.

A *comment* is text that documents or explains what a section of code does. Comments are not executable code. In VBA, a comment appears in green and begins with an apostrophe or the keyword Rem followed by a space. When you insert comments, keep them brief yet descriptive, such as the following:

```
'Sorts the list by faculty names in alphabetical order
```

Identify Objects and Methods

When you create objects, such as Excel macros and Access controls, the host application creates a procedure. Procedures are uniquely named and contain a sequence of programming statements to execute an algorithm. These procedures are contained within modules. VBA has two types of modules: standard modules and class modules. A *standard module* stores procedures that can be used by any object in the application. When you use the macro recorder in Excel or add a module to a workbook, the code for the macro is stored in a standard module. A *class module* enables you to create your own object template along with the properties and methods that decide how the object behaves. These custom objects can have properties and methods similar to the built-in objects, and you can create multiple copies of these objects as needed. Microsoft Access uses class modules to store the procedures associated with objects on a form or report. You can also create class modules in Excel to store procedures for specific objects, such as forms that a VBA procedure displays in a workbook.

A standard module stores procedures available to an object or by any event in the application.

A class module stores public code definitions of a class, such as properties and methods.

An object-oriented programming language uses methods to manipulate objects.

A method is an action that can be taken for an object.

VBA is an *object-oriented programming language* in which methods revolve around objects and actions that manipulate those objects. For example, Excel objects include worksheets, charts, and ranges. In Access, objects include tables, queries, forms, and reports. *Methods* are actions pertaining to the objects. Think of objects as nouns (an Excel range) and methods as verbs (Select). When you record a macro to select cell A4 or range B4:B10 in an Excel worksheet, the VBA code identifies the object, such as Range("A4"), and then the action, such as Select. In Access, you can manage macros in dialog boxes or convert macros to VBA code. The first line of code in Code Window 1 shows how to select a cell or a range in Excel. The second line of code shows how to use the ClearContents method to clear the data in the selected range. The last line of code shows the statement to open a form in Access.

```
Range("A4").Select
Range("B4:B10").ClearContents
DoCmd.OpenForm "Employees", acNormal, "", "", , acNormal
```

CODE WINDOW 1 ➤

In some cases, you need to qualify methods with the hierarchy of objects. For example, a workbook object contains a worksheet object, and a worksheet object contains range objects. When you specify the hierarchy of objects, separate the object names with periods. Code Window 2 shows an example of using Excel objects and methods. *ActiveWorkbook* is the main object. *Worksheets* is an object within the ActiveWorkbook. *("Sheet3")* defines which worksheet object you are referring to. *Sort* is a method acting on the Sheet3 data, *SortFields* is an object referring to the list of data to sort, and *Clear* is a method or an action acting on the SortFields object.

CODE WINDOW 2 ➤

```
ActiveWorkbook.Worksheets("Sheet3").Sort.SortFields.Clear
```

 TIP Auto List Members

When you type a period, the Auto List Members feature displays a list of potential objects, properties, or methods that can logically complete the statement. For example, after you type *ActiveWorkbook*, VBA displays a list of applicable items that relate to the active workbook. If you type W, VBA will scroll through the list to the first item starting with a W. You can continue typing the object, property, or method name, or you can double-click the word in the list to insert it into the code.

Creating Procedures

An **event** is an action at run time that triggers the execution of code.

Custom applications use VBA to process information or perform actions in response to events. An ***event*** is an action, such as the user clicking a button at run time that triggers a program instruction. For example, you can write VBA code to specify what an object does in response to the event. The system triggers some events, such as when Access opens a form. Users trigger other events by performing specific actions, such as selecting an item in a list or a menu option. VBA is an event-driven language, meaning that the program statements run in response to specific events.

A **sub procedure** performs an action but does not return a specific value.

A **function procedure** performs an action and returns a value.

A **property procedure** creates or manipulates a custom property.

A **public procedure** is available to any object in the application.

A **private procedure** is available only to a specific object or module.

VBA supports three kinds of procedures. A ***sub procedure*** is a procedure that performs an action but does not return a specific value, such as *Sub FacultySort* in Figure 1. A ***function procedure*** is a procedure that performs an action and returns a value, similar to how functions return values in Excel. A ***property procedure*** is a procedure that creates or manipulates a custom property. Most procedures you create with VBA will be sub procedures or function procedures.

All procedures are either public or private. A ***public procedure*** is available to any object in an application; the code for an object anywhere in the application can use the code statements. A ***private procedure*** is available only to a specific object or module. Procedures are public by default, unless the procedure is associated with a specific event, such as clicking a button.

Sub procedures begin with the Sub statement and end with End Sub. The code for a procedure must be contained between these two statements. In Figure 1, the Sub FacultySort() statement begins the procedure, which is contained in a standard module. The procedure is public and is available to any object in the Class Schedule1 workbook. This is useful when more than one procedure must perform the same action, such as changing user preferences or validating an action before closing the application. Rather than writing the code in each procedure that performs the action, you can write the code once and access the procedure from multiple objects.

Creating a Message Box

A common task for programmers is to display a message to the user. For example, you might want to display a message that announces that changes were saved to a database table, or that the user entered an incorrect value in an Excel cell. Programmers also create message boxes

A **message box** is a dialog box that displays a message or information and contains buttons for the user to click to perform alternative actions.

to display intermediate or final calculations in a process. *Message boxes* are small dialog boxes that contain a title bar, message, an icon, and one or more buttons. During run time, the program halts until the user clicks a button. When the user clicks a button on the message box, the message box closes, and a specific action programmed to that button executes.

Use the MsgBox Statement and Function

The **MsgBox statement** displays a message box onscreen with optional buttons, icons, and title bar text.

To create a message box in VBA, use either the MsgBox statement or the MsgBox function. The *MsgBox statement* displays a message onscreen. This statement is useful when you need to provide a message, such as a confirmed change or error alert, to the user. The default options for a message box include the title of the application in the title bar, the message, and an OK button. The code statement that defines a message box is identical in Access and Excel. Code Window 3 illustrates the code to display a message box. Figure 4 shows an example of a message box created using the MsgBox statement in Access.

CODE WINDOW 3 ➤

```
Sub Display_Message()
'Display a message box with a prompt
    MsgBox "Welcome to ACME Consulting!"
End Sub
```

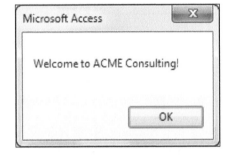

FIGURE 4 Message Box in Access ➤

The **MsgBox function** displays a message box onscreen and returns an integer to indicate which button the user clicked.

The *MsgBox function* displays a message on the screen and returns an integer value indicating which button the user clicked in the message box. The MsgBox function is useful when the program needs to have the user make a choice by clicking a particular button, such as OK or Cancel, and you need to store a specific value depending upon that choice. In addition, the MsgBox function enables you to customize the title bar, include an icon, and specify which buttons to display. Like Excel functions, VBA functions include a function name and the arguments. An *argument* is a value in the form of a constant, variable, or expression that provides necessary information to a procedure or function, similar to how arguments provide necessary data for Excel functions. The MsgBox function contains four arguments in a specific sequence. If you omit an argument, VBA assigns a default value.

An **argument** is a value that provides necessary information to a procedure or a function.

MsgBox("prompt"[, buttons] [, "title"] [, helpfile, context])

The *prompt argument* is the message or information that appears within the main area of the message box. It is called the prompt argument because it prompts the user to click a button within the message box. Prompt is the only required argument; the other arguments—indicated by brackets above—are optional but typically included. You must type the text for the prompt and title arguments within quotation marks. If you omit an optional argument that occurs before another argument you define, you must enter a comma as a placeholder for the omitted argument.

Display Buttons and Icons in a Message Box

The second argument in the MsgBox function enables you to specify buttons and icons you want to display in the message box. If you want to use the default OK button only but want to specify the message box title, type the prompt, two commas, and then the title. Table 2 lists some of the button syntax and the buttons displayed by the syntax.

TABLE 2	Message Box Button and Icons
Button Syntax	**Displays**
vbOKOnly	OK
vbOKCancel	OK Cancel
vbAbortRetryIgnore	Abort Retry Ignore
vbYesNoCancel	Yes No Cancel
vbYesNo	Yes No
vbRetryCancel	Retry Cancel
vbCritical	(critical icon)
vbQuestion	(question icon)
vbExclamation	(exclamation icon)
vbInformation	(information icon)

You can specify buttons, icons, or both. For example, you might want to display the default OK button and the Exclamation icon. Because the default displays the OK button, you can specify only vbExclamation for the second argument. The vb prefix indicates that the item, such as vbExclamation, is part of the VBA object library, which is a collection of objects with designated purposes. Code Window 4 shows a few sample individual buttons or icons and sample combinations. Note that you cannot combine two or more button sets (such as both vbYesNo and vbRetryCancel) or two or more icon sets (such as both vbCritical and vbInformation) in the same statement. Type a + between the constants, such as vbYesNo + vbExclamation.

CODE WINDOW 4 ➤

```
MsgBox("Welcome!", vbExclamation, "VBA in Access")
MsgBox("Welcome!", vbYesNo, "VBA in Access")
MsgBox("Welcome!", vbYesNo + vbExclamation, "VBA in Access ")
```

Because the MsgBox function returns an integer value based on which button the user clicks, you must assign the returned value to a variable or do something else with the returned integer. Table 3 lists the buttons and their return values.

TABLE 3	Integers Returned by Button
Button	**Integer Returned**
OK	1
Cancel	2
Abort	3
Retry	4
Ignore	5
Yes	6
No	7

Code Window 5 illustrates the use of the MsgBox function. The first argument "Welcome to ACME Consulting!" contains the text for the message box shown in Figure 5. Because the statement is long, you can divide it into two physical lines by typing the *line-continuation character*, which is a space followed by an underscore (_). The second argument "vbYesNo + vbInformation" creates the Yes and No buttons and the Information icon, respectively. The third argument "VBA in Access" displays the text for the message box title bar. When the message box displays, the user clicks Yes or No. If the user clicks Yes, the MsgBox function returns the integer 6. If the user clicks No, the MsgBox function returns the integer 7. The integer is stored in the intMsgBoxReturn variable, and you can execute different statements depending on the value of 6 or 7 that is stored in that variable.

The **line-continuation charac-ter** is a space followed by an underscore that programmers manually insert to display one statement on two or more physical lines in the Visual Basic Editor.

CODE WINDOW 5 ➤

```
'MsgBox Function
Sub Custom_Message()
    Dim strMessage As String
    strMessage = MsgBox("Welcome to ACME Consulting!", _
                    vbYesNo + vbInformation, "VBA in Access")
End Sub
```

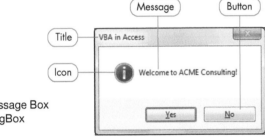

FIGURE 5 Message Box Created by MsgBox Function ➤

TIP MsgBox Function Integer

Remember that the MsgBox function returns an integer value based on which button the user clicks. The statement must do something with that returned value. Often, you will assign that value to a variable. Variables are discussed after Hands-On Exercise 1.

Getting Help and Debugging Errors

Use Help to learn more about VBA, explain terminology, or provide examples of programming code. For specific context assistance, click on a keyword, such as Sub, and then press F1. VBA will display specific help for that keyword.

The **Immediate window** is a window to enter and run small segments of code.

You can test out small segments of code by displaying the *Immediate window*, copying code into that window, and then running the code. To display the Immediate window, click View on the menu bar, and then select Immediate Window. This approach enables you to test small segments of code in isolation when building a larger program instead of running an entire procedure and then trying to debug the exact location of an error.

The Debug menu helps you identify errors in programming code. You can step through a procedure, step-by-step, until you identify the error, or you can select options to run the code to a particular breakpoint. Use Help to learn more about the Debug options.

1 Introduction to VBA

McKynlee and Anthony provided you with an Excel workbook and an Access database so that you can experiment with implementing VBA code. They want to make sure you can succeed on some basic VBA commands before having you work on larger files.

Skills covered: Display VBA and Get Help • Create a Procedure to Sort Records in Excel • Run VBA Procedures • Create a Procedure to Close a Form in Access • Create a Procedure to Display a Message Box in Access

---

STEP 1 ▶ **DISPLAY VBA AND GET HELP**

You will open an Excel workbook and use the Help menu to find a glossary of VBE terms. Refer to Figure 6 as you complete Step 1.

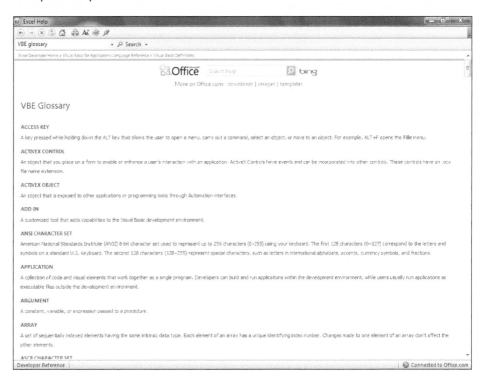

FIGURE 6 VBE Glossary in Help ➤

a. Start Excel, open *v1h1acme.xlsm* (an Excel macro-enabled workbook), and then save it as **v1h1acme_LastnameFirstname.xlsm**.

> TROUBLESHOOTING: If you make any major mistakes in this exercise, you can close the file, open *v1h1acme.xlsm* again, and then start this exercise over. If the Security Warning toolbar appears, click Enable Content.

b. Click the **Developer tab**, and then click **Visual Basic** in the Code group.

> TROUBLESHOOTING: If the Developer tab is not displayed, click the File tab, click Options, click Customize Ribbon, click the Developer tab check box in the Main Tabs list on the right side, and then click OK. Maximize the VB Editor if necessary.

The VB Editor opens and shows existing VBA code for a macro.

Getting Started with VBA

c. Click **Microsoft Visual Basic for Applications Help** (the question mark) on the toolbar.

   The Excel Help window opens so that you can search for a topic.

d. Type **VBE glossary** in the **Search help box**, and then click **Click to search**.

   The Excel Help window displays a potential Help topic.

e. Click the **VBE Glossary link** to open a window containing the glossary of terms. Scroll through the list and print a copy for reference, if you want.

f. Adapt steps d and e to search for **Create a Procedure** and **MsgBox Function**. Read a few articles from each of the search results. Close the Help window after reading about each topic.

g. Leave the VB Editor open to continue with the next step.

STEP 2 ▶ CREATE A PROCEDURE TO SORT RECORDS IN EXCEL

The Excel workbook contains a macro to sort the list by last name in alphabetical order and then to further sort by first name in alphabetical order. You will study this macro code to create a new procedure that sorts the list by salary in descending order. Refer to Figure 7 as you complete Step 2.

FIGURE 7 SortSalary Procedure ➤

a. Press **Ctrl+End** to position the insertion point on the line below the SortName procedure's End Sub statement, and then press **Enter**.

b. Type **Sub SortSalary()** and then press **Enter**.

   The VB Editor creates a corresponding End Sub statement and displays a horizontal line between the SortName procedure's End Sub statement and the Sub SortSalary() statement to separate the procedures visually.

c. Type ' **Sort by salary in descending order** and then press **Enter**.

   The Code window formats the comment in green.

d. Press **Tab**. Type **Range("B4").Select** and then press **Enter**.

   You indented the main code to offset it from the Sub and End Sub statements for readability. After you type *Range(*, VBA's Auto List Members feature displays a list of potential items to complete the statement.

e. Type **ActiveWorkbook.Worksheets("ACME").Sort.SortFields.Clear** and then press **Enter**.

After you type ActiveWorkbook and the period, VBA displays a list of potential objects that relate to the ActiveWorkbook object. You can select from the list or continue typing the programming statement.

f. Select **Ln 8 through Ln 19** of code in the SortName procedure (look at Figure 7 and the toolbar to identify the line numbers) stopping after the *End With* statement, click **Copy** on the Standard toolbar, click below the line of code you typed in the SortSalary procedure, and then click **Paste** on the Standard toolbar.

> **TROUBLESHOOTING:** Depending on what you selected and where you pasted exactly, you may need to press Tab to indent the first line of the pasted code in the SortSalary procedure. Check your code with Figure 7 to ensure correct placement and indenting of pasted code.

You copied most of the code from the SortName procedure to the SortSalary procedure to minimize time typing code and to avoid creating syntax errors. Now you need to edit the code so that the procedure will sort by salary instead of by names.

> **TIP** Location Status
>
> Look at the toolbar to identify lines (Ln) within the Visual Basic Editor.

g. Select **B4:B24** on Ln 26 in the SortSalary procedure, and then type **F4:F24**.

The range F4:F24 in the worksheet contains the salary data.

h. Select **xlAscending** on Ln 27 in the SortSalary procedure, and then type **xlDescending**.

> **TROUBLESHOOTING:** Make sure you type the letters *xl*, not the letter x and the number 1. The *xl* prefix refers to an object in the Excel object library that you can use in your code.

Steps g and h will sort the list of salaries so that the largest value is listed first.

i. Select **C4:C24** on Ln 28 in the SortSalary procedure, and then type **B4:B24**.

The range B4:B24 contains the last names in worksheet. Step i will further sort the list by last names in alphabetical order when employees have identical salaries.

j. Click **Save** on the toolbar.

STEP 3 ▶ RUN VBA PROCEDURES

You want to run the SortSalary procedure to ensure it sorts the list correctly. Refer to Figure 8 as you complete Step 3.

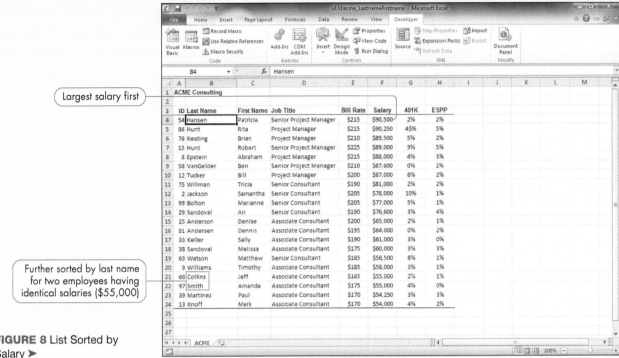

Largest salary first

Further sorted by last name for two employees having identical salaries ($55,000)

FIGURE 8 List Sorted by Salary ➤

a. Make sure the insertion point is within the SortSalary procedure you just created.

b. Click **Run Sub/UserForm** (the green triangle) on the toolbar.

   Nothing changes in VBA; however, the procedure runs in the Excel workbook.

c. Minimize the VB Editor, and then look at the Excel workbook.

   The list is sorted in descending order (largest to smallest) by salary. For the two employees who earn $55,000, the list is further sorted by last name so that Collins appears before Smith.

d. Click **Macros** in the Code group on the Developer tab, select **SortName** in the dialog box, and then click **Run**.

   The list is sorted in alphabetical order by last name and then by first name. You can run procedures from either the Macros dialog box or from within the VB Editor.

e. Click **Macros** in the Code group on the Developer tab, select **SortSalary** in the dialog box, and then click **Run**.

f. Save the workbook. Exit Excel, which will also close the VB Editor.

<hr />

STEP 4   **CREATE A PROCEDURE TO CLOSE A FORM IN ACCESS**

Anthony's Access database contains one table and one form. He has created five buttons on the form; however, only the Quit button works. He has asked you to write the VBA code for the Close Form button. Refer to Figure 9 as you complete Step 4.

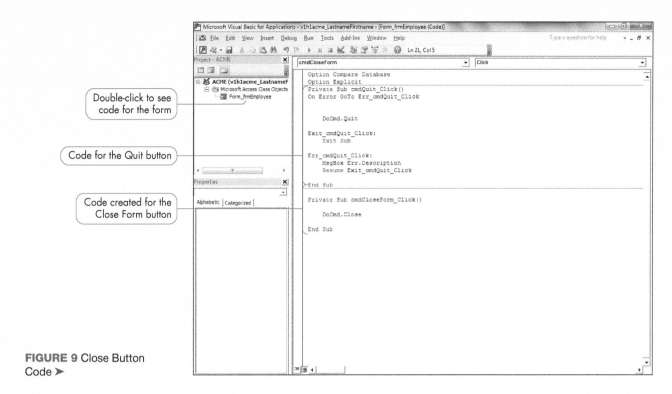

Double-click to see code for the form

Code for the Quit button

Code created for the Close Form button

FIGURE 9 Close Button Code ➤

a. Start Access, open *v1h1acme.accdb*, and then save it as **v1h1acme_LastnameFirstname**.

> **TROUBLESHOOTING:** If you make any major mistakes in this exercise, you can close the file, open *v1h1acme.accdb* again, and then start this exercise over. Enable the content, if needed.

b. Open the frmEmployee form, and then click each button at the bottom of the form: **About**, **401K**, **Bonus**, **Close Form**, and **Quit**.

Only the Quit button has been programmed to quit or close the entire database.

c. Open *v1h1acme_LastnameFirstname.accdb* again, click the **Database Tools tab**, and then click **Visual Basic** in the Macro group to open the VB Editor.

d. Double-click **ACME** in the Project Explorer, double-click **Microsoft Access Class Objects**, and then double-click **Form_frmEmployee**.

The programming code displays in the Code window.

e. Click in the code window, and then press **Ctrl+End** to go to the end of the code. Type **Private Sub cmdCloseForm_Click()** and then press **Enter** twice.

VBA adds the End Sub statement. You created a procedure named cmdClose that corresponds to the Close Form button's name (cmdClose). After typing the command button name, you type an underscore, and then specify the event (Click). You are about to specify the action to take when the user clicks that button.

f. Press **Tab**. Type **DoCmd.Close** and then press **Enter**.

Compare your code to the code shown in Figure 9.

g. Click **Save** on the toolbar, and then close the VB Editor.

The frmEmployee form is open in Design view in Access.

h. Click **Form View** on the right side of the status bar to display the form in Form view. Click **Close Form** at the bottom of the form.

The form closes, but the database remains open (unlike when you click the Quit button).

i. Keep Access open.

STEP 5 ▶ CREATE A PROCEDURE TO DISPLAY A MESSAGE BOX IN ACCESS

Anthony wants a message box to appear when users click the About button. You need to add a MsgBox statement to do this. Refer to Figure 10 as you complete Step 5.

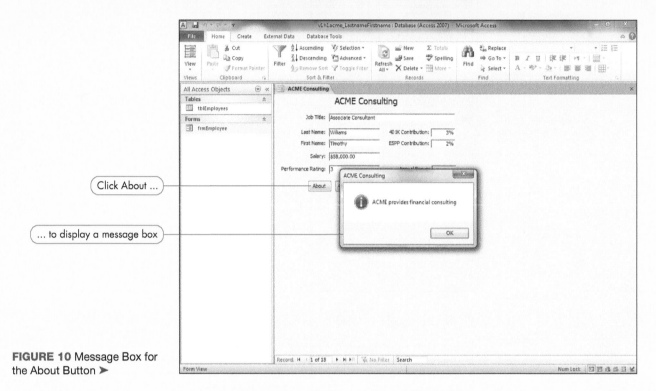

Click About ...

... to display a message box

FIGURE 10 Message Box for the About Button ➤

a. Click the **Database Tools tab** if necessary, and then click **Visual Basic** in the Macro group.

b. Press **Ctrl+End** to go to the end of the code, and then press **Enter**. Type **Private Sub cmdAbout_Click()** and then press **Enter** twice.

c. Press **Tab**. Type **MsgBox "ACME provides financial consulting", vbInformation, "ACME Consulting"** and then press **Enter**.

You used the MsgBox statement instead of the MsgBox function because you do not need a return value.

d. Click **Save** on the toolbar, and then close the VB Editor.

e. Click **Form View** on the right side of the status bar to display the form in Form view. Click **About** at the bottom of the form.

The MsgBox statement displays the message, an Information icon, and the title. By default, the message box will also display the OK button.

f. Click **OK** in the message box, click **Close Form** at the bottom of the form, and then exit Access.

Variables, Constants, Input, and Output

Programmers create variables and constants to store values that ... perform calculations or manipulate data during execution.

When a program is running, it needs to be able to accept input, perform calculations, and then display output. For example, in a payroll program, the inputs needed include an employee's name or ID, the hours worked, and the hourly pay rate. The processing would take the inputs to calculate the regular pay, overtime pay, total gross pay, income taxes and other deductions withheld, and the net pay. The output will display the results of the calculations. In addition to specifying the inputs, processing, and outputs, the program needs mechanisms for storing data. Programmers create variables and constants to store values that are then used in other statements to perform calculations or manipulate data during execution.

In this section, you will learn how to declare variables and constants, assign descriptive names, and select appropriate data types. In addition, you will learn how to obtain user input, store the input in variables, and display output.

Declaring and Using Variables and Constants

A **variable** is a programmer-defined name that stores values that can change or vary during run time.

Variables are programmer-defined names that store values that can change while the application is running. Variables store values in computer memory, and your code statement can change the value at any time. Because variables are stored in computer memory, a value for a variable exists only while a program is running. When the program ends, the ability to access the value in memory is lost. The advantage to using variables is that the value can change. For example, you might originally order one dessert at a restaurant and then change the order to two desserts.

A **constant** stores values that remain the same (or constant) during run time.

Constants store values that are specified at design time and that remain the same (or constant) while the application is running. Only a programmer can change a constant's value at design time; users cannot change a constant's value during run time. Declaring and using constants is important in a program because it prevents the use of raw, unidentified values within mathematical expressions. VBA supports three types of constants:

- *Intrinsic constant* is a constant specific to an application, such as Microsoft Excel or Microsoft Access. You can use the Object Browser to view constants in the object library. You cannot create a user-defined constant that uses the same name as an intrinsic constant.
- *Symbolic or user-defined constant* is a constant created by a programmer.
- *Conditional compiler constant* is defined in the host application. The compiler uses it to determine when or if specific Visual Basic code blocks are compiled. (Because this type of constant is more specialized, it will not be discussed or illustrated in this chapter.)

> **TIP** Variable or Constant?
>
> When deciding whether to create a variable or a constant, ask yourself if a user should be able to change a value. For example, if you want the user to specify hours worked, create a variable to accept and store that input. If the user should not be changing a value, such as a sales tax rate, create a constant to store the tax rate.

Select a Data Type

A **data type** specifies what type of data (such as text or value precision) can be stored in the variable or constant.

All variables and constants have a ***data type***, which refers to the kind of data the variable or constant can hold and how the data is stored in the computer's memory. Because variables and constants are stored in memory, good programmers select the appropriate data type that uses the least amount of memory necessary to store various kinds of information, such as text and numbers. Because each data type has different memory requirements, you can conserve computer memory, increase the speed of your application, and minimize programming errors by carefully selecting the most appropriate data type for the kind of data your application needs to store. The Reference Page lists the data types in VBA.

REFERENCE   Data Types

The characteristic of a variable determine what kind of data it can hold. Data types include *Boolean, Byte, Currency, Date, Decimal, Double, Integer, Long, Object, Single, String, Variant* (default), and user-defined types, as well as specific types of objects.

Data Type	Data Stored in the Variable	Memory Used
Boolean	Only two possible values: True (–1) or False (0).	2 bytes
Byte	A positive whole number from 0 to 255.	1 byte
Currency	Values ranging from –922,337,203,685,477.5808 to 922,337,203,685,477.5807 for calculations involving money and for fixed-point calculations in which accuracy is imperative.	8 bytes
Date	Date or time (where the value on the left side of the decimal is a date, and the value on the right side of the decimal point is time) in an eight-character format, such as 01/01/2013, ranging from 01/01/1000 to 12/31/9999.	8 bytes
Decimal	Value that contains decimal numbers scaled by a power of 10.	12 bytes
Double	Double-precision floating-point numbers with 14 digits of accuracy. Values –1.79769313486231E308 to –4.94065645841247E-324 for negative values and 4.94065645841247E-324 to 1.79769313486232E308 for positive values.	8 bytes
Integer	Whole numbers ranging from –32,768 to 32,767.	2 bytes
Long	Whole numbers ranging from –2,147,483,648 to 2,147,483,647.	4 bytes
Object	A reference to any application object.	4 bytes
Single	Single-precision floating-point numbers with six digits of accuracy. Values range from –3.402823E38 to –1.401298E-45 for negative values and 1.401298E-45 to 3.402823E38 for positive values.	4 bytes
String (fixed length)	Alphanumeric data including letters, numbers, spaces, punctuation, and other characters with a fixed length.	1 to approximately 63K characters
String (variable length)	Alphanumeric data including letters, numbers, punctuation, and other characters with variable length.	0 to 2 billion characters
Variant	Default type if no type is assigned.	Up to 22 bytes plus the length of a text string
Type (user defined)	Structured data that contains data appropriate to the required elements in a range.	Size depends upon the data definition

How do you determine the appropriate data type to use in your applications? If you are processing text or need to store a text string such as a person's name, use the String data type. If your application needs to perform calculations between dates, use the Date data type. If the variable holds data that requires only a simple Yes or No value, use the Boolean data type.

For numeric data that does not include dates, such as 100 items in stock, a tax rate of 5 percent, gross pay of $1,500, or a number expressed as an exponent, such as 3.2×10^{23}, the choice of the appropriate data type requires more consideration. Table 4 shows that the Integer and Long data types all store whole number (nondecimal) values. Because these data types store only whole numbers, they are called *integral data types*. Therefore, if you need to store a whole value for calculations, such as the number of items in stock or the term of a loan, use an integral data type.

An **integral data type** can store only whole numbers.

Nonintegral data types, such as Single and Double, represent numbers with integer and fractional parts. The Single and Double data types store floating-point numbers. You can use these types to store numbers that are extremely small (a number with a negative exponent, such as the thickness of a gold plating measured in microns) or extremely large (a number with a positive exponent, such as the national debt).

Floating point (Single and Double) numbers have larger ranges but can be subject to rounding errors. Thus, if you use two decimal point numbers in calculations, very small rounding errors might occur. The errors are too small to be of any significance, unless you are working with complex monetary calculations. If your application makes complex calculations using money, use the Currency or Decimal data type.

> **TIP** Variables for Currency Values
>
> For simple calculations involving money, such as calculating the value of inventory or a monthly loan payment, some programs perform best if you use the Single data type, whereas others perform best with the Currency data type. This book uses the Currency data type for monetary calculations.

Choosing the appropriate data type for variables is important. Table 4 provides examples of the recommended data types for various kinds of data.

TABLE 4 Recommended Data Types		
Data to Store	**Recommended Data Type**	**Example**
Employee address	String	100 Elm Street
Number of graduating students	Integer	1234
Marital status	Boolean	Married (–1) or Not Married (0)
Speed of light	Double	2.99 10^8
Age of a person in years	Integer	24
Population of a major metropolitan city	Integer	157000
Gross pay for a pay period	Currency	2526.41
Net 30 payment due	Date	12/01/2013
Term of a loan in months	Integer	360
Total sale amount	Currency	360.27
Constant *pi*	Double	3.1415926535897
Local sales tax rate	Single	0.065
Estimated world population in 2012	Long	7000000000

Name Variables and Constants

In addition to choosing a data type, you must choose a name for your variables and constants. You will then use those names to store and retrieve values to manipulate when the program is running. The standards for naming variables and constants in VBA follow requirements and recommendations.

Requirements

- Use a letter as the first character for a variable or constant name.
- Avoid disallowed characters: space, period (.), exclamation mark (!), @, &, $, and #.
- Create names that are 255 or fewer characters in length.

Recommendations

- Use descriptive names that tell the purpose of a variable or constant and the kind of data it contains.
- Begin the name with the first three characters indicating the data type (in lowercase) and the remainder specifying the variable's purpose (beginning with an uppercase letter). For example, a variable for storing the number of units might be named *intQuantity*, where *int* indicates the data type (Integer) and *Quantity* is a descriptive name for the values the variable holds (number of units). The first three characters appear in lowercase, with the remaining part of the variable name appearing as descriptive words that begin with uppercase letters. If the descriptive name includes more than one word, the first character of each word is capitalized. (This is known as CamelCase.) Table 5 lists the three-character designation for each data type and gives an example of how to apply the CamelCase convention.

TABLE 5 Variable Prefixes and Same Names		
Data Type	**Prefix**	**Example Variable Name**
Boolean	bln	blnMaritalStatus
Currency	cur	curNetPay
Date	dtm	dtmNet30
Double	dbl	dblSpeedOfLight
Integer	int	intQuantity
Long	lng	lngPopulation
Object	obj	objCurrent
Single	sng	sngSalesTax
String	str	strAddress

In previous versions of Visual Basic, programmers capitalized constant names and used an underscore between words, such as TAX_RATE. However, the current naming convention for user-defined constants is CamelCase, such as TaxRate.

Intrinsic constants defined by an application for specific objects use a two-character prefix and mixed-case format. For example, the prefix *vb* represents a constant in the VBA object library, and *xl* represents a constant from the Microsoft Excel object library.

Declare Variables and Constants

A **declaration** is a statement that creates a variable or constant and specifies its data type and name.

Scope specifies which statements can access a variable or constant.

When you want to define a variable, you must include a declaration statement. The **declaration** statement assigns a name and data type and allocates memory to store a value for the variable or constant. When you declare a variable or a constant, you can specify its accessibility or **scope**. The scope specifies which program statements can access the value stored in the variable or constant. If you declare a variable or constant within a procedure that you want to be available to only that procedure, it is a local variable or constant and has procedure scope. This means that other procedures cannot access directly the variable or constant. If you want to make a variable or constant accessible to any procedure within an Access form, for example, you create a module-level (or form-level) variable or constant, which has module scope.

Declare a local variable at the top of a procedure or declare a module-level variable at the top of the module code in the Code window using the *Dim* statement. After you type the Dim keyword, type the variable name, type As, and then type the data type. Code Window 6 provides example variable declarations.

CODE WINDOW 6 ➤

```
Dim blnMaritalStatus As Boolean
Dim curNetPay As Currency
Dim intQuantity As Integer
Dim strAddress As String
```

To declare a user-defined constant, start with the keyword Const and include the constant name. In addition, you must assign a value that will not change during the run time of the application. The value must match the data type you specify. For example, if you declare an integer constant, you cannot assign a value of 0.065 to it because integers store whole numbers only. Code Window 7 shows sample constant declarations.

CODE WINDOW 7 ➤

```
Const SalesTaxRate As Double = 0.065
Public Const Taxrate As Double = 0.065
Private Const CityTaxRate As Double = 0.065
```

To be able to use a value stored in a variable or constant in all procedures in a project, use the *Public* statement instead of the *Dim* statement. To ensure that variables are properly declared before being used, you should type the statement *Option Explicit* at the top of the code window. If Option Explicit is on, you must explicitly declare a variable before assigning a value to it. If you do not enter that statement, VBA allows you to create variables on the spot, which can lead to problems in an application. It is good programming practice to always declare variables before using them.

By default, constants are private. You cannot change a constant's availability within a procedure. However, in a standard module, you can add the keyword Public at the beginning of the declaration statement to make a constant available to "all procedures in all modules." You can limit a constant's availability to a specific module only by including the keyword Private at the beginning of the declaration. Help further explains Public and Private and the usage in class modules.

TIP Auto Syntax Corrections

VBA checks for and corrects some errors for you if the Auto Syntax Check check box is selected in the Options dialog box. For example, if you forget to space before and after the assignment operator (=), VBA will insert the spaces for you when you press Enter. Other automatic corrections include changing case, such as changing *as integer* to *As Integer* or making a variable's case match its case in the declaration statement. Select Tools on the menu, and then select Options to verify the Auto Syntax Check setting.

Assign Values to Variables

An assignment statement is one that assigns a value to a variable or constant. With constants, the declaration and assignment must occur within one statement because once the constant is declared and assigned a value that value cannot change during run time. For variables, you create separate declaration and assignment statements. Code Window 8 shows example variable declaration and assignment statements for an integer and a string. The variable name goes on the left side of the = operator, and the value being assigned goes on the right side of the = operator. When you assign text to a string, you must enclose the text within quotation marks.

CODE WINDOW 8 ➤

```
Dim intQuantity As Integer
intQuantity = 100

Dim strLastName As String
strLastName = "Johnson"
```

 TIP Date Literals

When you assign dates to a Date variable or constant, you must enclose the date in a mm/dd/yyyy (two digits for the month and day, and four digits for the year) format within two pound sign (#) characters, such as #07/01/2013#. This value, known as a date literal, assigns the proper date to the variable or constant.

Creating an Input Box

An **input box** is a dialog box that prompts the user to enter data.

Variables and constants simplify the calculations your applications perform. However, you need to plan how the data assigned to variables gets into an application. An application can include specific controls, such as a text box, to obtain data from the user. You create an *input box*, a dialog box that displays on the screen to prompt the user to enter for a value. Like a message box, the program halts after displaying an input box until the user enters data, and then clicks OK. Unlike message boxes, input boxes do not have icons.

Programmers use functions to simplify program code statements. VBA includes numerous functions to return values. Predefined VBA functions often require one or more arguments, similar to Excel functions such as the IF function. A code statement with a function contains the function name and one or more arguments. The arguments are the values supplied to the function. Arguments can be required or optional. If an argument is required, it must be included in the code statement. As you type a function in the code window, the Visual Basic Editor displays a pop-up window listing the required functions.

Obtain User Input with the InputBox Function

The **InputBox function** displays a prompt dialog box to the user to enter a value.

The *InputBox function* (InputBox) prompts the user to enter a value that the application needs to perform an action. This function returns the value supplied by the user as a string. The syntax for the InputBox function is as follows:

InputBox(prompt[, title] [, default] [, xpos] [, ypos] [, helpfile, context])

The *prompt* is the message inside the input box; the *title* is an optional argument. When specified, it displays the text that appears on the input box title bar. The optional *xpos* and *ypos* arguments specify the horizontal distance from the left edge of the screen and the vertical distance from the top of the screen, respectively, to display the input box.

Code Window 9 shows the InputBox function used to get a person's name and store it in a string variable and then display a message box that contains a text string and the contents of the strLastname variable. Because the InputBox statement is long, it is divided into two lines by using the line-continuation character. If you do not use a line-continuation character at the end of the first line or if you use a line-continuation within string quotes enclosed within quotation marks, VBA will display an error. To combine two text strings together into one string, type & between them. Figure 11 shows the input box, and Figure 12 shows the resulting message box.

CODE WINDOW 9 ➤

```
'Declare string variable
Dim strLastName As String
     'Display input box, get user input,& store in variable
     strLastName = InputBox("Please enter your last name.", _
                       "Data Entry: Last Name")

     'Display results in a message box
     MsgBox "Last Name is: " & strLastName

End Sub
```

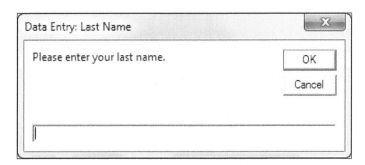

FIGURE 11 Input Box ➤

FIGURE 12 Message Box ➤

> **TIP** Concatenation Character
>
> Use the ampersand character (&) or plus sign (+) to *concatenate*, or join, two values, such as *MsgBox "Last Name is: " & strLastName* shown in Code window 9. Figure 12 displays the result of the code, Last Name is: Johnson. The message box displays the text string Last name is: and the value of the strLastName variable, which in this case is Johnson. Concatenation is useful for joining text strings.

Concatenate is the process of joining two or more text strings.

Convert Strings to Numeric Values Using the Val Function

When you obtain user input using the InputBox function, the value that the user supplies is returned to the procedure as a text string by default. This is fine for text data, but if you need to perform calculations on numbers entered into an input box, you need to use the *Val function*, which converts the value into numeric data for calculations.

The **Val function** converts text into a numeric value.

The Val function stops reading the string when it encounters the first character it does not recognize as part of a number. Symbols and characters frequently added to numeric values (like currency symbols and commas) are not recognized. When the Val function encounters a nonnumeric character, it ignores the remaining characters in the string.

You can use the Val function in conjunction with the InputBox function to convert the string value into a numeric value for calculations. For example, Code Window 10 shows a procedure that uses the Val function to convert numbers entered as text into numeric values that can be used in calculations. This code declares and assigns text to string variables so that you can use the string variable names in the InputBox() function to simplify that line of code.

CODE WINDOW 10 ➤

```
Dim strMessage As String
Dim strTitle As String
Dim curSalary As Currency

strMessage = "Please enter your annual salary."
strTitle = "Salary Data Entry"

    curSalary = Val(InputBox(strMessage, strTitle, "45000"))
    MsgBox "You entered: " & curSalary
```

This procedure prompts the user for his or her salary. The title of the input box uses the strTitle variable contents, *Salary Data Entry*, and the message uses the strMessage variable contents, *Please enter your annual salary.* Including 45000 as the third argument in the InputBox function displays that value as a default value in the input box when the program runs. However, the user can type over that value. The Val function converts the user's entry from a text string to a numeric value, assigns it to the variable curSalary, and a message box displays the entry.

> **TIP** Val Function and Text Entries
>
> What happens if you enter a text string into the input box that requires a value? The Val function converts any values it cannot interpret as a number to the value of zero. If you enter nonnumeric characters into the input box, the Val function returns a value of zero. If you enter leading numbers followed by characters, the Val function converts the numeric values to numbers. When a custom application has an input box for data input, programmers often include a sentence or two explaining how to enter data. You can include these instructions as a part of the prompt for the input box.

Performing Calculations

To perform calculations within a procedure using variables, you need to create an arithmetic expression. Expressions use operators to perform calculations and join text strings. You can also format the results of calculations.

Use Operators and Order of Precedence

An **operator** is one or more characters that performs a calculation.

Many of the expressions you create to perform calculations contain functions and operators. An *operator* is a character or combination of characters that accomplishes a specific computation. VBA supports six kinds of operators: arithmetic, assignment, comparison, concatenation, logical, and miscellaneous. Table 6 lists the arithmetic operators supported in VBA.

TABLE 6	VBA Arithmetic Operators	
Operator Symbol	**Operator Name**	**Purpose**
^	Exponentiation	Raises a number to the power of another number.
*	Multiplication	Multiplies two numbers.
/	Division	Divides two numbers and returns a floating-point result.
\	Integer Division	Divides two numbers and returns an integer result.
Mod	Modulus arithmetic	Modulus arithmetic, which divides two integer numbers and returns only the remainder.
+	Addition, concatenation	Adds two numbers. Also used to concatenate two strings.
–	Subtraction, negation	Yields the difference between two numbers or indicates the negative value of a numeric expression.
+ or &	String concatenation	Combines two strings.

An **order of precedence** is a rule that controls the sequence in which arithmetic operations are performed.

When several operations occur in an expression, each part is evaluated and used in a predetermined order called operator precedence. ***Order of precedence*** is the order in which arithmetic expressions are performed. Understanding operator precedence is important for creating expressions that produce the results you want. VBA performs arithmetic calculations left to right in the order: parentheses, exponentiation, multiplication or division, and finally addition or subtraction.

You can use parentheses to override the order of precedence and force some parts of an expression to evaluate before others. When you use parentheses, operations within parentheses occur before those outside. Expressions with parentheses occur according to operator precedence (multiplication, division, addition, subtraction). Code Window 11 shows example expressions that perform calculations using constants that have already been declared and variable values obtained from worksheet cells:

```
'Declare constants
Const conStTax As Single = 0.065
Const conCityTax As Single = 0.035

'Declare variables
Dim curSaleAmount As Currency
Dim curTotalTax As Currency
Dim curTotalSale As Currency

'Obtain the sale amount
curSaleAmount = Val(InputBox("Ener the sale amount: "))

' Calculate taxes and total sale amount
curTotalTax = curSaleAmount * (conStTax + conCityTax)
curTotalSale = curSaleAmount + curTotalTax

'Display result
MsgBox "The total sale is " & curTotalSale
```

CODE WINDOW 11 ➤

Given the two constants in Code Window 11, if a user enters 123.45 as the sales amount, the result is 135.795. The addition operation within parentheses occurs first: conStTax (0.065) is added to the conCityTax (0.035). The result of 0.1 is then multiplied by the curSaleAmount (123.45) to calculate the curTotalTax (12.345). Then, the curSaleAmount (123.45) is added to the curTotalTax (12.345); the result (135.795) is then stored in the curTotalSale variable and displayed in the message box.

Format Output Results

When you perform calculations, you should format the results. Unformatted results might display more decimal places than required or not include a currency symbol when you are displaying monetary units. For example, the result of the calculation appears as a decimal value with three digits to the right of the decimal: 135.795.

The **Format function** formats the first argument (such as a value) into a particular appearance, such as a monetary format or date format.

You can use the *Format function* to format the results of calculations. This function uses predefined formats to change the appearance of text. In its simplest form, the Format function has the following syntax:

Format (expression, style)

Expression refers to the string you want to format, and *style* refers to a named format. Table 7 lists the named number styles that you can use with the Format function. VBA also includes named formats for dates. Use Help to learn about other named formats.

TABLE 7	Named Styles for Number Formats
Format Name	**Description**
General Number	Displays number without a thousand separator.
Currency	Displays number with thousand separators, if appropriate; displays two digits to the right of the decimal point.
Fixed	Displays at least one digit to the left and two digits to the right of the decimal point.
Standard	Displays numbers with thousand separators, at least one digit to the left and two digits to the right to the decimal point.
Percent	Displays numbers multiplied by 100 with a percent sign (%) appended to the right. Always displays two digits to the right of the decimal point.
Scientific	Uses standard scientific notation.
Yes/No	Displays No if the number is 0; otherwise, displays Yes.
True/False	Displays False if the number is 0; otherwise, displays True.
On/Off	Displays Off if the number is 0; otherwise, displays On.

Code Window 12 illustrates the use of Format functions.

```
Dim curSalary As Currency
Dim sngBonus As Single
Dim blnExempt As Boolean

curSalary = 47000
sngBonus = 0.065
blnExempt = 21

MsgBox "Salary: " & Format(curSalary, "Currency") _
       & Chr$(10) & Chr$(13) _
       & "Bonus: " & Format(sngBonus, "Percent") _
       & Chr$(10) & Chr$(13) _
       & "Exempt: " & Format(blnExempt, "Yes/No")
```

CODE WINDOW 12 ➤

The procedure in Code Window 12 declares three variables and then assigns each a value. The MsgBox statement returns each variable formatted using a named style. To make the code easier to read, the statement uses the line-continuation character. Figure 13 displays the formatted results.

Salary: $47,000.00
Bonus: 6.50%
Exempt: Yes

FIGURE 13 Message Box ➤

TIP Chr Function

The Chr function requires an integer as its argument and then returns a character associated with that integer. For example, Chr$(10) returns a line feed, and Chr$(13) returns a carriage return. You can create a hard return in a text string by combining the line feed and carriage return characters, as in the previous code example.

HANDS-ON EXERCISES

2 Variables, Constants, Input, and Output

McKynlee and Anthony need you to create procedures that perform calculations in the Excel workbook and Access database. You will utilize your knowledge of message boxes, input boxes, variables, and constants to add the desired functionality. McKynlee asks you to create a procedure to automate the Excel workbook so that she can search for an employee by unique ID, locate that person's salary, and then calculate a 5% bonus for that person.

Skills covered: Declare a Constant and Three Variables • Enter the ID to Select the Salary • Calculate and Display the Bonus • Create a Sub Procedure in Access

---

STEP 1 ▶ DECLARE A CONSTANT AND THREE VARIABLES

You need to create a procedure and declare a constant to store the 5% bonus rate and three variables: ID selection, salary, and bonus amount. Refer to Figure 14 as you complete Step 1.

```
(General)                                      ▼    CalculateBonus                          ▼

  Sub CalculateBonus()

      ' Declarations
      Const BonusRate As Double = 0.05
      Dim intID As Integer
      Dim curFindSalary As Currency
      Dim curBonus As Currency

  End Sub
```

FIGURE 14 Declarations ➤

a. Open the macro-enabled *v1h1acme_LastnameFirstname* workbook in Excel, save it as **v1h2acme_LastnameFirstname**, and then display the VB Editor.

> **TROUBLESHOOTING:** If the Security Warning toolbar appears, click Enable Content.

b. Click at the top of the Code window, type **Sub CalculateBonus**() and then press **Enter** twice.

c. Press **Tab**. Type ' **Declarations** and then press **Enter**.

It is good programming practice to enter comments for blocks of code.

d. Type **Const BonusRate As Double = 0.05** and then press **Enter**.

You declared a constant to store the bonus rate. You must enter 5% as a decimal point equivalent in programming code: 0.05.

e. Type **Dim intID As Integer** and then press **Enter**. Type **Dim curFindSalary As Currency** and then press **Enter**. Type **Dim curBonus As Currency** and then press **Enter**.

Compare your declarations to those in Figure 14. You declared an Integer to store the employee ID, a Currency variable to store the employee's salary, and a Currency variable to store the calculated bonus amount.

f. Click **Save** on the toolbar.

STEP 2 ▶ ENTER THE ID TO SELECT THE SALARY

The procedure needs to prompt the user to enter an employee's ID, store it in a variable, and use that variable to find the ID in the list. After the procedure finds the ID, it must make the respective salary the active cell. With the salary as the active cell, the procedure saves the salary value in a variable. Refer to Figure 15 as you complete Step 2.

FIGURE 15 Code to Enter ID and Select the Salary ➤

```
(General)                                         ▼   CalculateBonus                                              ▼

    Sub CalculateBonus()

        ' Declarations
        Const BonusRate As Double = 0.05
        Dim intID As Integer
        Dim curFindSalary As Currency
        Dim curBonus As Currency

        ' Set the active cell to A3
        Application.Goto Reference:="R3C1"

        ' Display input to get employee ID
        intID = Val(InputBox("Enter ID", "Find Employee's Data"))

        ' Use Find dialog box to find ID and then select respective salary
        Cells.Find(What:=intID, After:=ActiveCell, LookIn:=xlFormulas, LookAt:= _
            xlWhole, SearchOrder:=xlByColumns, SearchDirection:=xlNext, MatchCase:=False _
            , SearchFormat:=False).Activate
        ActiveCell.Offset(0, 5).Select
        curFindSalary = ActiveCell.Value

    End Sub
```

a. Press **Enter**. Type ' **Set the active cell to A3** and then press **Enter**. Type **Application.Goto Reference:="R3C1"** and then press **Enter** twice.

The code makes the third row (R3) in the first column (C1) the active cell. In Excel, you typically refer to cells with the column letter first, such as A1; however, in VBA, use the abbreviations R and C for row and column respectively.

b. Type ' **Display input to get employee ID** and then press **Enter**. Type **intID = Val(InputBox("Enter ID", "Find Employee's Data"))** and then press **Enter** twice.

> **TROUBLESHOOTING:** Look at Figure 15 carefully as you type each statement. Pay close attention to spaces, periods, and spelling to avoid syntax errors.

This code displays an input box with the message *Enter ID* and the title *Find Employee's Data*. The data entered by the user is a string and must be converted to a value; therefore, you use the Val function to surround the InputBox function. Once the input is converted to a value, you must assign it to the intID variable.

c. Use Figure 15 to type the *Use Find dialog box* comment and the three lines of the *Cells.Find* statement. Make sure you use the line-continuation character, a space followed by the underscore, at the end of the first two lines.

What:=intID is the equivalent of typing a value in the Find dialog box. In this situation, you want to use the value in the intID variable. LookAt:=xlWhole requires that the entire cell must be identical to the data entered. If you search for 8, it finds 8 and not 86. SearchOrder:=xlByColumns searches down the current (ID) column rather than across by rows.

> **TROUBLESHOOTING:** A syntax error will occur if you forget to use a line-continuation character to continue a line of code. If you get a syntax error, check to see if the line-continuation character is missing. If so, insert it at the end of each line (except the last) of a complete programming statement. In addition, make sure you type the letters *xl*, not x and the number 1.

d. Type **ActiveCell.Offset(0,5).Select** and then press **Enter**.

This statement keeps the active cell on the same row (0) and moves over to the right by five cells (5) and makes that cell the active cell. That cell contains the salary for the ID you found.

e. Type **curFindSalary = ActiveCell.Value**.

This statement uses the active cell's value and then assigns it to the curFindSalary variable.

f. Click **Save** on the toolbar.

To complete the procedure, you need to add an expression to calculate the bonus amount based on the identified salary and the constant bonus rate. After calculating the bonus, you need to format it and display it in a message box. Refer to Figure 16 as you complete Step 3.

```
(General)                                        ▼    CalculateBonus                        ▼

    Sub CalculateBonus()

        ' Declarations
        Const BonusRate As Double = 0.05
        Dim intID As Integer
        Dim curFindSalary As Currency
        Dim curBonus As Currency

        ' Set the active cell to A3
        Application.Goto Reference:="R3C1"

        ' Display input to get employee ID
        intID = Val(InputBox("Enter ID", "Find Employee's Data"))

        ' Use Find dialog box to find ID and then select respective salary
        Cells.Find(What:=intID, After:=ActiveCell, LookIn:=xlFormulas, LookAt:= _
            xlWhole, SearchOrder:=xlByColumns, SearchDirection:=xlNext, MatchCase:=False _
            , SearchFormat:=False).Activate
        ActiveCell.Offset(0, 5).Select
        curFindSalary = ActiveCell.Value

        ' Calculate bonus based on salary and display output
        curBonus = curFindSalary * BonusRate
        MsgBox "Your bonus is " & Format(curBonus, "Currency"), vbInformation, "Bonus"

    End Sub
```

FIGURE 16 Code to Calculate and Display the Bonus ➤

a. Press **Enter** twice. Type ' **Calculate bonus based on salary and display output** and then press **Enter**.

b. Type **curBonus = curFindSalary * BonusRate** and then press **Enter**.

The expression takes the value in curFindSalary and multiplies it by 0.05 in the constant BonusRate. The result is then assigned to the curBonus variable.

c. Type **MsgBox "Your bonus is " & Format(curBonus, "Currency"), vbInformation, "Bonus"**. Click **Save**.

This statement uses the Format() function to format the curBonus value in Currency format. That result is displayed with the text *Your bonus is* and then displayed in a message box. The message box also contains the Information icon.

> **TROUBLESHOOTING:** Check your code with Figure 16 to ensure you entered the statements correctly. The code should contain a space between *is* and the quotation mark to ensure a space displays between the word *is* and the actual salary value.

d. Click **Run Sub/UserForm** on the toolbar.

The Find Employee's Data message box opens.

e. Type **75** and then click **OK**.

The procedure finds 75 in the ID column, goes to the right by five cells to find the $81,000 salary, multiplies it by 5%, and displays $4,050.00 in the message box (see Figure 17).

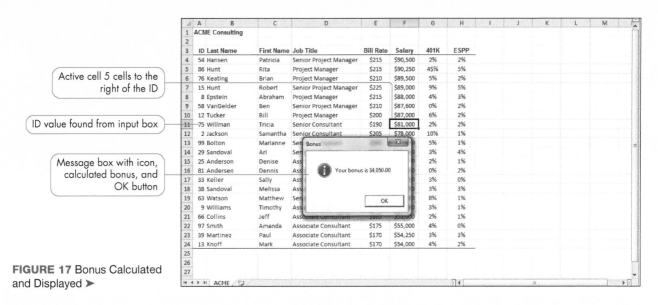

Active cell 5 cells to the right of the ID

ID value found from input box

Message box with icon, calculated bonus, and OK button

	A	B	C	D	E	F	G	H	I	J	K	L	M
1	ACME Consulting												
2													
3	ID	Last Name	First Name	Job Title	Bill Rate	Salary	401K	ESPP					
4	54	Hansen	Patricia	Senior Project Manager	$215	$90,500	2%	2%					
5	86	Hunt	Rita	Project Manager	$215	$90,250	45%	5%					
6	76	Keating	Brian	Project Manager	$210	$89,500	5%	2%					
7	15	Hunt	Robert	Senior Project Manager	$225	$89,000	9%	5%					
8	8	Epstein	Abraham	Project Manager	$215	$88,000	4%	3%					
9	58	VanGelder	Ben	Senior Project Manager	$210	$87,600	0%	2%					
10	12	Tucker	Bill	Project Manager	$200	$87,000	6%	2%					
11	75	Willman	Tricia	Senior Consultant	$190	$81,000	2%	2%					
12	2	Jackson	Samantha	Senior Consultant	$205	$78,000	10%	1%					
13	99	Bolton	Marianne	Sen			5%	1%					
14	29	Sandoval	Ari	Ser			3%	4%					
15	25	Anderson	Denise	Ass			2%	1%					
16	81	Andersen	Dennis	Ass			0%	2%					
17	33	Keller	Sally	Ass			3%	0%					
18	38	Sandoval	Melissa	Ass			3%	3%					
19	63	Watson	Matthew	Ser			8%	1%					
20	9	Williams	Timothy	Ass			3%	1%					
21	66	Collins	Jeff	Associate Consultant			2%	1%					
22	97	Smith	Amanda	Associate Consultant	$175	$55,000	4%	0%					
23	39	Martinez	Paul	Associate Consultant	$170	$54,250	3%	3%					
24	13	Knoff	Mark	Associate Consultant	$170	$54,000	4%	2%					
25													
26													
27													

Bonus — Your bonus is $4,050.00 — OK

FIGURE 17 Bonus Calculated and Displayed ➤

f. Click **OK** in the message box. Close the VB Editor, and then save and close the workbook.

CREATE A SUB PROCEDURE IN ACCESS

Anthony wants to expand the frmEmployee form so that it calculates and displays the monthly 401k contribution for an employee. Refer to Figure 18 as you complete Step 4.

```
Private Sub cmd401K_Click()
    'Declare three variables
    Dim cur401K As Currency
    Dim curSalary As Currency
    Dim sng401K As Single

    ' Obtain values from text boxes on the form
    txtSalary.SetFocus
    curSalary = txtSalary.Text

    txt401K.SetFocus
    sng401K = Val(txt401K.Text) / 100

    ' Calculate and display the monthly 401K contribution
    cur401K = curSalary / 12 * sng401K
    MsgBox "Your monthly 401K contribution is: " _
        & Format(cur401K, "Currency"), vbInformation, "401K"

End Sub
```

FIGURE 18 Procedure in Access ➤

a. Open the *v1h1acme_LastnameFirstname* database in Access, and then save the database as **v1h2acme_LastnameFirstname**.

> TROUBLESHOOTING: If the Security Warning toolbar appears, click Enable Content.

b. Click the **Database Tools tab**, and then click **Visual Basic** in the Macro group.

> TROUBLESHOOTING: If you do not see the Visual Basic Editor containing code, double-click Microsoft Access Class Objects in the Project Explorer, and then double-click Form_frmEmployee to display its code.

c. Click in the Code window, press **Ctrl+End** to position the insertion point after all existing code, and then press **Enter**.

Getting Started with VBA

31

d. Type **Private Sub cmd401K_Click**() and then press **Enter** twice. Press **Tab**.

e. Type the first comment and the three variable declarations shown in Figure 18, making sure you type it exactly as shown.

You declared two Currency variables and one Single variable.

f. Type the second comment and the four statements after it as shown in Figure 18, making sure you type it exactly as shown.

The *txtSalary.SetFocus* code makes the txtSalary box have the focus during run time. That is, when a user clicks the 401K button, the procedure makes the txtSalary box active to select its current value. The *curSalary = txtSalary.Text* code uses the Text property, which contains the current value of the txtSalary box and then assigns that value to the curSalary variable.

The *txt401K.SetFocus* code then sets the focus to the txt401K box. The *sng401K = Val(txt401K.Text) / 100* statement uses the Text property that contains the current value in the txt401K box, converts it to a value, divides that value by 100, and then assigns the result to the sng401K variable.

g. Type the third comment and the two statements after it as shown in Figure 18, making sure you type it exactly as shown.

The first statement calculates the 401K value, and the second statement displays a message box with the value in the cur401K variable formatted as Currency.

h. Click **Save** on the toolbar, and then close the VB Editor.

i. Click **Form View** on the status bar to display the open form in Form view, and then click **401K** in the form.

Timothy Williams' 401k contribution is $145.00 (see Figure 19).

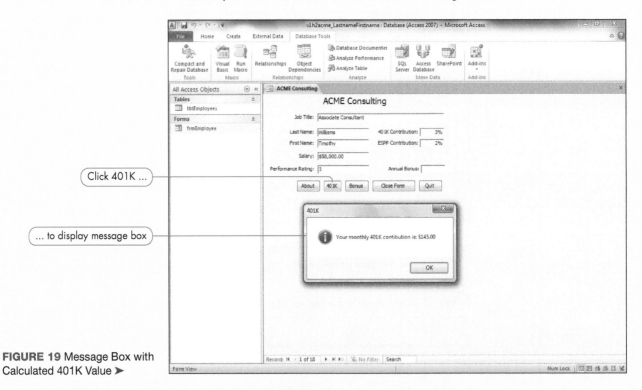

FIGURE 19 Message Box with Calculated 401K Value ➤

j. Click **OK**, and then exit Access.

Decision Structures

When you customize applications with VBA, you write code using program statements that tell the computer exactly what to do based on a programming structure. A ***programming structure*** is the sequence in which the program statements execute at run time. Programmers use programming structures to organize code statements in one of three ways: with a sequence structure, a decision structure, or a repetition structure.

If the program executes statements in the order that they appear, it uses the ***sequence structure***. All of the sub procedures you have written up to this point use the sequence structure because the program statements execute in a direct sequence when the procedure runs. That is, the first statement runs, followed by each successive statement until all statements have run, with no statements skipped. Sequence structures are the simplest programming structures.

In this section, you will learn how to use decision structures in VBA procedures. Specifically, you will create procedures that use the If...Then, If...Then...Else, and Select Case decision structures.

Using Decision Structures

A ***decision structure*** is a programming structure that makes a comparison between values, variables, and/or constants. Based on the result of that comparison, the program executes statements in a certain order. If the result of the comparison is true (or yes), one statement executes, but if the result of the comparison is false (or no), an alternative statement executes. Thus the result of the comparison determines which path the program takes.

By phrasing the conditions in terms of a question, you can determine the appropriate course of action. A ***condition*** is an expression that uses a ***relational operator*** (such as = and <=) to compare two values (through variables, constants, or expressions) and determine whether the result of the comparison is true or false. An expression is a combination of variables and operators that performs a calculation or returns a value. A comparison that uses relational operators is a ***logical test***, which is always contained within a decision structure. In programming, you can use a logical test within your program statements to respond to conditions that vary. VBA uses the relational operators listed in Table 8.

TABLE 8	Relational Operators	
Relational Operator	**Tests whether the value of ...**	**Example**
=	two operands are equal.	`txtLastName.Text = Smith`
<>	two operands are not equal.	`Val(txtLoanAmont.Text)<>0`
<	the first operand is less than the value of the second operand.	`Val(txtLoanAmount.Text)<25000`
>	the first operand is greater than the value of the second operand.	`Val(txt401K.Text)>100000`
<=	the first operand is less than or equal to the second operand.	`sngConversionResult<=300`
>=	the first operand is greater than or equal to the second operand.	`curGrossPay>=500`

Decision structures use relational operators to make comparisons that perform a logical test. You can use a decision statement to test whether a condition is true or false, to test a series of conditions, or to make a selection when a condition is true. Table 9 lists the decision statements supported in VBA.

A **programming structure** is the sequence in which the program statements execute at run time.

A **sequence structure** executes the statements in the sequence they are listed in the procedure.

A **decision structure** is a block of code that uses relational operators to make comparisons and then executes alternative statements based on the outcome.

A **condition** is an expression that determines if a situation is true.

A **relational operator** is a symbol or word that determines the relationship between two statements.

A **logical test** evaluates the truth of the stated relationship.

TABLE 9 Decision Statements Supported in VBA	
Decision Statement	**Usage**
If...Then	Performs a logical text. If the test evaluates to True, the program executes a specific statement or block of statements.
If...Then...Else	Performs a logical test. If the test evaluates to True, the program executes a specific statement or block of statements. If the test evaluates to False, the program executes a different statement or block of statements.
Select Case	Compares the same expression to several different values. The Select statement evaluates a single expression only once and uses it for every comparison. When the test evaluates to True, the case is applied.

Create an If...Then Statement

The **If...Then statement** performs a logical test and executes one or more statements if the test is True.

The *If...Then statement* represents the simplest kind of decision structure. An If.....Then statement performs a logical test; if the test evaluates to True, the program code specifies what action to take. No alternative statements are executed if the logical test is false, however.

Suppose an employer wants to encourage its employees to make a year-end contribution to the company's 401k retirement plan. The standard match is 25%. If an employee contributes more than $500, the company will match the contribution at 50%. You can phrase this decision as a question:

- Is the contribution greater than $500?
- Yes: Match is 50%
- No: Match is 25% (keep the original 25% match)

Code Window 13 shows how to implement this decision in a VBA procedure.

```
Dim sngContribution As Single
Dim sngMatch As Single
sngMatch = 0.25

sngContribution = Val(InputBox("Enter the contribution amount", _
                  "401K Contribution"))

' Test if contribution is greater than 500
' If true, assign 0.5 to sngMatch
' If false, maintain existing value (0.25)
If sngContribution > 500 Then
    sngMatch = 0.5
End If

MsgBox "We will match your contribution by " & _
       Format(sngMatch, "Percent")
```

CODE WINDOW 13 ⋀

This procedure declares two variables: a Single data type for contribution amount and a Single data type for the match percentage, which is assigned a default value of 0.25. An input box prompts the user to enter a contribution amount. The If...Then statement performs the logical test; if the contribution exceeds 500, it assigns a new value to the sngMatch variable. A message box displays the match percentage. For example, if a user types 600 in the input box, the message box will display 50.00%. If the user types 500 in the input box, the message box will display 25.00%.

Create an If...Then...Else Statement

The **If...Then...Else statement** performs a logical test and executes different statements based on whether the test is True or False.

You can use an *If...Then...Else statement* to test for a condition and specify one option if the test evaluates to True and another if it evaluates to False.

Use the If...Then...Else structure to determine the appropriate matching percentage for an employee's 401k contribution. Because the statement tests a condition and specifies a path for a True and a False result, you do not need to set a default value for the sngMatch variable. Figure 20 illustrates the process using a flowchart, and Code Window 14 shows the code.

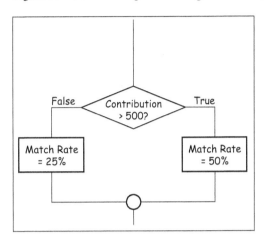

FIGURE 20 If...Then...Else Flowchart ➤

```
Dim sngContribution As Single
Dim sngMatch As Single

sngContribution = Val(InputBox("Enter the contribution amount", _
                 "401K Contribution"))

' Test if contribution is greater than 500
' If true, assign 0.5 to sngMatch
' If false, assign 0.25 to sngMatch
If sngContribution > 500 Then
    sngMatch = 0.5
Else
    sngMatch = 0.25
End If

MsgBox "We will match your contribution by " & _
       Format(sngMatch, "Percent")
```

CODE WINDOW 14 ⬆

The statement begins with *If* and ends with *End If*. The word *Then* must appear after the logical test. In this example, the procedure performs the logical test before assigning a value to the sngMatch variable. Note that the logical test sngContribution > 500 is executed only once. The test evaluates to either True or False. If the result is True, the statement after Then is executed. If the result is false, the statement after the Else is executed.

> **Using the ElseIf Statement**
>
> At times, you need to test additional conditions when the first logical test evaluates to False. You can add additional conditions using the ElseIf statement. You can combine multiple ElseIf conditions, as long as the final condition uses the Else statement. You can also nest If statements within one another to test multiple conditions. Because nested If statements can become difficult to manage, the Select Case statement is often used as an alternative.

Create a Select Case Statement

The conditions you need to test sometimes become complex and require one or more If statements nested within another If statement. Suppose ACME Consulting pays employees an annual bonus that is a percentage of the employee's salary. The percentage used is determined by the employee's performance rating. Managers rate employee performance on a 10-point scale (see Table 10). For example, if an employee gets a rating between 1 and 3, that person earns a 5% bonus.

TABLE 10 Ratings and Bonus Percentages	
Performance Rating	**Bonus Percentage**
0	No Bonus
1–3	5%
4–8	7.5%
9 and above	10%

You can determine each employee's rating using nested If statements. Figure 21 models this decision in a flowchart.

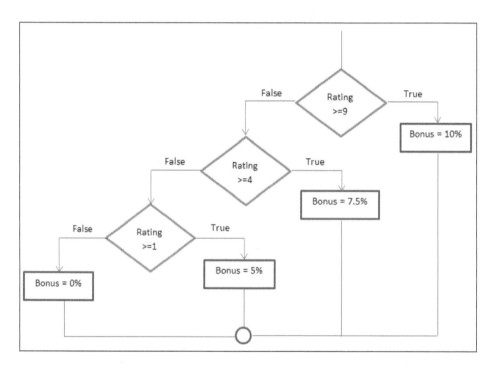

FIGURE 21 Flowchart Modeling Nested If Statement ➤

You can nest as many levels of If statements as your application requires; however, nesting too deeply makes code hard to model, write, and manage. The Select Case statement is a good alternative to nested If statements when you need to test a single variable or expression for multiple values, such as testing for an employee's performance rating and returning one of four possible values depending upon the rating. The Select Case structure is simpler than a nested If structure; the code is more concise for testing one value against multiple conditions.

The *Select Case statement* compares an expression or a value to a case block, which is the set of cases that might apply. A case is an individual condition to test. You can easily code this complex decision structure using the Select Case statement. Figure 22 models this decision with a flowchart, and Code Window 15 illustrates the use of a Select Case statement.

The **Select Case statement** compares an expression and then executes the code for the matching case.

Getting Started with VBA

36

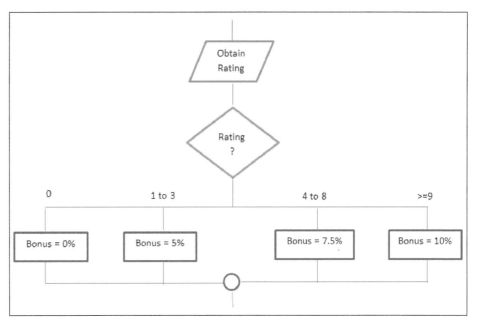

FIGURE 22 Flowchart Modeling Select Case Statement ➤

CODE WINDOW 15 ➤

```
Dim curSalary As Currency
Dim curBonusPay As Currency
Dim sngBonus As Single
Dim intRating As Integer

curSalary = InputBox("Enter your salary", "Salary")
intRating = InputBox("Enter your performance rating", "Rating")

Select Case intRating
    Case Is < 1
        sngBonus = 0
    Case 1 To 3
        sngBonus = 0.05
    Case 4 To 7
        sngBonus = 0.075
    Case Is > 7
        sngBonus = 0.1
End Select

curBonusPay = curSalary * sngBonus
MsgBox "Your bonus is " & Format(curBonusPay, "Currency")
```

The case block begins with the Select Case statement and ends with End Select. The Select Case statement uses the case block to determine the appropriate bonus rate based on the performance rating value. When the structure tests a single value, the Case Is statement is used. When the structure tests a range of values, the word *Case* is followed by the range of values. If a user enters 45500 for the salary and 5 for the performance rating, the calculated bonus is $3,412.50. Not shown in the example is an optional Case Else statement. You can use this statement after all Case Is statements to catch all other conditions and perform an action.

Performing Data Validation

In the decision structures discussed thus far, we have assumed that the data entered into an input box is entered correctly. However, users can inadvertently enter text where a number is required, which can produce unintended results. Because computer output depends on the quality of the data the user supplies, programmers need to check the values entered in Windows forms to make sure the data is appropriate for its intended use.

The process of checking data entered by a user to ensure it meets certain conditions, such as a value within a particular range or values instead of text, is called **data validation**. You can use decision structures to display a message if the user fails to enter the required data or to ensure that users enter numbers where they are needed to perform calculations.

Data validation is the process of checking data entered to ensure it meets certain requirements.

Check for a Required Value

A common data validation task is checking to make sure users input required data. You can use a simple If…Then…Else statement and a message box to confirm the data entered or to warn the user that required data is missing. Code Window 16 checks to make sure that users have entered an annual salary greater than 25000.

```
Dim curSalary As Currency

curSalary = Val(InputBox("Enter your salary", "Salary"))
If curSalary > 25000 Then
    MsgBox "You entered " & curSalary
Else
    MsgBox "Not a valid entry", vbCritical, "Invalid Data"
End If
```

CODE WINDOW 16 ➤

The Val function converts the user's entry into a numeric value. If text is entered instead of a valid number, the function returns a value of zero. The decision structure displays one of two messages, depending upon the value supplied.

Check for a Numeric Value

You have used the Val function to convert data entered into a text box to a numeric value for performing calculations. However, if the Val function encounters an empty text string, it converts the empty string to a value of zero. Therefore, it is important to validate numeric data before performing calculations.

VBA includes a function designed to determine whether data entered is a numeric value. The **IsNumeric function** checks a text string and determines whether it evaluates as a number. If the string does evaluate as a number, the function returns a Boolean value of True. Otherwise, the function returns False. The function requires one argument: the expression to evaluate. The required argument can be a variable, a property of a control, or a text string. Code Window 17 illustrates the use of the IsNumeric function.

The **IsNumeric function** checks a string and returns True if the string can evaluate to a value or False if the string cannot evaluate to a value.

```
Dim varSalary
varSalary = InputBox("Enter your salary", "Salary")

If IsNumeric(varSalary) = False Then
    MsgBox "Enter your salary as a number"
Else
    MsgBox "You entered " & varSalary
End If
```

CODE WINDOW 17 ➤

This procedure declares a variable for the salary without specifying a data type, so the default data type is variant. The If…Then…Else statement checks the value. If the user has not made an entry or if the user enters invalid characters, the function returns False. A numeric or decimal value returns a Boolean result of True. For example, if the user enters 25000, the return value is True. If the user enters nothing, the return value is False.

Using Logical Operators

A **logical operator** uses Boolean logic to perform a logical test.

The **And operator** is a logical operator that requires that two or more conditions be met to evaluate to True.

The **Or operator** is a logical operator that requires that only one condition be met to evaluate to True.

You can test for more than one condition in a decision structure by using logical operators. A *logical operator* is an operator that uses Boolean logic to test conditions. Programmers often use two logical operators: the And operator and the Or operator. The ***And operator*** requires that all conditions included in the statement evaluate to True. The ***Or operator*** requires that any one of the conditions evaluate to True.

Use the Or Logical Operator

Code Window 18 shows a procedure that declares a string variable and then prompts the user for a text string to assign to the variable. The procedure then uses the Or operator to validate the text string as being either Smith or Jones.

```
Dim strText As String
strText = InputBox("Enter either 'Smith' or 'Jones'")
If strText = "Smith" Or strText = "Jones" Then
    MsgBox "Your data entry passes the test: " & strText
Else
    MsgBox "Invalid Data", vbCritical, "Error"
End If
```

CODE WINDOW 18 ➤

   If the user enters Smith or Jones, a message appears indicating that the data is valid. If the user enters anything else or does not make an entry, a message appears indicating that the data is invalid. Note that text comparisons are case sensitive. If the user enters smith or sMiTh, the data entry does not match the text string specified in the logical test; therefore, the Invalid Data message box would appear.

Use the And Logical Operator

You might need to perform a logical test to ensure that two or more conditions are true. For example, you might need the user to enter a value within a particular range. Therefore, you must use the And logical operator to ensure the user input meets the minimum value and another test to ensure the user input does not exceed the maximum value. Code Window 19 declares an integer variable and then prompts the user for a value between 10 and 90. The procedure then uses the And operator to validate the entry as being greater than or equal to 10 and less than or equal to 90.

```
Dim intvalue As Integer
intvalue = InputBox("Enter an integer between 10 and 90")

If Val(intvalue) >= 10 And Val(intvalue) <= 90 Then
    MsgBox "Your data passes the test: " & intvalue
Else
    MsgBox "Invalid Data", vbCritical, "Error"
End If
```

CODE WINDOW 19 ➤

   If the user enters a number that is greater than or equal to 10 and less than or equal to 90, a message appears indicating that the data is valid. If the user enters anything else or does not make an entry, a message appears indicating that the data is invalid.

HANDS-ON EXERCISES

3 Decision Structures

Anthony wants you to complete the programming code for the buttons on the frmEmployee form in the Access database. Specifically, you need to write procedures for the Quit, 401K, and Bonus buttons.

Skills covered: Create an If...Then Decision Structure • Create an If...Then...Else Decision Structure • Create a Select Case Structure

---

STEP 1 ▸ CREATE AN IF...THEN DECISION STRUCTURE

Anthony wants a confirmation message box to display when the user clicks Quit. Currently, when a user clicks Quit, the database closes without any confirmation. Refer to Figure 23 as you complete Step 1.

```
cmdQuit                                    ▼   Click                                   ▼

Option Compare Database
Option Explicit
Private Sub cmdQuit_Click()

    Dim intResponse As Integer
    intResponse = MsgBox("Do you want to exit this application?", _
                    vbYesNo + vbCritical, "Exit?")

    If intResponse = 6 Then
        DoCmd.Save
        DoCmd.Quit
    End If

End Sub
```

FIGURE 23 Message Box Code with If...Then Statement ➤

a. Open the *v1h2acme_LastnameFirstname* database, and then save it as **v1h3acme_LastnameFirstname**.

> **TROUBLESHOOTING:** If the Security Warning toolbar appears, click Enable Content.

b. Open the VB Editor, and then display the code in the Code window.

c. Select the code for the Private Sub cmdQuit_Click() procedure. Do not select this header or the End Sub statements. Press **Delete** to delete the statements within this procedure.

d. Type the code shown in Figure 23.

The MsgBox function returns an integer that is assigned to the intResponse variable. You use the If...Then decision structure to determine if the user clicked Yes, which is assigned an integer of 6. If so, the procedure saves the current record and quits the application. If the user clicks No, nothing special happens. The form remains onscreen, and of course, the database does not close.

e. Click **Save** on the toolbar, and then close the VB Editor.

f. Click **Form View** on the status bar to display the form in Form view, and then click **Quit** in the form (see Figure 24).

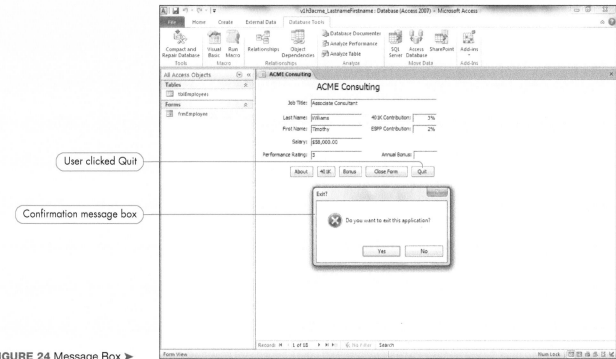

User clicked Quit

Confirmation message box

FIGURE 24 Message Box ➤

g. Click **No**.

The form and Access remain open.

h. Click **Quit** again, and then click **Yes** in the message box to close the database.

STEP 2 **CREATE AN IF...THEN...ELSE DECISION STRUCTURE**

Your next task is to create a procedure for the 401K button. You need to create an If...Then...Else decision structure to determine whether to add a 5% contribution to the existing percent for senior project managers or add a 3% contribution to the existing percent for other employees. Refer to Figure 25 as you complete Step 2.

```
Private Sub cmd401K_Click()
    'Declare three variables
    Dim cur401K As Currency
    Dim curSalary As Currency
    Dim sng401K As Single
    Dim strTitle As String

    ' Obtain values from text boxes on the form
    txtSalary.SetFocus
    curSalary = txtSalary.Text

    txt401K.SetFocus
    sng401K = Val(txt401K.Text) / 100
    If strTitle = "Senior Project Manager" Then
        sng401K = sng401K + 0.05
    Else
        sng401K = sng401K + 0.03
    End If

    ' Calculate and display the monthly 401K contribution
    cur401K = curSalary / 12 * sng401K
    MsgBox "Your monthly 401K contribution is: " _
        & Format(cur401K, "Currency"), vbInformation, "401K"
End Sub
```

FIGURE 25 If...Then...Else Statement ➤

Getting Started with VBA

41

a. Open the *v1h3acme_LastnameFirstname* database.

b. Open the VB Editor, and then display the code in the Code window.

c. Place the insertion point after the last variable declaration statement for the Sub cmd401K_Click() procedure, and then press **Enter** to start a new line.

d. Type **Dim strTitle As String** to declare a string variable.

e. Place the insertion point after the *sng401K = Val(txt401K.Text) / 100* statement, and then press **Enter**.

f. Type the If…Then…Else statement as shown in Figure 25. Click **Save**, and then close the VB Editor.

g. Click **Form View** on the status bar to display the form in Form view, and then click **401K** in the form.

   The current employee is an associate consultant. Therefore, the conditional expression is false. The procedure adds 3% to the current 401k contribution of 3% and then multiplies it by the salary and divides by 12. The result is $290.00.

h. Click **OK**, and then navigate to the fifth record in the form. Click **401K** again.

   Patricia is a senior project manager. Therefore, the conditional expression is true. The procedure adds 5% to the current 401k contribution of 2%. The result of 7% is multiplied by the salary and divided by 12. The result is $377.08.

i. Click **OK** to close the message box, and then click **Close Form**.

STEP 3 ▶ CREATE A SELECT CASE STRUCTURE

Anthony wants to create a set of rules to calculate employees' bonuses based on their respective performance ratings. A rating of 0 means no bonus. A rating of 1–3 earns a 5% bonus, a rating of 4–7 earns a 7.5% bonus, and a rating of 8–10 earns a 10% bonus. You will create a Select Case decision structure to identify the correct bonus rate and use that rate to calculate the bonus amount. Refer to Figure 26 as you complete Step 3.

```
Private Sub cmdBonus_Click()

    ' Declare variables
    Dim curSalary As Currency
    Dim intRating As Integer
    Dim sngBonus As Single
    Dim curBonus As Currency

    ' Obtain salary and performance rating
    txtSalary.SetFocus
    curSalary = txtSalary.Text

    txtRating.SetFocus
    intRating = txtRating.Text

    ' Calculate the bonus
    Select Case intRating
        Case Is = 0
            sngBonus = 0
        Case 1 To 3
            sngBonus = 0.05
        Case 4 To 7
            sngBonus = 0.075
        Case 8 To 10
            sngBonus = 0.1
    End Select

    ' Calculate the bonus and assign to the txtBonus text box
    curBonus = curSalary * sngBonus
    txtBonus.SetFocus
    txtBonus.Text = curBonus

End Sub
```

FIGURE 26 Select Case Structure ➤

Getting Started with VBA

a. Open the VB Editor again.

b. Position the insertion point after the last procedure's End Sub statement, and then press **Enter**. Type **Private Sub cmdBonus_Click**() and then press **Enter** twice.

c. Type the code shown in Figure 26.

    You declared four variables to store values. The second block of code sets the focus to text boxes to obtain their values and assign those values to two variables. The Select Case statement uses the performance rating to determine which bonus rate to select. The last block of code multiplies the selected bonus rate by the current salary, calculates the bonus, and then displays the bonus on the form.

d. Click **Save** on the toolbar, and then close the VB Editor.

e. Click **Form View** on the status bar to display the form in Form view, and then click **Bonus** in the form.

    The Bonus textbox displays $2,900 for the first employee. The performance rating of 3 qualifies Timothy for the 5% bonus rate. Five percent of his $58,000 salary equals his $2,900 bonus. This value is added to Timothy's record in the tblEmployees table (see Figure 27).

f. Close the form, close the database, and then exit Access.

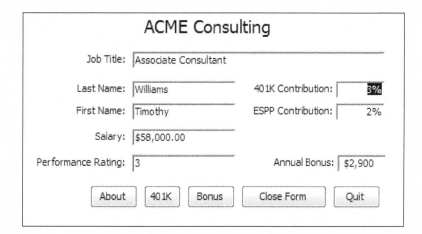

FIGURE 27 Results of the Select Case Structure ➤

TIP Assigning a Value to a Text Box

The procedures you have written to obtain a value from a text box use the SetFocus method to set the focus to the text box and then assign the text value to a variable. In this procedure, you assigned the value of a variable to the Text property of a text box by setting the focus to the text box, and then assigning the value of the variable to the Text property of the text box.

Repetition Structures

Sometimes ... you need to complete an operation a specific number of times while a certain condition is true or until a condition is true.

Programmers use decision structures when an application requires a program to analyze conditions. Sometimes, however, you need to complete an operation a specific number of times while a certain condition is true or until a condition is true. For example, a payroll application may need to calculate employee bonuses for all eligible employees. To accomplish this, you can use a *repetition structure*, which repeats the execution of a series of program statements. You can use two types of statements to define repetition structures: For...Next and Do...Loop.

In this section, you will learn how to use For...Next and Do...Loop repetition structures.

A **repetition structure** is one that repeats the execution of a series of statements at run time.

Using the For...Next Loop Statement

The **For...Next statement** is a repetition structure that repeats statements a specific number of times.

A **loop** is the set of statements that repeat for a repetition structure.

An **iteration** is one execution of a loop statement.

A **counter variable** is a variable used to count the number of times a loop repeats.

The **step value** is the number by which the counter is incremented or decremented during each iteration of the loop.

The *For...Next statement* repeats a *loop*—a set of statements or a procedure—a specific number of times. As the computer processes the statements, one execution of the loop is an *iteration*. When you use looping, which is the process of repeating a procedure until a condition is met, the statements repeat until the condition is true, until the condition is false, or until they have repeated for a specified number of times.

The For...Next statement requires a *counter variable*, which is used to count the number of times the loop repeats. The counter increases or decreases in value during each repetition of the loop. An increment is an increase in the value of the counter; a decrement is a decrease in the value of the counter. The start value is the value at which it begins incrementing. The end value is the final value of the counter. When the counter reaches this value, the loop ends. The *step value* is the amount by which the counter is incremented during each cycle of the loop. The step value, which is optional, can be positive or negative. If it is omitted, VBA supplies a default value of 1.

Code Window 20 shows an incrementing For...Next loop and a decrementing For...Next loop. In the first loop, the intCounter counter variable starts at 1 and ends at 5, incrementing by 1 each time. During each iteration, the loop produces a message box that displays the counter variable's value. After five iterations, the loop ends. In the second loop, the intCount counter variable starts at 5 and ends at 1, decreasing by 1 each time. During each iteration, the loop produces a message box that displays the counter variable's value. After five iterations, the loop ends. When one procedure uses two loops, you should declare two separate counter variables, each with its own name such as intCount and intCounter.

CODE WINDOW 20 ➤

```
' Counter increments by 1 each time
Dim intCounter As Integer
For intCounter = 1 To 5 Step 1
    MsgBox intCounter
Next

' Counter decrements by 1 each time
Dim intCount As Integer
For intCount = 5 To 1 Step -1
    MsgBox intCount
Next
```

> **TIP** Avoiding Infinite Loops
>
> As you create For...Next loops, it is important to consider under which conditions a loop will never reach the end value. For example, you could inadvertently add a statement that resets the counter, as shown in the following code statements:
>
> ```
> For intCounter = 1 To 4
>     strName = strName & InputBox("Please enter a name.")
>     intCounter = 1
> Next
> ```
>
> This loop is infinite, meaning that it will never reach the end value, because the counter value is reset to 1 during each iteration of the loop. Avoid introducing an infinite loop into your programs; this is considered a poor programming practice. Test your loops to make sure they will not run endlessly.

Using the Do...Loop Statement

For...Next loops are an appropriate choice when you know how many iterations the loop will require. However, sometimes, you do not know in advance when a loop will end because the loop will continue until a certain condition is met. Do...Loops are appropriate when you do not know in advance how many times you need to execute the statements in the loop. A *Do...Loop statement* differs from the For...Next structure in that it executes a block of statements while a condition remains true or *until* a condition is true. In either case, you do not define an end value for the loop. Do...Loop statements execute a series of statements an indefinite number of times, depending on the Boolean value of the condition. The Do...Loop structure uses the keywords *While* or *Until*.

The **Do...Loop statement** is a repetition structure that repeats designated statements as long as a condition is true or until a condition is satisfied.

Loop While a Condition Is True

Use the While keyword in a Do...Loop to repeat the iterations of the loop *while* the condition is true. VBA provides two ways to use the While keyword to check the condition: by specifying the condition *before* entering the loop or by checking for the condition *after* the loop runs. Because the loop performs a test to check for the condition, specifying the condition before entering the loop uses a *pretest* to test for the condition, and testing the condition after entering the loop uses a *posttest* to check the condition. In either case, looping continues for as long as the condition remains true.

A **pretest** performs the logical test first and executes the code within the loop if the test is true.

A **posttest** executes the code within the loop one time and then performs the logical test to determine if the loop iterates again.

Code Window 21 illustrates pretest and posttest Do While loop structures. In both examples, the loops iterate five times.

```
' Pretest Loop
Dim intCounter As Integer
intCounter = 1
Do While intCounter <= 5
    MsgBox "intCounter is " & intCounter, _
            vbInformation, "Do While Pretest"
    intCounter = intCounter + 1
Loop

' Posttest Loop
Dim intCount As Integer
intCount = 1
Do
    MsgBox "intCount is " & intCount, _
            vbInformation, "Do While Posttest"
    intCount = intCount + 1
Loop While intCount <= 5
```

CODE WINDOW 21 ➤

Loop Until a Condition Becomes True

Use the Until keyword in a Do...Loop to repeat the iterations of the loop *until* the specified condition evaluates to True. The structure is similar to the While keyword. As with the While keyword, you can check the condition before you enter the loop by using a pretest or after the loop has run at least once by using a posttest. In either case, looping continues until the condition evaluates to True.

Code Window 22 illustrates pretest and posttest Do Until loop structures. In the pretest loop, the logical test intCounter > 5 is False to start because intCounter starts at 1. The loop iterates until the logical test is true. After the fifth iteration, intCounter is 6. When the logical test is performed again, the condition is met and the loop does not iterate a sixth time. In the posttest loop, the loop iterates at least one time before performing the logical test. After the first iteration, intCount is 2, the logical test intCount > 5 is False, so the loop iterates again. After the fifth iteration, intCount is 6. When the logical test is performed again, the condition is met, and the loop does not iterate a sixth time.

```
' Pretest Loop
Dim intCounter As Integer
intCounter = 1
Do Until intCounter > 5
    MsgBox "intCounter is " & intCounter, _
            vbInformation, "Do Until Pretest"
    intCounter = intCounter + 1
Loop

' Posttest Loop
Dim intCount As Integer
intCount = 1
Do
    MsgBox "intCount is " & intCount, _
            vbInformation, "Do Until Posttest"
    intCount = intCount + 1
Loop Until intCount > 5

End Sub
```

HANDS-ON EXERCISES

4 Repetition Structures

McKynlee wants you to create two procedures in the Excel workbook to display cumulative monthly salary data. You will use the For...Next loop structure to create a procedure to show cumulative gross salary for a 12-month period. You will then use a Do...Loop structure to display cumulative gross salary, cumulative taxes, and cumulative net pay for a 12-month period.

Skills covered: Create a For...Next Loop • Create a Do While Loop

STEP 1 ▶ CREATE A FOR...NEXT LOOP

McKynlee wants a user to enter an employee's ID, look up the salary, and then display a message box that shows the cumulative salary for a 12-month period. You can copy some code you created in Hands-On Exercise 2 to find a salary for a particular ID. Then you need to create a For...Next repetition structure to store the data in a string and then display the string in a message box. Refer to Figure 28 as you complete Step 1.

```
(General)                                              DisplayMonthlySalary

Sub DisplayMonthlySalary()

    ' Declarations
    Dim curSalary As Currency
    Dim curGrossPay As Currency
    Dim intCounter As Integer
    Dim strMessage As String

    ' Set the active cell to A3
    Application.Goto Reference:="R3C1"

    ' Display input to get employee ID
    intID = Val(InputBox("Enter ID", "Find Employee's Data"))

    ' Use Find dialog box to find ID and then select respective salary
    Cells.Find(What:=intID, After:=ActiveCell, LookIn:=xlFormulas, LookAt:= _
        xlWhole, SearchOrder:=xlByColumns, SearchDirection:=xlNext, MatchCase:=False _
        , SearchFormat:=False).Activate
    ActiveCell.Offset(0, 5).Select
    curSalary = ActiveCell.Value

    ' Calculate monthly pay and display cumulative pay
    intCounter = 1
    curGrossPay = curSalary / 12

    For intCounter = 1 To 12
        strMessage = strMessage & vbCrLf & "Month: " & intCounter & " " _
                    & Format(curGrossPay * intCounter, "Currency")
    Next

    MsgBox strMessage, vbInformation, "Monthly Salary"

End Sub
```

FIGURE 28 For...Next Loop Structure ➤

a. Open *v1h2acme_LastnameFirstname.xlsm* in Excel, save it as **v1h4acme_LastnameFirstname.xlsm**, and then open the VB Editor.

b. Position the insertion point before the Sub CalculateBonus() statement. Type **Sub DisplayMonthlySalary()** and then press **Enter** twice.

c. Type the declarations comment and the four declarations shown in Figure 28.

d. Scroll to the CalculateBonus() procedure, start selecting with the comment *Set the active cell to A3* through *curFindSalary = ActiveCell.Value*. Copy the selected statements, and then paste them after the declarations in the Sub DisplayMonthlySalary() procedure.

You copied the statements that set cell A3 as the active cell, display a dialog box to enable the user to find an ID, locate the respective salary for that ID, and then save it in a variable.

e. Change *curFindSalary* to **curSalary** in the copied procedure statement.

   The CalculateBonus() procedure declared and used a variable named curFindSalary. However, you need to edit the variable name in the current procedure, which uses curSalary as a variable name instead.

f. Click at the end of the curSalary statement, press **Enter** twice, and then type the rest of the code shown in Figure 28.

   The code initializes the counter variable, intCounter, to 1 and then divides the annual salary by 12 to get a monthly salary. The For...Next loop adds to the existing string, which accumulates during each iteration. The vbCrLf inserts a carriage return within the string, adds the text Month, and enters the current counter variable's value. The monthly salary is multiplied by the current loop's iteration for the month number, formats the value as currency and adds that to the string. After the twelfth iteration, the loop ends, and a message box displays the cumulative salary by month. You indented the carryover line for the strMessage assignment statement so that the & is below the first character on the right side of the assignment operator = so that the variable name stands out.

g. Click **Save** on the toolbar, click **Run** on the toolbar, and then select **Run Sub/UserForm**.

h. Type **38** in the **input box**, and then click **OK**.

   The procedure finds the ID containing 38, identifies and stores the respective salary ($60,000), and uses that salary to calculate the monthly pay and then calculate the cumulative pay for 12 months. The message box displays a string containing the entire 12-month data (see Figure 29).

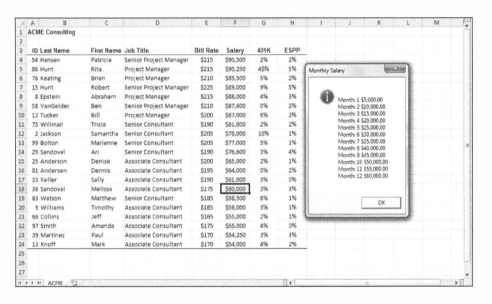

FIGURE 29 Results of For...Next Loop Structure ➤

i. Click **OK** in the message box.

STEP 2 ⟩ CREATE A DO WHILE LOOP

Anthony and McKynlee like the last procedure you wrote and want one that displays cumulative taxes and cumulative net pay. You will use the Do While repetition structure this time.

```
(General)                                          ▼  DisplayMonthlyDetails                          ▼

  Sub DisplayMonthlyDetails()

       ' Declarations
       Dim curSalary As Currency
       Dim curGrossPay As Currency
       Dim curTaxes As Currency
       Dim intCounter As Integer
       Const TaxRate As Single = 0.125
       strMessage = "Month" & vbTab & "Gross" & vbTab & "Taxes" & vbTab & "Net"

       ' Set the active cell to A3 and displays input to get ID
       Application.Goto Reference:="R3C1"
       intID = Val(InputBox("Enter ID", "Find Employee's Data"))

       ' Use Find dialog box to find ID and then select respective salary
       Cells.Find(What:=intID, After:=ActiveCell, LookIn:=xlFormulas, LookAt:= _
           xlWhole, SearchOrder:=xlByColumns, SearchDirection:=xlNext, MatchCase:=False _
           , SearchFormat:=False).Activate
       ActiveCell.Offset(0, 5).Select
       curSalary = ActiveCell.Value

       ' Calculate monthly pay, taxes, and net pay
       intCounter = 1
       curGrossPay = curSalary / 12
       curTaxes = curGrossPay * TaxRate
       curNetPay = curGrossPay - curTaxes

       ' Calculate, store, and display cumulative salary data
       Do While intCounter <= 12
           strMessage = strMessage & vbCrLf & intCounter & " " _
                       & vbTab & Format(curGrossPay * intCounter, "$#,###") _
                       & vbTab & Format(curTaxes * intCounter, "$#,###") _
                       & vbTab & Format(curNetPay * intCounter, "$#,###")
           intCounter = intCounter + 1
       Loop

       MsgBox strMessage, vbInformation, "Monthly Salary Details"

  End Sub
```

FIGURE 30 Do While Repetition Structure ➤

a. Display the VB Editor in Excel again, if necessary. Position the insertion point before the Sub DisplayMonthlySalary() statement, type **Sub DisplayMonthlyDetails** () and then press **Enter** twice.

b. Press **Tab**. Type ' **Declarations** and then press **Enter**. Type the four variable and one constant declaration statements shown in Figure 30.

c. Type the statement that assigns text to the strMessage variable as shown in Figure 30, and then press **Enter** twice.

   The assignment statement adds the words *Month*, *Gross*, *Taxes*, and *Net*. You use the vbTab character constant to insert tabs between the words within the string variable.

d. Select and copy the '*Set the active cell* comment through *curGrossPay = curSalary / 12* in the DisplayMonthlySalary procedure, and then paste it below the strMessage assignment statement in the DisplayMonthlyDetails procedure. Edit the first pasted comment; delete the second pasted comment and blank line as shown in Figure 30.

e. Position the insertion point after the *curGrossPay = curSalary / 12* statement, press **Enter**, and then type **curTaxes = curGrossPay * TaxRate**.

   This expression multiplies the employee's gross pay by the constant tax rate. The product is then stored in the curTaxes variable.

f. Press **Enter**, and then type **curNetPay = curGrossPay – curTaxes**.

   This expression subtracts the value in the curTaxes variable from the value in the curGrossPay variable. The result is then stored in the curNetPay variable.

g. Press **Enter** twice. Type ' **Calculate, store, and display cumulative salary data** and then press **Enter**.

h. Type the Do While statement block and the MsgBox statement shown in Figure 30.

The loop iterates 12 times, once for each month. The loop continues to add to the existing strMessage variable using the & concatenation character. The vbCrLf character constant inserts a carriage return to store each month's data on a separate line in the string variable.

For each iteration, the current intCounter's value is added to the string to indicate month 1, month 2, etc. The vbTab character constant inserts tabs between data. The Format function formats values with a custom Currency type: $#,### to avoid zeros for cents. The last line of the loop increments the counter.

After the loop terminates, the MsgBox statement displays the contents of the strMessage.

i. Click **Save**, and then run the DisplayMonthlyDetails procedure.

j. Type **38** in the **input box**, and then click **OK** (see Figure 31).

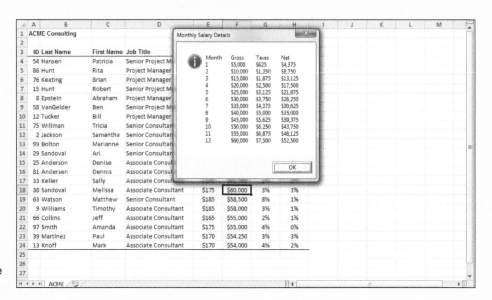

FIGURE 31 Result of Do While Repetition Structure ➤

k. Click **OK** in the message box, close the VB Editor, and then exit Excel.

CHAPTER OBJECTIVES REVIEW

After reading this chapter, you have accomplished the following objectives:

1. **Use the VBA interface.** The interface includes a menu bar and toolbar to select options and perform commands. The left side contains the Project Explorer, a window similar to Windows Explorer, in that it displays a hierarchy of objects for a particular project or file. Below the Project Explorer is the Properties window, which contains a list of properties or attributes for the selected object in the Project Explorer. The Visual Basic Editor is a text editor in which you create, modify, and view programming code in design time. When you execute a procedure, the program is in run time.

2. **Identify code in the Visual Basic Editor.** Procedures start with Sub and end with End Sub. Code between these points provides the instructions for executing an algorithm. VBA color-codes words: black for most code, blue for keywords, green for comments, and red for errors. Keywords are reserved by the system and can be used only for their intended purposes. Comments are non-executable code, but they provide descriptive documentation on what blocks of code do. Code is typically written with an object name in the form of a noun, followed by a period and an action that is performed on the object.

3. **Create procedures.** Procedures are classified as either sub procedures that programmers create or function procedures, which often require arguments to execute, similar to the Excel function PMT that requires at least three arguments.

4. **Create a message box.** A message box is a window that displays a message or information to the user, optional icons, and optional buttons. You can write a MsgBox statement or a MsgBox function. The difference is that the function returns an integer based on which button the user clicks. Message boxes can have an OK button, Yes/No buttons, or other combinations of buttons. In addition, you can display icons, such as the Critical icon or the Information icon.

5. **Get Help and debug errors.** The Help feature provides information to explain VBA programming syntax. Press F1 when the insertion point is within a keyword to obtain help about that particular keyword. In addition, you can display the Immediate window to run small portions of code to test its accuracy. Furthermore, you can use the Debug menu to run a program to detect and correct bugs or errors.

6. **Declare and use variables and constants.** While a program is running, it often needs to store values and text. Create constants for values that should not change during run time, such as a tax rate. Create variables for values that might change during run time. When you declare (create) a variable or constant, you specify a name and the data type. The data type is important in that it specifies what type of data (text, values, number of decimal points, etc.) that you can store in that variable or constant. With constants, you must also assign a value in the declaration statement.

7. **Create an input box.** To obtain data from a user during program execution, create an input box using the InputBox function. The function arguments include a message and a title. When the user enters data, the function returns a value. On the same line of code, you must assign that returned value to a variable or use it in some way. When the program asks for a value as input, enclose the InputBox function inside a Val function to convert the data into a numerical value.

8. **Perform calculations.** Procedures often include expressions, or mathematical statements that perform calculations. Expressions are similar to Excel formulas. Type the appropriate operators, and create expressions that build accurate results using the order of precedence rules. You can then use the Format function to format the results of the calculations onscreen.

9. **Use decision structures.** A decision structure is a programming structure that makes a comparison between program statements. After making the comparison, the structure selects the appropriate statements to execute. The If...Then statement performs a logical test and then performs an action if the result of the test is true. No specific action is taken if the statement is false. For more robust decision structures, use the If...Then...Else structure. This statement also provides statements to execute if the logical test is false. You can also create nested If...Then...Else statements for complex decisions. The Select...Case structure is also useful for complex decisions or when needing to perform a calculation if a value falls within a particular range.

10. **Perform data validation.** You can use If...Then...Else statements to check data entered by the user to ensure it is valid or falls within a particular range. The IsNumeric function checks data to determine if it is a value or not.

11. **Use logical operators.** Logical operators use Boolean logic to test conditions. Use the Or operator to test to see if at least one of two or more conditions is true. Use the And operator to test to see if *both* conditions are true.

12. **Use the For...Next loop statement.** Programs use loops for repetition structures. The For...Next loop uses a counter variable to count the number of iterations during the loop. The loop specifies a starting value, ending value, and step value. The body of the loop either increments or decrements the counter variable's value from the starting point until the ending point.

13. **Use the Do...Loop statement.** The Do While structure loops while a logical test is true. Once the test is false, the loop terminates. The Do Until structure loops until a statement becomes true; that is, it continues looping when a condition is not met. The Do While and Do Until loops are pretest loops. They test a condition upfront. If the conditions are not met, the statements in the loop never execute. On the other hand, the Do...Loop While and Do...Loop Until structures perform at least one loop before testing the condition.

KEY TERMS

And operator	Format function	Method	Property procedure
Argument	Function procedure	Module	Public procedure
Class module	If...Then statement	MsgBox function	Relational operator
Code window	If...Then...Else statement	MsgBox statement	Repetition structure
Comment	Immediate window	Object-oriented programming	Run time
Concatenate	Input box	language	Scope
Condition	InputBox function	Operator	Select Case statement
Constant	Integral data type	Or operator	Sequence structure
Counter variable	IsNumeric function	Order of precedence	Standard module
Data type	Iteration	Posttest	Step value
Data validation	Keyword	Pretest	Sub procedure
Decision structure	Line-continuation character	Private procedure	Syntax error
Declaration	Logical operator	Procedure	Val function
Design time	Logical test	Programming structure	Variable
Do...Loop statement	Loop	Project	Visual Basic for Applications
Event	Message box	Property	(VBA)
For...Next statement			

MULTIPLE CHOICE

1. VBA cannot be used:
   (a) To create code in Access.
   (b) To create stand-alone applications.
   (c) To create code in PowerPoint.
   (d) To create code in Excel.

2. Which of these components is not part of the VB Editor?
   (a) Expression Builder
   (b) Project Explorer
   (c) Properties Window
   (d) Immediate Window

3. Which statement should be used to create a procedure that can only be accessed from a specific object?
   (a) Public Sub MySubroutine
   (b) Const Sub MySubroutine
   (c) Private Sub MySubroutine
   (d) Sub MySubroutine

4. The difference between a MsgBox statement and an InputBox statement is:
   (a) InputBox allows the user to enter data.
   (b) MsgBox is easier to use.
   (c) Only InputBox can be customized.
   (d) No difference.

5. The purpose of declaring variables in VBA is:
   (a) To make it easier to debug the code at a later date.
   (b) Because it is required by VBA.
   (c) To follow standard programming techniques.
   (d) To use the variables later in calculations.

6. When creating VBA procedures, calculations in Excel and Access are:
   (a) Exactly the same in both applications.
   (b) Not the same because Excel has cells and Access does not.
   (c) Not the same because Access has records and Excel does not.
   (d) Slightly different because Access is object oriented.

7. Which statement can be used to determine which code to execute in a VBA procedure?
   (a) InputBox()
   (b) If...Next
   (c) Select Case...End Select
   (d) Else...Then

8. Which of these operations does not require a Do...Loop?
   (a) Repeating the same code 10 times.
   (b) Repeating the same code until a variable reaches a certain value.
   (c) Looping until a certain condition is met.
   (d) Adding two variables that are obtained from user input.

9. Data validation is used in all cases except:
   (a) Prohibiting incorrect data from being used in procedures.
   (b) Creating a procedure with the correct logic.
   (c) Ensuring only string variables are used.
   (d) Helping users catch data entry errors.

10. A For...Next loop:
    (a) Allows the code to execute from top to bottom.
    (b) Is required in all subroutines.
    (c) Can only be used when incrementing by 1.
    (d) Allows a section of the code to repeat x number of times.

1 Library Budget

You have been appointed to the executive board of your local library. As part of your duties, you need to create the budget for the next fiscal year. Using the previous year's budget worksheet, you decide to create a procedure that will ask for the percent increase (or decrease) from the previous year, and then create the next fiscal year's budget amounts. This exercise follows the same set of skills as used in Hands-On Exercises 1 and 2 in the chapter. Refer to Figures 32 and 33 as you complete this exercise.

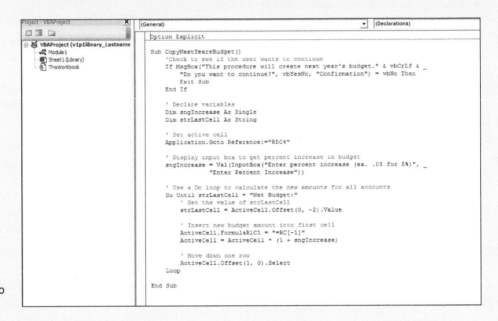

FIGURE 32 VBA Procedure to Calculate the New Budget ➤

FIGURE 33 New Budget after Running the VBA Procedure ➤

	A	B	C	D	E	F	G
1	Library Budget						
2							
3	Category	Account	2011	2012	2013	2014	
4	Revenue						
5		Federal Funding	$120,560	$126,588			
6		Real Estate Tax	$95,000	$99,750			
7		Local Fundraising	$27,800	$29,190			
8		Fees	$3,687	$3,871			
9		Total:	$247,047	$259,399			
10	Personnel						
11		Librarian	$45,000	$47,250			
12		Other Professionals	$25,000	$26,250			
13		Clerical Staff	$15,000	$15,750			
14		Custodians	$10,500	$11,025			
15		Benefits	$12,340	$12,957			
16		Total:	$107,840	$113,232			
17	Expenses						
18		Books	$50,500	$53,025			
19		Periodicals	$37,805	$39,695			
20		Audio/Video	$29,658	$31,141			
21		Insurance	$3,525	$3,701			
22		Utilities	$5,988	$6,287			
23		Maintenance	$7,500	$7,875			
24		Supplies	$2,965	$3,113			
25		Total:	$137,941	$144,838			
26							
27		Net Budget:	$1,266	$1,329			

Getting Started with VBA

a. Open the *v1p1library.xlsm* Excel workbook, and then save it as **v1p1library_ LastnameFirstname.xlsm**.

> **TROUBLESHOOTING:** If the Security Warning toolbar appears, click Enable Content.

b. Type =**C5*1.05** in **cell D5**, and then press **Enter**.
This represents a 5% increase in the Federal Funding account compared to the previous year.

c. Click the **Developer tab**, and then click **Visual Basic** in the Code group to open the VB Editor. You will create a VBA procedure to automate what you did in step b.

d. Type **Sub CopyNextYearsBudget()** in the Code window, and then press **Enter**. The End Sub statement appears, as shown in Code Window 23.

```
Sub CopyNextYearsBudget()

End Sub
```

CODE WINDOW 23 ▲

e. Type the code shown in Code Window 24 to verify that the user wants to continue.

```
Sub CopyNextYearsBudget()
    'Check to see if the user wants to continue
    If MsgBox("This procedure will create next year's budget." & vbCrLf & _
        "Do you want to continue?", vbYesNo, "Confirmation") = vbNo Then
        Exit Sub
    End If

End Sub
```

CODE WINDOW 24 ▲

f. Press **Enter**, and then type the code shown in Code Window 25. This code declares a variable, sets the active cell, obtains the percent increase in the budget from the user, and inserts the new amount into the first row.

```
Sub CopyNextYearsBudget()
    'Check to see if the user wants to continue
    If MsgBox("This procedure will create next year's budget." & vbCrLf & _
        "Do you want to continue?", vbYesNo, "Confirmation") = vbNo Then
        Exit Sub
    End If

    ' Declare variables
    Dim sngIncrease As Single

    ' Set active cell
    Application.Goto Reference:="R5C4"

    ' Display input box to get percent increase in budget
    sngIncrease = Val(InputBox("Enter percent increase (ex. .05 for 5%)", _
            "Enter Percent Increase"))

    ' Insert new budget amount into first cell
    ActiveCell.FormulaR1C1 = "=RC[-1]"
    ActiveCell = ActiveCell * (1 + sngIncrease)

End Sub
```

CODE WINDOW 25 ▲

Getting Started with VBA

g. Click **Save** on the toolbar, and then minimize the VB Editor. Type **0** in **cell D5** to reset the Federal Funding amount, and then click **VBA** in the taskbar to restore the VB Editor. Make sure the insertion point is within the CopyNextYearsBudget procedure you just created. Click **Run Sub/Userform** on the toolbar. Click **Yes** to confirm you want to continue, type **.05** in the **input box**, and then click **OK**.

Next, you will modify the procedure to calculate the new budget for all accounts.

h. Place the insertion point after the Dim sngIncrease As Single statement in the *Declare variables* section, and then press **Enter**. Type **Dim strLastCell As String**.

i. Place the insertion point below the *sngIncrease = Val(InputBox("Enter percent increase (ex. .05 for 5%)", "Enter Percent Increase"))* statement, and then press **Enter** twice. Type the remaining code as shown in Code Window 26 to create a Do...Loop that will calculate the new budget amounts for all accounts. Save the code.

```
Sub CopyNextYearsBudget()
    'Check to see if the user wants to continue
    If MsgBox("This procedure will create next year's budget." & vbCrLf & _
        "Do you want to continue?", vbYesNo, "Confirmation") = vbNo Then
        Exit Sub
    End If

    ' Declare variables
    Dim sngIncrease As Single
    Dim strLastCell As String

    ' Set active cell
    Application.Goto Reference:="R5C4"

    ' Display input box to get percent increase in budget
    sngIncrease = Val(InputBox("Enter percent increase (ex. .05 for 5%)", _
            "Enter Percent Increase"))

    ' Use a Do loop to calculate the new amounts for all accounts
    Do Until strLastCell = "Net Budget:"
        ' Set the value of strLastCell
        strLastCell = ActiveCell.Offset(0, -2).Value

        ' Insert new budget amount into first cell
        ActiveCell.FormulaR1C1 = "=RC[-1]"
        ActiveCell = ActiveCell * (1 + sngIncrease)

        ' Move down one row
        ActiveCell.Offset(1, 0).Select
    Loop

End Sub
```

CODE WINDOW 26 ⋀

j. Type **0** in **cell D5** in the worksheet to reset the Federal Funding amount. In the VB Editor, make sure the insertion point is within the CopyNextYearsBudget procedure you just created. Click **Run Sub/Userform** on the toolbar, click **Yes**, and then enter **.05** in the **input box**. Close the VB Editor.

k. Delete the zeros in **cells D10, D17,** and **D26**.

Sometimes, manual manipulation of a worksheet is still needed after a VBA procedure runs. Additional code could be added to remove the contents of these cells.

l. Compare your results to Figure 33.

m. Save the workbook, and then close Excel.

n. Submit the workbook based on your instructor's directions.

The owner of Zach's Coffee Shop needs your help creating an address for customer letters. Zach has a database that contains the addresses of all of his customers. He would like you to create a VBA procedure to create a mailing address that he can easily copy into a Word document. You decide to create a command button that will create the mailing address when clicked. This exercise follows the same set of skills as used in Hands-On Exercises 1 and 2 in the chapter. Refer to Figure 34 as you complete this exercise.

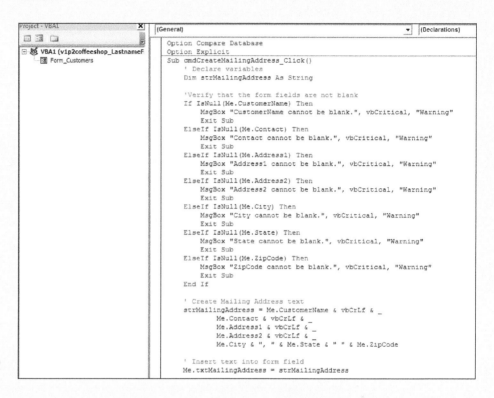

FIGURE 34 VBA Procedure to Create a Mailing Address ➤

a. Open *v1p2coffeeshop*. Click the **File tab**, click **Save Database As**, and then type **v1p2coffeeshop_LastnameFirstname**. Click **Save**. Enable the content.

b. Open the Customers form, and then click the **Create Address command button**. Nothing happens because the VBA code has not yet been created.

c. Click the **Create tab**, and then click **Visual Basic** in the Macros & Code group to open the VB Editor.

d. Press **F1**, and then type **Option Explicit** in the **search box**. Click **Search**. Review the purpose of the Option Explicit statement. Close the Help window.

e. Type **Option Compare Database**. Press **Enter**, and then type **Option Explicit**. Press **Enter**.

f. Type **Sub cmdCreateMailingAddress_Click**() and then press **Enter**. The End Sub statement appears as shown in Code Window 27.

```
Sub cmdCreateMailingAddress_Click()

End Sub
```

CODE WINDOW 27 ▲

g. Press **Tab**. Type **' Declare variables** and then press **Enter**. Type **Dim strMailingAddress As String** and then press **Enter** twice. Continue typing the remainder of the code as shown in Code Window 28. Press **Enter** and **Tab** as necessary to achieve the formatting shown.

```
Sub cmdCreateMailingAddress_Click()
    ' Declare variables
    Dim strMailingAddress As String

    'Verify that the form fields are not blank
    If IsNull(Me.CustomerName) Then
        MsgBox "CustomerName cannot be blank.", vbCritical, "Warning"
        Exit Sub
    ElseIf IsNull(Me.Contact) Then
        MsgBox "Contact cannot be blank.", vbCritical, "Warning"
        Exit Sub
    ElseIf IsNull(Me.Address1) Then
        MsgBox "Address1 cannot be blank.", vbCritical, "Warning"
        Exit Sub
    ElseIf IsNull(Me.Address2) Then
        MsgBox "Address2 cannot be blank.", vbCritical, "Warning"
        Exit Sub
    ElseIf IsNull(Me.City) Then
        MsgBox "City cannot be blank.", vbCritical, "Warning"
        Exit Sub
    ElseIf IsNull(Me.State) Then
        MsgBox "State cannot be blank.", vbCritical, "Warning"
        Exit Sub
    ElseIf IsNull(Me.ZipCode) Then
        MsgBox "ZipCode cannot be blank.", vbCritical, "Warning"
        Exit Sub
    End If

End Sub
```

CODE WINDOW 28 ᴧ

> h. Type ' **Create Mailing Address text** and then press **Enter**. Type **strMailingAddress =**
>   **Me.CustomerName & vbCrLf & _** and then press **Enter**. (The Me object enables you to choose the
>   field names from a list.)
>
> i. Press **Tab** twice. Type **Me.Contact & vbCrLf &** and then press **Enter**.
>
> j. Type the remaining address lines as shown in Code Window 29.

```
Sub cmdCreateMailingAddress_Click()
    ' Declare variables
    Dim strMailingAddress As String

    'Verify that the form fields are not blank
    If IsNull(Me.CustomerName) Then
        MsgBox "CustomerName cannot be blank.", vbCritical, "Warning"
        Exit Sub
    ElseIf IsNull(Me.Contact) Then
        MsgBox "Contact cannot be blank.", vbCritical, "Warning"
        Exit Sub
    ElseIf IsNull(Me.Address1) Then
        MsgBox "Address1 cannot be blank.", vbCritical, "Warning"
        Exit Sub
    ElseIf IsNull(Me.Address2) Then
        MsgBox "Address2 cannot be blank.", vbCritical, "Warning"
        Exit Sub
    ElseIf IsNull(Me.City) Then
        MsgBox "City cannot be blank.", vbCritical, "Warning"
        Exit Sub
    ElseIf IsNull(Me.State) Then
        MsgBox "State cannot be blank.", vbCritical, "Warning"
        Exit Sub
    ElseIf IsNull(Me.ZipCode) Then
        MsgBox "ZipCode cannot be blank.", vbCritical, "Warning"
        Exit Sub
    End If

    ' Create Mailing Address text
    strMailingAddress = Me.CustomerName & vbCrLf & _
            Me.Contact & vbCrLf & _
            Me.Address1 & vbCrLf & _
            Me.Address2 & vbCrLf & _
            Me.City & ", " & Me.State & " " & Me.ZipCode

    ' Insert text into form field
    Me.txtMailingAddress = strMailingAddress

End Sub
```

CODE WINDOW 29 ⬆

k. Click **Save** on the toolbar, and then minimize the VB Editor. Open the Customers form in Form view, and then click the **Create Address command button** to test the procedure. The Customer Name and Address appears in the text box at the bottom of the form.

l. Advance to the next Customer using the Record Navigation bar. The previous customer is still showing in the text box; this problem requires an additional VBA procedure.

m. Return to the VB Editor.

n. Place the insertion point after the End Sub statement, and then press **Enter**. Type **Sub Form_Current**() and then press **Enter**. Continue typing the remainder of the code as shown in Code Window 30.

```
Sub Form_Current()
    ' Clear the mailing address text box for each new customer
    Me.txtMailingAddress = Null
End Sub
```

CODE WINDOW 30 ▲

o. Click **Save** on the toolbar. Minimize the VB Editor, and then click the **Create Address command button** to test the procedure. The Customer Name and Address appears in the text box at the bottom of the form. Advance to the next customer using the Record Navigation bar view and verify the previous customer is no longer showing in the text box.

p. Click the **Create Address command button** to test the procedure.

q. Save and close the form.

r. Exit Access.

s. Submit the database based on your instructor's directions.

MID-LEVEL EXERCISES

1 Food Service Company

A food service company needs to increase the price of its products based on category. Categories include Beverages, Condiments, Confections, etc. The company's database contains a list of products and the corresponding category for each product. You need to create a new VBA procedure to display the new price based on the category. Refer to Figure 35 as you complete this exercise.

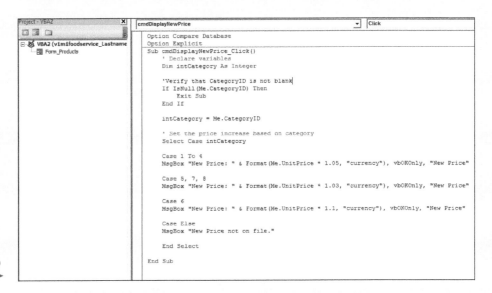

FIGURE 35 VBA Procedure to Count Products by Category ➤

a. Open *v1m1foodservice*. Save the database as **v1m1foodservice_LastnameFirstname**. Enable the content.

b. Open the Categories table and review the categories. Close the table.

c. Open the Products table and review the products. Take note that each product has a CategoryID designation. Close the table.

d. Open the Average Price query to review the average price of products in each category. Close the query.

e. Open the VB Editor.

f. Place the insertion point under *Option Compare Database*, type **Option Explicit** and then press **Enter**.

g. Type **Sub cmdDisplayNewPrice_Click()** and then press **Enter**.

h. Press **Tab**, type **' Declare variables** and then press **Enter**. Type **Dim intCategory As Integer** and then press **Enter** twice. Continue typing the remainder of the code shown in Code Window 31. This section establishes the VBA category variable.

```
Sub cmdDisplayNewPrice_Click()
    ' Declare variables
    Dim intCategory As Integer

    'Verify that CategoryID is not blank
    If IsNull(Me.CategoryID) Then
        Exit Sub
    End If

    intCategory = Me.CategoryID

End Sub
```

CODE WINDOW 31 ▲

Getting Started with VBA

i. Type ' and then set the price increase based on category. Type **Select Case intCategory** and then press **Enter**. Continue typing the code as shown in Code Window 32.

```
Sub cmdDisplayNewPrice_Click()
    ' Declare variables
    Dim intCategory As Integer

    'Verify that CategoryID is not blank
    If IsNull(Me.CategoryID) Then
        Exit Sub
    End If

    intCategory = Me.CategoryID

    ' Set the price increase based on category
    Select Case intCategory

    Case 1 To 4
    MsgBox "New Price: " & Format(Me.UnitPrice * 1.05, "currency"), vbOKOnly, "New Price"

    Case 5, 7, 8
    MsgBox "New Price: " & Format(Me.UnitPrice * 1.03, "currency"), vbOKOnly, "New Price"

    Case 6
    MsgBox "New Price: " & Format(Me.UnitPrice * 1.1, "currency"), vbOKOnly, "New Price"

    Case Else
    MsgBox "New Price not on file."

    End Select

End Sub
```

CODE WINDOW 32 ▲

j. Save the file. Open the Products form in Form view, and then click the **New Price command button** to test the procedure. The new price should appear in a message box. Use a calculator to verify the new price is correct.

k. Advance to the next record and test the New Price button again. Repeat for several more records.

DISCOVER

l. Create a new category in the Categories table, and then assign any product in the Products table to the new category. Test the New Price procedure to verify it displays the *New Price not on file* message.

m. Exit Access.

n. Submit the database based on your instructor's directions.

---

2 Loan Calculation

You are the manager of a used car dealership. You need to calculate loan payments for your customers. You are currently using an Excel worksheet to calculate payments, but you decide that a VBA procedure may allow your customers to calculate their own payments. Using the existing worksheet, you will write a new procedure that will collect information from the user and then provide the monthly payment. Refer to Figure 36 as you complete this exercise.

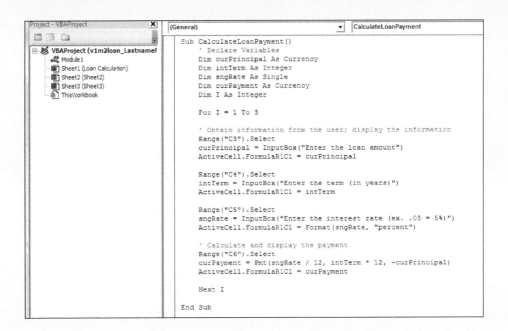

FIGURE 36 Loan Payment Procedure ➤

a. Open the *v1m2loan* workbook, and then save it as **v1m2loan_LastnameFirstname**. Enable the content.

b. Open the Visual Basic Editor. You will create a VBA procedure to automate the monthly loan payment shown in column B of the worksheet.

c. Type **Sub CalculateLoanPayment** () in the Code window, and then press **Enter**.

d. Press **Tab**. Type ' **Declare Variables** and then press **Enter**. Continue typing the remainder of the code as shown in Code Window 33 to set up the procedure's variables.

```
Sub CalculateLoanPayment()
    ' Declare Variables
    Dim curPrincipal As Currency
    Dim intTerm As Integer
    Dim sngRate As Single
    Dim curPayment As Currency
    Dim I As Integer

End Sub
```

CODE WINDOW 33 ▲

e. Type the lines of code shown in Code Window 34 to obtain the loan amount from the user. The code will enable the user to enter variables for three loans.

```
Sub CalculateLoanPayment()
    ' Declare Variables
    Dim curPrincipal As Currency
    Dim intTerm As Integer
    Dim sngRate As Single
    Dim curPayment As Currency
    Dim I As Integer

    For I = 1 To 3

    ' Obtain information from the user; display the information
    Range("C3").Select
    curPrincipal = InputBox("Enter the loan amount")
    ActiveCell.FormulaR1C1 = curPrincipal

    Range("C4").Select
    intTerm = InputBox("Enter the term (in years)")
    ActiveCell.FormulaR1C1 = intTerm

    Range("C5").Select
    sngRate = InputBox("Enter the interest rate (ex. .05 = 5%)")
    ActiveCell.FormulaR1C1 = Format(sngRate, "percent")

    ' Calculate and display the payment
    Range("C6").Select
    curPayment = Pmt(sngRate / 12, intTerm * 12, -curPrincipal)
    ActiveCell.FormulaR1C1 = curPayment

    Next I

End Sub
```

CODE WINDOW 34 ▲

f. Save the procedure. Run the procedure using the same amounts shown in column B of the Loan Payment Calculation worksheet. Verify the payment in column C matches the payment in column B. Enter a different interest rate or term when the procedure repeats two or more times.

g. Remove the period in the **Range("C3").Select** statement to see how VBA handles an error. Click **Run** on the toolbar. When the code stops at the error, type the period again, and then click **Run** again.

h. Save the workbook, and then close Excel.

DISCOVER

i. Submit the workbook based on your instructor's directions.

CAPSTONE EXERCISE

You work as a sales manager of a local real estate company. The sales agents are responsible for entering key data into the computer whenever they list or sell a property. You decide to display some key statistics about each property whenever the employee clicks a command button. As you complete this project, make sure the procedure "works" after each step and again at the end of the project.

Setup the Database

You need to save a database with a new name, and then enable the content to start this capstone exercise. You will then create a new form and add a command button.

a. Open the *v1c1homes* database.

b. Save the database as **v1c1homes_LastnameFirstname**, and then enable the content.

c. Select the Properties table.

d. Create a new form. Save the form as **Properties**.

e. Switch to Design view. Add a button under the Roof field in the Properties form. Cancel the Command Button Wizard when it opens.

f. Open the Property Sheet, and then change the Name property of the button to **cmdCheckKeyStatistics**. (*Hint*: To open the Property Sheet, double-click the button.)

g. Change the Caption property of the button to **Key Statistics**.

h. Save the form.

Test the Command Button

You need to test the new command button using the MsgBox statement. Add a procedure in Visual Basic to verify the command button is working.

a. With the Key Statistics button selected, click the **Event tab** on the Property Sheet, and then click **On Click Event**.

b. Click **Build**, select **Code Builder** from the Choose Builder dialog box, and then click **OK**.

c. A new subroutine, *Sub cmdCheckKeyStatistics_Click()*, appears along with the End Sub statement. Add the statement **MsgBox "Test"** to the contents of the subroutine.

d. Save the code, and then minimize the VB Editor.

e. Switch to Form view, and then click **Key Statistics** to verify *Test* appears in a message box. Click **OK** to close the box.

f. Return to the VB Editor, and then remove the test MsgBox.

Declare Key Data Variables

You need to define six variables that are required for the key statistics calculations. Four variables are used to store the current record field data and two variables are used for calculations.

a. Add a comment that indicates ' **Declare Variables**.

b. Declare four variables to hold the form data: **datDateListed** as Date, **datDateSold** as Date, **curListPrice** as Currency, **curSalePrice** as Currency.

c. Declare two variables to hold the calculated data: **intDaysOnMarket** as Integer, **curSalePriceDiscount** as Currency.

d. Declare the **strYourName** as String variable.

e. Declare two Boolean variables: **blnInvalidFlag1** and **blnInvalidFlag2**.

f. Compare your work to Code Window 35.

```
Sub cmdCheckKeyStatistics_Click()
    ' Declare Variables
    Dim datDateListed As Date
    Dim datDateSold As Date
    Dim curListPrice As Currency
    Dim curSalePrice As Currency
    Dim intDaysOnMarket As Integer
    Dim curSalePriceDiscount As Currency
    Dim strYourName As String
    Dim blnInvalidFlag1 As Boolean
    Dim blnInvalidFlag2 As Boolean

End Sub
```

CODE WINDOW 35 ▲

Check for Data and Set Key Data Variables

You need to ensure that data exists in the four form fields and then set the variables. If the form fields are blank, warn the user using a message box.

a. Add a comment that indicates ' **Check the form fields for data and then set the variables**.

b. Add the decision structure shown in Code Window 36 to verify and set the first variable. The decision structure contains the IsNull function, which determines if there is data in the form field. The code also contains the Exit Sub statement, which stops the procedure from running if any key data is blank.

```
Sub cmdCheckKeyStatistics_Click()
    ' Declare Variables
    Dim datDateListed As Date
    Dim datDateSold As Date
    Dim curListPrice As Currency
    Dim curSalePrice As Currency
    Dim intDaysOnMarket As Integer
    Dim curSalePriceDiscount As Currency
    Dim strYourName As String
    Dim blnInvalidFlag1 As Boolean
    Dim blnInvalidFlag2 As Boolean

    ' Check the form fields for data and then set the variables
    If IsNull(Me.DateListed) Then
        MsgBox "DateListed is blank." & vbCrLf & "Key statistics cannot be displayed.", _
                vbCritical, "Warning"
        Exit Sub
    Else
        datDateListed = Me.DateListed
    End If

End Sub
```

CODE WINDOW 36 ⋀

c. Press **Enter** twice, and then add three additional decision
    structures as shown in Code Window 37.

```
' Check the form fields for data and then set the variables
If IsNull(Me.DateListed) Then
    MsgBox "DateListed is blank." & vbCrLf & "Key statistics cannot be displayed.", _
            vbCritical, "Warning"
    Exit Sub
Else
    datDateListed = Me.DateListed
End If
If IsNull(Me.DateSold) Then
    MsgBox "DateSold is blank." & vbCrLf & "Key statistics cannot be displayed.", _
            vbCritical, "Warning"
    Exit Sub
Else
    datDateSold = Me.DateSold
End If
If IsNull(Me.ListPrice) Then
    MsgBox "ListPrice is blank." & vbCrLf & "Key statistics cannot be displayed.", _
            vbCritical, "Warning"
    Exit Sub
Else
    curListPrice = Me.ListPrice
End If
If IsNull(Me.SalePrice) Then
    MsgBox "SalePrice is blank." & vbCrLf & "Key statistics cannot be displayed.", _
            vbCritical, "Warning"
    Exit Sub
Else
    curSalePrice = Me.SalePrice
End If
```

CODE WINDOW 37 ⋀

Getting Started with VBA

66

d. Create an InputBox() that enables you to enter your name and then store the information in the strYourName variable.

e. Compare your statement to Code Window 38, and then save the code.

```
If IsNull(Me.SalePrice) Then
    MsgBox "SalePrice is blank." & vbCrLf & "Key statistics cannot be displayed.", _
            vbCritical, "Warning"
    Exit Sub
Else
    curSalePrice = Me.SalePrice
End If

' Ask for the user's name
strYourName = InputBox("Enter your name", "Information required")
```

CODE WINDOW 38 ▲

f. Test the code by clicking the command button on the form. Try a variety of conditions by advancing forward to a different record.

Perform Calculations and Display the Key Statistics

If all the key fields have data, display the key statistics using a message box.

a. Add a comment that indicates ' **Perform the calculations; display the Key Statistics using a Message Box**.

b. Add the calculations shown in Code Window 39.

```
' Ask for the user's name
strYourName = InputBox("Enter your name", "Information required")

' Perform the calculations; display the Key Stastistics using a Message Box
intDaysOnMarket = datDateSold - datDateListed
curSalePriceDiscount = curListPrice - curSalePrice

' Display warning if invalid data exists
If intDaysOnMarket < 0 Then
    'Set invalid flag
    blnInvalidFlag1 = True
ElseIf curSalePriceDiscount < 0 Then
    'Set invalid flag
    blnInvalidFlag2 = True
End If
If blnInvalidFlag1 = True Or blnInvalidFlag2 = True Then
    MsgBox "Data is invalid. Check the raw data.", vbOKCancel, "Warning"
    Exit Sub
End If
```

CODE WINDOW 39 ▲

c. Display the key statistics to the user using a message box as shown in Code Window 40.

```
    If blnInvalidFlag1 = True Or blnInvalidFlag2 = True Then
        MsgBox "Data is invalid. Check the raw data.", vbOKCancel, "Warning"
        Exit Sub
    End If


    MsgBox "This property was on the market for " & intDaysOnMarket & _
            vbCrLf & "days when it was sold." & vbCrLf & _
            "It was sold for " & curSalePriceDiscount & _
            " less than " & vbCrLf & "the original price.", _
            vbOKOnly, "Key Statistics for " & strYourName

End Sub
```

CODE WINDOW 40 ⏶

d. Format the discount sale price as **Currency**.

e. Save the code.

f. Switch to Form view, and then test the code by clicking the command button on the form. Try a variety of conditions by advancing forward to several different records, including a record with a DateSold.

g. Close the database, and then exit Access.

h. Submit the database based on your instructor's directions.

Check for Scholarship Eligibility

GENERAL CASE

The *v1b1eligible* file contains student data from your local two-year college. The database contains a list of students who have applied for a tuition scholarship. You need to determine the eligibility for each student, and then display whether or not the student is eligible (or the reason why they are not). Open the *v1b1eligible* file, and then save the database as **v1b1eligible_LastnameFirstname**. Create a new form based on the Students table. Add a command button, and then create a subroutine that checks the scholarship eligibility of a student when clicked.

When creating the VBA code, declare the variables first, and then verify that the key fields contain data. Next, check to make sure that a student meets the following eligibility requirements: 1) resides in CA, 2) age <=24 as of 1/1/2011, 3) GPA > 2.50, and 4) application has been completed. If a student does not meet one of the requirements, display a message to the user that includes which requirement has not been met. Display a message when the command button is clicked if the student is eligible. Close the database. Submit based on your instructor's directions.

Case Sensitive Input

RESEARCH CASE

When using input boxes in VBA, you can create strings that function as security codes for users. For example, if only "Smith" and "Jones" are allowed to see certain data or run a certain program, you could ask the user to enter a security code (similar to a password). Open the *v1b2logical.xlsm* workbook, and then save it as **v1b2logical_LastnameFirstname.xlsm**. Open the VB Editor, and then run the two procedures. Enter a few responses to test the code. Is your input case sensitive? Run a search on the Internet and find out how to change the code so that it is NOT case sensitive. Modify the first procedure so the procedure enables the user to have three attempts. Save the workbook with any changes you make. Submit based on your instructor's directions.

Revise the Scholarship Database

IMPROVE CODE

You decide to review the scholarship database to see if you can improve the code. You decide that the message box text could be more efficient if the repeating phrases were assigned to constants. Open the *v1b3scholarship* file, and then save the database as **v1b3scholarship_LastnameFirstname**. Open the VBA code, and then review the message box components. Declare a new variable, and then assign the repeating text phrases to the new variable. Replace the text phrases in the message boxes with the new variable; join the phrase using the "&" character. Test your results and make corrections if necessary. Test the procedure further by introducing an error into the code. Insert a space between the first ElseIf statement so it becomes *Else If*. Click **Debug** in the toolbar, and then select **Compile** from the list. The compile process should stop at the Else If error. Correct the error, and then run the compile process again. Close the database. Submit based on your instructor's directions.

VBA

EXCEL AND VBA

Creating an Excel Application

CASE STUDY | Expert Financial Services

Expert Financial Services (EFS) offers an array of financial services, one of which is providing home mortgages. Several factors affect the interest rate EFS charges. In particular, the interest rate depends upon the amount borrowed and the length of time of the loan repayment. EFS offers fixed interest rates from 4.25% to 5.25% based on the term (10 to 30 years) and the loan amount ($100,000 to $500,000).

All loans have closing costs, which are fees paid to obtain and process the loan. The original fees paid vary based on the mortgage scenario. All EFS loans have a 2% origination fee and additional points that vary depending upon the loan term and the initial loan amount. Customers who open a personal investment account with EFS qualify for a discount on the origination fees.

Cassandra Wilson, vice president of EFS, asked you to oversee the design, development, and implementation of a custom Excel workbook for representing mortgage loan options to customers. Your job is to create a simple interface to manage customer information, loan details, loan repayment schedule, etc. You will finish creating a customer information form and write the VBA code behind it. Next, you will insert buttons and write VBA code on an instructions worksheet to enable users to efficiently use the application. In addition, Cassandra wants the application to show a loan repayment schedule that lists the monthly principal payment, interest payment, cumulative principal, and cumulative interest payments for each monthly payment until the loan is paid in full. Finally, you will create a Truth-in-Lending disclosure form that summarizes the amount to be financed (the principal), the total finance charge (cumulative interest payments), the total payments (principal and finance charge), the interest rate, the term, and the dates the first and last payments are due.

OBJECTIVES AFTER YOU READ THIS CHAPTER, YOU WILL BE ABLE TO:

1. Complete a software development life cycle
2. Use the Excel Object Model in VBA code
3. Create forms
4. Use financial functions

5. Create function procedures
6. Initialize, display, and close forms
7. Create or search a list in a worksheet
8. Prepare an application for distribution

From Chapter 2 of *Exploring Getting Started with VBA for Microsoft® Office 2010*, First Edition, Robert T. Grauer, Keith Mulbery, Keith Mast, Mary Anne Poatsy. Copyright © 2012 by Pearson Education, Inc. Published by Pearson Prentice Hall. All rights reserved.

Objects and Forms

You can use VBA to make programs more user-friendly and to automate repetitive tasks, such as calculating the principal and interest payments for the term of a loan. Before you customize an Excel workbook, it is a good practice to follow a structured application development process in which you define the application requirements, build the user interface, write the code procedures, and test and distribute the application.

... it is a good practice to follow a structured application development process....

As you develop a VBA application, you create and manipulate objects within a particular program, such as Excel. Therefore, you must understand how VBA works within the particular Microsoft Office program in order to design an application to run within that program. Often, application development includes building forms to obtain user information and interfaces to display results to the users.

In this section, you will learn about the system development life cycle, the Excel object model for creating VBA code, how to design forms, and how to write code for forms within Excel.

Completing a Software Development Life Cycle

Custom Excel applications use forms and built-in functions to solve business problems. For software developers, the process for planning, designing, testing, and implementing software is called the *software development life cycle (SDLC)*. To create custom applications, you need to determine the following:

The **software development life cycle (SDLC)** is a structured process for planning, designing, testing, and implementing an application.

- What information and instructions to obtain from the user
- How to manage and store user input
- How the applications act upon this information (calculations, data storage, and so on)
- How to return the program results to the user

Addressing these questions helps you design a custom application. Although the applications you customize in this chapter are relatively simple, getting into the practice of following the SDLC will help you as you learn to design more complex applications. The SDLC is a systematic methodology for planning, designing, and implementing applications that involves the following four steps:

1. Plan the application.
2. Design the user interface.
3. Write code to handle events.
4. Run and test the application to verify that it produces the intended results.

Plan the Application

Planning an application includes determining the inputs and outputs. Table 1 lists the inputs and outputs for this application.

TABLE 1 Inputs and Outputs	
Inputs	**Outputs**
Customer Information	Customer name and address, other pertinent information entered on a form and displayed in the Customer Information worksheet
Loan Principal, Rate, and Term	Monthly principal and interest (PI) Closing fees Loan repayment schedule Truth-in-Lending disclosure

Design the User Interface

The user interface includes all the controls that provide access to your application. Custom Excel applications often include forms for entering and editing data, and other controls, such as buttons for performing actions and navigating between worksheets or exiting the application. The EFS application includes four worksheets:

- **Instructions:** This worksheet (see Figure 1) displays instructions for entering customer and loan information, calculating the loan repayment schedule, and displaying the Truth-in-Lending disclosure. It also includes buttons and a custom menu for entering and displaying customer and loan information. You will write VBA procedures for each command button.

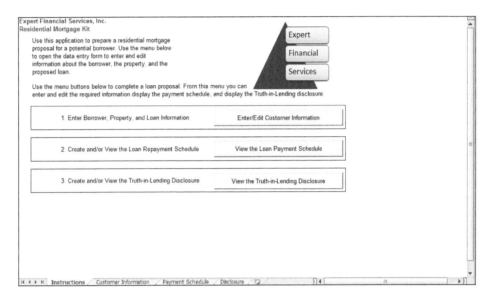

FIGURE 1 Instructions Worksheet ➤

- **Customer Information:** This worksheet (see Figure 2) stores information about the borrower, the address and location of the property, and other loan details. It also stores a Yes/No value indicating whether the borrower has opened or will open an investment account with EFS. The Customer Information worksheet has worksheet protection enabled so that users make changes to the worksheet by using the data entry form. The default values appearing in the form are $150,000 for the loan principal and a term of 30 years. The calculated interest rate for the default settings is 5.75%.

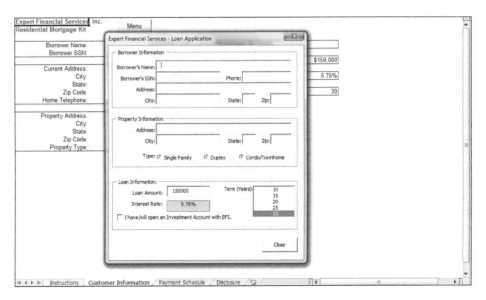

FIGURE 2 Customer Information Worksheet and Form ➤

Excel and VBA

- **Payment Schedule:** This worksheet (see Figure 3) lists the monthly principal payment, interest payment, cumulative principal, and cumulative interest payments for each monthly payment until the loan is paid in full. This worksheet is protected so that users cannot change it directly. However, users can click the Menu button to return to the Instructions worksheet.

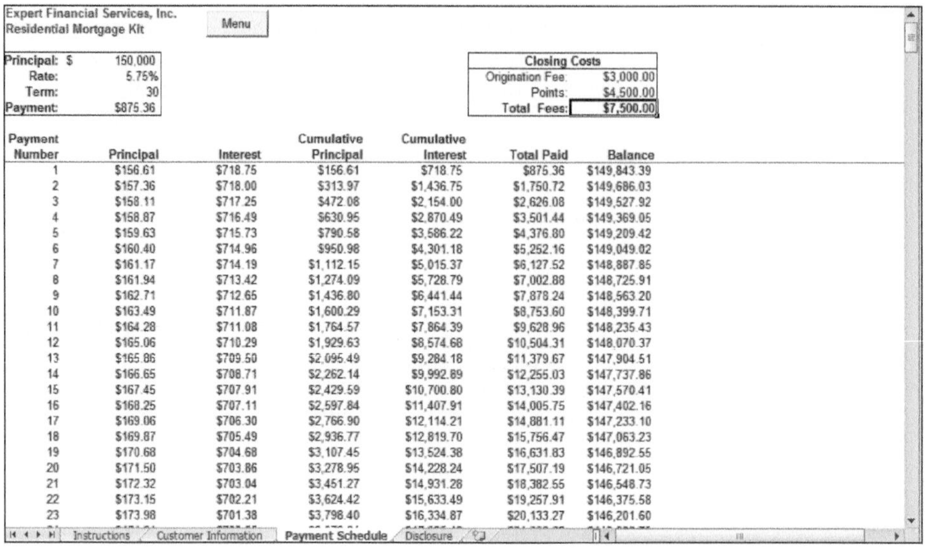

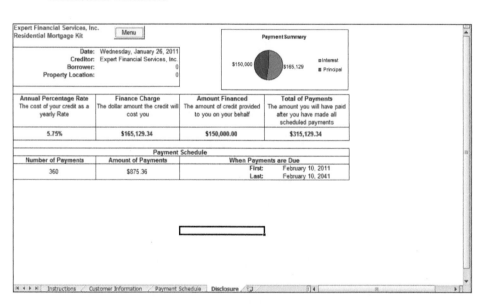

FIGURE 3 Payment Schedule
Worksheet ➤

- **Disclosure:** This worksheet (see Figure 4) summarizes the amount to be financed, the total finance charges, the total payments, the interest rate, the term, and the dates the first and last payments are due. Users can click the Menu button to return to the Instructions worksheet.

FIGURE 4 Disclosures
Worksheet ➤

Write the Code

The third step in designing an application is writing the VBA code procedures that handle events and perform actions. The procedures you create will be associated with each button's Click event and, in the case of the form for entering data, the Change events for two controls.

Excel and VBA

74

Run and Test the Application

After you write the procedures to handle the buttons' Click events, you are ready to run the application to test its accuracy. When testing a custom application, check for the following:

- **Usability:** the interface is intuitive and easy to use, controls are clearly labeled, and the flow of controls is easy to read
- **Accuracy:** the calculations produce correct values based on input values entered
- **Protection:** the application anticipates user events and protects the application from modification that adversely impacts its use

Test your applications thoroughly before distributing them. You can prepare test cases in which you define particular input values to enter to determine if the application produces the expected output. For example, if you are testing a payroll calculator program, you can test 40 hours at $10 per hour to see if the program produces the calculated output of $400.

Using the Excel Object Model in VBA Code

As you develop custom applications, you will work with numerous objects that are central to VBA. By definition, an *object* represents an element of the host application. Any part of the host application that you can identify as an entity or an element and therefore reference with a noun is an object. In Excel, objects can include worksheets, cells, charts, forms, etc. All code statements and the Excel objects that you reference in them fit into a logical framework called an *object model*. The object model organizes all objects into an object hierarchy, which defines how objects are related to one another. Objects in the hierarchy are organized in collections. A *collection* is a group of objects with similar characteristics and behaviors.

An **object** is an element, such as a worksheet cell, within a host application.

The **object model** is a framework that organizes objects into a hierarchy.

A **collection** is a group of objects with similar characteristics and behaviors.

Understand Object Hierarchy

Understanding how objects relate to one another is essential to working with VBA, because VBA statements refer to objects by name and in order according to their position in the object hierarchy. Figure 5 shows a workbook named Loan Calculator, which includes one worksheet named Payment.

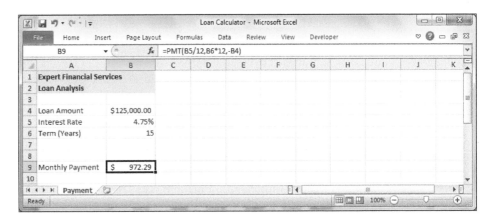

FIGURE 5 Loan Calculator Workbook ➤

Assume you are creating a VBA procedure that needs to obtain a value from the Payment worksheet. The worksheet is a member of the Worksheets collection. Therefore, you specify the Worksheets object with the worksheet object name enclosed in quotation marks within the parentheses. If you are working with two workbooks that both have a worksheet named Payment, you need to indicate which worksheet you want to manipulate, by indicating the name of the workbook. When you reference multiple objects in a hierarchy, the top-level object is referenced first. A period (dot) separates the object references. To refer to a specific cell or group of cells, use the Range object after the Workbooks and Worksheets objects.

The object highest in the hierarchy is the Application object. To reference every object in the hierarchy to which a specific cell belongs (such as a specific worksheet range), your code must include the Application object. Code Window 1 displays four statements that illustrate different levels of depth in referencing objects. To ensure the correct object is being used from the correct worksheet in a specific workbook, you can explicitly or directly state the entire hierarchy.

```
' Only one workbook open with a Payment worksheet
Worksheets ("Payment")

' Two or more workbooks open with a Payment worksheet
Workbooks("Loan Calculator.xlsx").Worksheets ("Payment")

' A range in a particular worksheet object
Workbooks("Loan Calculator.xlsx").Worksheets("Payment").Range ("B9")

' Explicit statement showing hierarchy
Application.Workbooks("Loan Calculator.xlsx").Worksheets("Payment").Range ("B9")
```

CODE WINDOW 1 ⮝

The way you reference an object depends on several factors. First, determine whether other objects in the application have a similar name. For example, referencing a cell range in a worksheet when two workbooks with different names are open and both workbooks have a worksheet with the same name requires an explicit or complete reference that names the workbook, the worksheet, and the range. If your object references omit any part of the hierarchy, Excel uses the active object. For that reason, most programmers do not include a reference to the Application object in code, because by default the application is running. The best principle is to keep your code as simple as possible, while also anticipating how the code will run when multiple workbooks might be open. The more explicit you are by specifying the hierarchy, the less the potential for conflicts, but more coding is required. Therefore, you should explicitly include as many elements in the hierarchy as you think the application will require for typical usage.

Manipulate Object Properties, Methods, and Events

You need to know about the characteristics of objects (properties), the actions that objects can perform (methods), and the actions that cause program statements to act upon objects (events). The first line of code in Code Window 2 shows how to write code to change the value in a range (cell B5) in a specific worksheet (Payment) in a specific workbook (Loan Calculator). The second line of code uses ActiveCell.Offset to move the active cell to the same row (0) and to the right one cell (1) and use the Activate method to activate that cell. The third line of code uses ActiveCell.FormulaR1C1 to assign the content of the variable strFirst to the active cell. The fourth line of code uses the Activate method to activate a specific worksheet (Customer Information). The last block of code applies several Font property values (Bold, Color, Name, and Size) to a selected range at one time.

```
' Assign a value of $150,000 to cell B5 of the active workbook
Workbook("Loan Calculator.xlsx").Worksheets("Payment").Range("B5").Value = 150000

' Move the active cell to the same row (0) and to the right by one cell (1)
ActiveCell.Offset(0, 1).Activate

' Assign a value stored in a variable to the active cell
ActiveCell.FormulaR1C1 = strFirst

' Use the Activate method to make a particular worksheet active
Worksheets("Customer Information").Activate

' Apply several attribute settings to a selected range
With Selection.Font
    .Bold = True
    .Color = -16776961
    .Name = "Calibri"
    .Size = 12
End With
```

CODE WINDOW 2 ▲

TIP Multiple Settings for One Property

In Code Window 2, several values are applied to the Font property (bold, color, font, and size). To apply several attribute values to the same range, you can use *With Selection* and *End With* and indent the specific lines. This approach keeps the code simpler without having to repeat *Selection.Font* for each individual property setting. The indented lines indicate all the properties being assigned values for the same selection. The indented lines start with a period and the name of the specific Font property, such as Bold. After the property name, such as Bold, type = and the value, such as True. To apply red color, use the Font Color property by typing *.Color = -16776961*.

- A property is an attribute of an object that defines one of the object's characteristics—such as size or color—or an aspect of its behavior—such as whether it is enabled or visible. To change an object's characteristics, you can use an assignment statement to set the value of a property. The object reference and property name are separated by a period, and an equal sign assigns a value to the property.
- A method is an action that an object can perform while the application is running. For example, *Worksheet* objects have an *Activate* method, which makes a specified worksheet the active sheet. *Range* objects have a *Clear* method, which clears all the cells in a range. VBA Help includes information about the properties and methods for specific objects.
- An event is an action occurring at run time that triggers a program instruction. Recall that VBA is an event-driven language in which program statements execute at run time to process information or perform actions in response to events. The code specifies what the object will do in response to the event. The system triggers some events, such as when a user opens a workbook. Users trigger other events, such as clicking the mouse or pressing a key.

TIP VBA Help

Use VBA Help to search for and find information on specific Excel objects and properties. You can use the table of contents within Help to find the section on the Microsoft Excel Object Model and read about specific objects, such as the Workbook object. Many Help screens show sample code.

Creating Forms

Some workbooks or worksheets provide an effective user interface by displaying controls, such as command buttons or list boxes, on specific worksheets. In the Windows environment, forms are an important component of a program's user interface. Custom Excel applications often include forms to obtain user input or to manage program functionality. VBA has an object model that is specific to forms. The Forms Object Model includes the objects and collections programmers use to create custom forms.

The UserForm object contains the Control collection, which manages the individual controls, such as buttons, text boxes, list boxes, and images that provide a form with its functionality. To add a UserForm object to an Excel workbook, click Insert on the VBA menu bar, and then select UserForm. By default, a UserForm is given the name *UserForm1* or another integer value if more than one form has been added to an application. Adding a UserForm to an application also opens the Control Toolbox so that you can add controls to your form. Figure 6 shows a new form added to the Loan Calculator macro-enabled workbook.

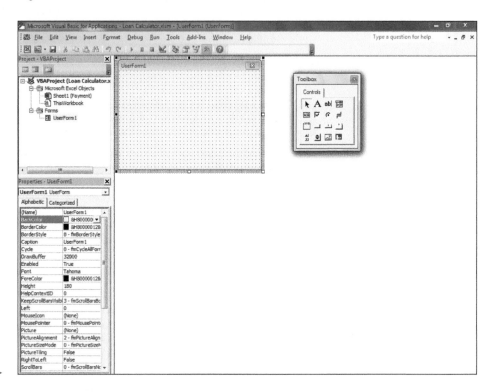

FIGURE 6 UserForm Object ➤

Set the Form Properties

After you insert a new UserForm object, you should set the form's properties. Most of the form properties control the appearance of the form. Figure 6 shows a form immediately after it was created. The Properties window reflects the original form property settings. Table 2 lists selected properties, their settings, and their purposes for the Expert Financial Services – Residential Loan Application form that you will create.

TABLE 2	Properties of the frmData UserForm	
Property	**Setting**	**Purpose**
Name	frmData	The name by which the form is referenced in code.
Caption	Expert Financial Services – Loan Application	The caption appearing in the form's title bar.
Height	369.75	The height of the form in points where 72 points create one vertical inch.
ShowModal	True	Sets the modality of the form. A modal form must be closed before control is returned to any other object in the application; a non-modal form allows other objects in the application to be activated while the form is open.
Width	333	The width of the form in points, where 72 points create one horizontal inch.

TIP Custom Forms

Technically, a custom form is an instance of the UserForm object. However, many developers refer to a UserForm simply as a form. The rest of this chapter uses the term *form* when referencing a UserForm object.

Add Controls to Forms

The **Toolbox** is a palette that contains the standard controls.

Forms usually contain controls for entering data, displaying information, or evoking events. You can add controls to a form using the *Toolbox*, which is a palette that contains the standard controls. Common form controls include labels, text boxes, buttons, list boxes, check boxes, options buttons, image control, etc. Each control provides specific functionality to a form. The Reference page lists the purpose of each standard control available in the Toolbox. Figure 7 shows a form with several common controls.

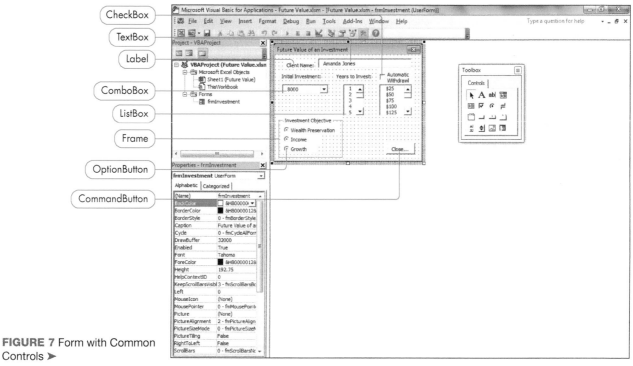

FIGURE 7 Form with Common Controls ➤

Excel and VBA

TIP Toolbox

You can use the View menu to display and hide the Toolbox. To show or hide the Toolbox, select Toolbox on the View menu to toggle it on or off. The Toolbox also toggles on and off depending on whether the form is selected; click the form's title bar to turn it on if it is hidden. Or, click Toolbox on the VBA window toolbar to show or hide the Toolbox.

To add a control to a form, click a control icon in the Toolbox, and then drag to create the control on the form. Use the sizing handles to resize the control. You can also adjust the alignment, spacing, and appearance of the control using commands on the Format menu.

REFERENCE

Control	Icon	Purpose
Select Objects	▸	Selects a control on a form. After you add a control to a form, use the Selection Tool to select the control to modify it.
Label	A	Appears as text on a form, usually for the purpose of identifying controls. Use this for text that the user will not change.
TextBox	abl	Appears as a box in which text can be entered and changed by the user. A text box is often bound to an object in the application (such as an Excel range).
ComboBox	▤	Combines the functionality of a list box and a text box. The user can either choose an item from the list or enter a value in the text box.
ListBox	▤	Displays a list of items from which the user can make a choice. If there are more items in the list than will fit in the control space, a scrollbar appears.
CheckBox	☑	Creates a square box that can be checked or unchecked, to indicate a yes/no condition or a selection.
OptionButton	◉	Displays a small circular button for toggling options on or off. When multiple option buttons (also called radio buttons) are used together, only one selection can be made (see frame).
ToggleButton	⇄	Displays a button for toggling (turning on or off) a selection.
Frame	☐	Displays a rectangular panel for grouping other controls. When option buttons are added to a frame, only one selection can be made.
CommandButton	⌐	Displays a button that evokes an event when clicked.
TabStrip	⊔	Displays tabs along the top of the window so that you can insert different controls on different tabs, similar to how the Page Setup dialog box in Excel has four tabs with each tab having a different set of controls.
MultiPage	⊔	Allows a form to store controls that appear on multiple pages in the form, much like a TabStrip control.
ScrollBar	≜	Enables you to change a set of continuous values using a horizontal or vertical bar. The values are changed by dragging the button appearing in the scrollbar.
SpinButton	≜	Increases and decreases values using up and down arrows. The values in the control are normally bound to a range in an Excel worksheet.
Image	🖾	Displays a bitmap graphic.
RefEdit	▣	Allows the user to select a range in a worksheet when the button is clicked.

Excel and VBA

Name Objects and Controls

The **Name property** is an object or control's attribute with which you reference that object in code.

An important property of all objects and controls is the Name property. The ***Name property*** of an object or control is what you use to reference the object in the program code. The naming scheme you choose for objects helps users understand the logical flow of an application.

You should make names long enough to be meaningful but short enough to be easily understood.

You should make names long enough to be meaningful but short enough to be easily understood. Unique names differentiate the objects in your application. Expressive names function as an aid to a human reader. You might want to use names that a reader can easily comprehend. The rules for naming objects are simple: The first character of the name must be an alphabetic character or an underscore. Most programmers follow a specific naming convention for Visual Basic objects so that the objects can easily be identified.

It is important to work by a standard so that the other programmers are familiar with the objects you create. The most common standard for naming controls in Visual Basic is Modified Hungarian Notation. This convention precedes the name of each instance of a control with a three-character prefix to the control and a descriptive title for the control. The three-character prefix appears in lowercase, and the descriptive title starts with an uppercase character. If the descriptive title has more than one word, CamelCase is used to differentiate the words, such as txtFirstName. Table 3 lists the Modified Hungarian Notation for naming conventions for common form controls.

TABLE 3	Naming Objects Using Hungarian Notation	
Object	**Prefix**	**Example**
Form	frm	frmClient
Command Button	cmd	cmdExit
Label	lbl	lblTitle
List Box	lst	lstInterestRate
Text Box	txt	txtFirstName
Combo Box	cbo	cboDays
Check Box	chk	chkSalariedEmployee
Option Button	opt	optTerm
Frame	fme	fmeLoan
Image	img	imgLogo

Change Property Controls

After you add a control to a form, use the Properties window to change the control's properties. When an object is active in VBA, you can view its properties by displaying the Properties window. You can open the Properties window using the View menu or by pressing F4. The Properties window displays the properties and current settings for the selected object. The Properties window in Figure 7 shows the associated properties of the Future Value of an Investment form.

By default, the properties are listed in alphabetical order, with the exception of the Name property, which appears at the top of the list in Alphabetic view. Click the Categorized tab to display the properties in categorical order, in which related properties are listed together.

Use Bound and Unbound Controls

A **bound control** is connected to a data source in the host application.

An **unbound control** is not connected to a data source in the host application.

A control can be either bound or unbound. A ***bound control*** is a control that is connected to a data source in the host application. In Excel, a bound control typically displays or changes the data in a worksheet cell or range. For example, a form might contain a text box for entering data and then assign the data to a worksheet range object. An ***unbound control*** is a control that is not connected to data in the host application. Labels are common examples of unbound controls because they do not store text that is changed by the user. Another example of an unbound control is the command button because it most often triggers events.

To bind controls to a worksheet range, you need to set the appropriate form properties. ListBox, ComboBox, and TextBox controls all have a ***ControlSource property*** that defines the cell to which the control is bound. VBA provides two ways to set control properties: the Properties window at design time or a code statement that executes at run time. To set the ControlSource property of a control using the Properties window, type the cell reference, such as A1 or D7, in the row for the ControlSource property. The column reference can be lower- or uppercase.

The **ControlSource property** is an attribute that defines the cell to which a control is bound.

You can set the ControlSource property for a control in code, by using an assignment statement that includes a reference to the object bound to a cell and the cell reference. The cell reference is enclosed in quotes, because the code statement refers to the cell as a string. Here's an example:

lstYears.ControlSource="B5"

The **RowSource property** specifies items through a worksheet range that will appear in a list box or combo box at run time.

ListBox and ComboBox controls have a ***RowSource property*** that specifies the range that contains a list of the items that will appear in the list box or combo box control at run time. You can set this property using either the Properties window at design time or in a code statement that executes at run time. The value of the RowSource property is a worksheet range, such as A1:B15, that contains the items that will populate the list. Valid settings include any worksheet range. Just like the ControlSource property, the column references in the RowSource property are not case-specific.

The Future Value worksheet contains a form with a ComboBox and two ListBox controls, all of which receive their values from specific worksheet ranges (in columns E, F, and G, respectively). Figure 8 displays the form at run time and, in the background, the worksheet ranges used to populate each list.

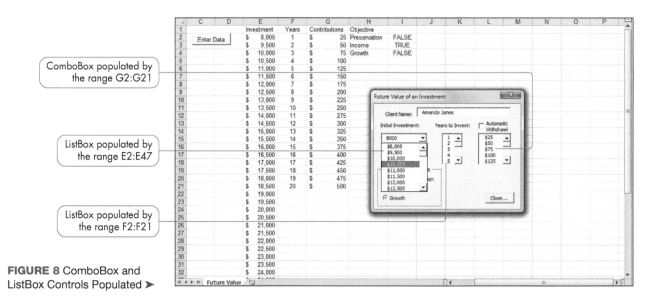

ComboBox populated by the range G2:G21

ListBox populated by the range E2:E47

ListBox populated by the range F2:F21

FIGURE 8 ComboBox and ListBox Controls Populated ➤

You can set the RowSource property for an object at design time using the Properties window, or at run time using program code. Code Window 3 shows three examples of code statements for setting the RowSource property for the controls.

```
cboInvestment.RowSource = "E2:E47"
lstYears.RowSource = "F2:F21"
lstContribution.RowSource = "G2:G21"
```

At times, you do not want a worksheet to display the values used to populate a list in a ListBox or ComboBox control, because displaying these ranges clutters the user interface. If the list obtains its value from a worksheet range, you can hide the worksheet column containing the range. You can also add items to a list at run time using the AddItem method in a code procedure. For example, a form can include a procedure to initialize the control with a list of items when the application loads the form into memory. Code Window 4 contains an example of an initialization procedure.

```
Sub Initialize_InvestmentForm()
' Populate the combo box and list box controls on the form
        cboInvestment.AddItem = "8000"
        cboInvestment.AddItem = "10000"
        cboInvestment.AddItem = "12000"
        cboInvestment.AddItem = "14000"
        cboInvestment.AddItem = "16000"

        lstYears.AddItem = "1"
        lstYears.AddItem = "2"
        lstYears.AddItem = "3"
        lstYears.AddItem = "4"
        lstYears.AddItem = "5"

        lstContribution.AddItem = "25"
        lstContribution.AddItem = "50"
        lstContribution.AddItem = "75"
        lstContribution.AddItem = "100"

End Sub
```

Set Other Control Properties

The EFS Residential Loan Application form (see Figure 9) contains frames, labels, text boxes, a check box, a list box, and a command button. After inserting the controls, you should set properties besides just the Name and Caption properties. Some important properties include Enabled, TabStop, TabIndex, and TextAlign.

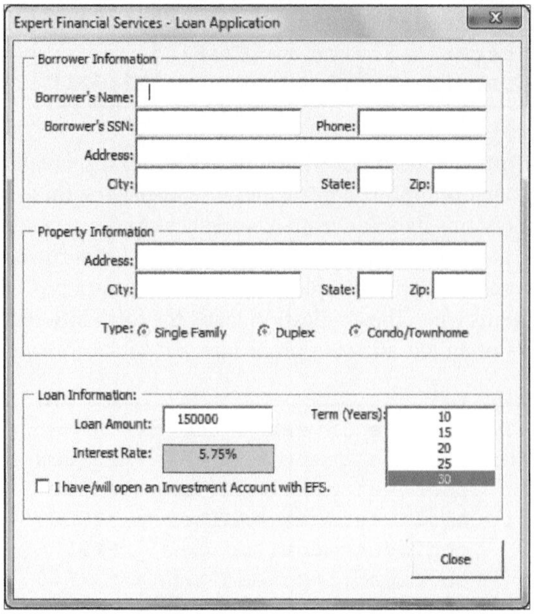

FIGURE 9 EFS Residential Loan Application Form ➤

The **Enabled property** has a value of True or False that determines whether a control can receive focus and respond to the user.

The *Enabled property* determines if a control can receive focus or attention and if that control can respond to the user. Commands on the Excel Ribbon exhibit Enabled status behavior. For example, the Enabled property of the Cut and Copy commands are set to False until you select something. After you select text, an image, or another object, the Enabled property of Cut and Copy changes to True. The following code shows how to disable a control's Enabled status:

```
cmdCut.Enabled=False
```

The **TabStop property** has a value of True or False that determines whether a control receives focus when the Tab key is pressed.

The **TabIndex property** determines the order in which a control receives the focus.

Controls on a form have two properties that determine the order in which the controls are activated as a user tabs through the form. The *TabStop property*, which accepts a value of True or False, determines whether the control receives the focus when the Tab key is pressed (True to receive the focus; False to skip the control when tabbing through the controls on the form). The *TabIndex property*, which accepts an integer value, determines the order in which a control receives the focus. A control with a TabIndex value of 0 receives the focus initially. The control with the next-highest value receives the focus when the Tab key is pressed.

The **TextAlign property** specifies the horizontal alignment of a caption appearing in a label.

The frame at the top of the form groups the controls for entering and editing information about the borrower. This frame has a Name property of fmeBorrowerInfo and a Caption property of Borrower Information. The TabStop property for the frame is set to True, and the TabIndex property is set to 0. The value of the *TextAlign property* specifies the alignment of the caption appearing in the label. Text box and list box controls have a Text property that you do not typically set in the Properties window. However, you can use the Text property in code to obtain the data entered in a text box or selected in a list box to assign those values to variables. You will do this in Hands-On Exercise 2. Table 4 lists the property settings for the controls on the frmData form.

TABLE 4	Properties for Controls in the Top Frame	
Control	**Property**	**Setting**
lblName	Caption	Borrower's Name:
txtName	TabStop TabIndex ControlSource	True 0 B4
lblSSN	Caption	Borrower's SSN:
txtSSN	TabStop TabIndex ControlSource	True 1 B5
lblAddress	Caption	Address:
txtAddress	TabStop TabIndex ControlSource	True 2 B7
lblCity	Caption	City:
txtCity	TabStop TabIndex ControlSource	True 3 B8
lblState	Caption	State:
txtState	TabStop TabIndex ControlSource	True 4 B9
lblZip	Caption	Zip:
txtZip	TabStop TabIndex ControlSource	True 5 B10
lblPhone	Caption	Phone:
txtPhone	TabStop TabIndex ControlSource	True 6 B11

The center frame groups the controls for entering and editing information about the property being financed. This frame has a Name property of fmePropertyInfo and a Caption property of Property Information. Table 5 lists the controls and properties used in the center frame on the form.

TABLE 5	Properties for Controls in the Center Frame	
Control	**Property**	**Setting**
lblAddress2	Caption	Address:
txtAddress2	TabStop TabIndex ControlSource	True 0 B13
lblCity2	Caption	City:
txtCity2	TabStop TabIndex ControlSource	True 1 B14
lblState2	Caption	State:
txtState2	TabStop TabIndex ControlSource	True 2 B15
lblZip2	Caption	Zip:
txtZip2	TabStop TabIndex ControlSource	True 3 B16
lblType	Caption	Type:
optSingle	Caption TabStop TabIndex ControlSource	Single Family True 4 B17
optDuplex	Caption TabStop TabIndex ControlSource	Duplex True 5 B17
optCondo	Caption TabStop TabIndex ControlSource	Condo/Townhome True 6 B17

TIP Option Buttons in Frames

When you place option buttons on a form, only one option button can be selected at a time. However, you can insert frames and then add option buttons inside the frame for different types of options. When you add option buttons inside a Frame control, only one option button within that frame can be selected at a time. Clicking an option button inside the frame changes that control's Value property to True. The Value property of the remaining option buttons in that frame is set to False.

The frame at the bottom of the form groups the controls for entering and editing information about the loan. This frame has a Name property of fmeLoanInfo and a Caption property of Loan Information. The TabStop property for the frame is set to True, and the TabIndex property is set to 2. Table 6 lists the controls and properties. This frame contains two Label controls for the interest rate. The first displays a descriptive label, and the second displays the calculated interest rate, which is determined by the loan amount (principal), loan term, and whether the applicant has opened or will open an investment account. You will create this frame, insert the controls, and set the properties in Hands-On Exercise 1.

Excel and VBA

TABLE 6	Properties for Controls in the Bottom Frame	
Control	**Property**	**Setting**
lblPrincipal	Caption	Loan Amount:
txtPrincipal	TabStop TabIndex ControlSource	True 0 F6
lblRate	Caption	Interest Rate:
lblRateValue	Caption BackColor BorderStyle TextAlign	None: Delete the default caption &H00FFFFC0& (Light Blue on the Color Palette) 1-fmBorderStyleSingle 2-fmTextAlignCenter
lblTerm	Caption	Term (Years):
lstTerm	BorderStyle ColumnWidths Height TabStop TabIndex TextAlign	0-fmBorderStyleNone 0.15 60 True 1 2-fmTextAlignCenter
chkAccount	Caption TabStop TabIndex Width	I have/will open an Investment Account with EFS. True 2 200

HANDS-ON EXERCISES

1 Objects and Forms

Cassandra's assistant created a workbook with the four main worksheets. In addition, she started to create the Residential Loan Application form. However, Cassandra asked you to finish creating the interface of the form.

Skills covered: Insert a Frame Control • Add Label and TextBox Controls • Insert ListBox, CheckBox, and Button Controls

---

STEP 1 ▶ INSERT A FRAME CONTROL

So far, the Residential Loan Application form contains the top two frames: Borrower Information and Property Information. The properties have been set to match the settings listed in Tables 4 and 5. You need to add the Loan Information frame and set its Name, Caption, Height, and Width properties. Refer to Figure 10 as you complete Step 1.

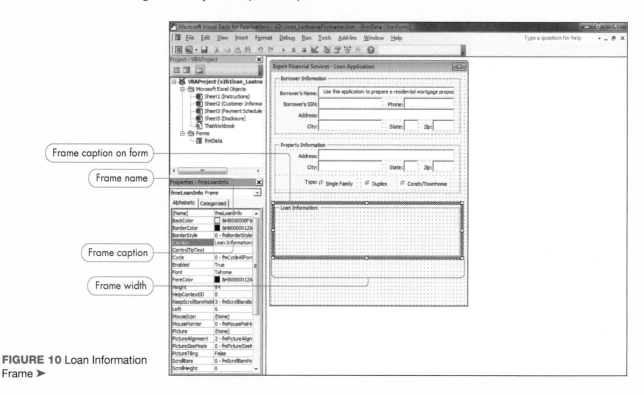

FIGURE 10 Loan Information Frame ▶

a. Start Excel, open *v2h1loan.xlsm* (an Excel macro-enabled workbook), and then save it as **v2h1loan_LastnameFirstname.xlsm**.

> **TROUBLESHOOTING:** If you make any major mistakes in this exercise, you can close the file, open *v2h1loan.xlsm* again, and then start this exercise over. If the Security Warning toolbar appears, click Enable Content.

b. Click the **Developer tab**, and then click **Visual Basic** in the Code group.

The VBA window opens and shows the worksheet names in the *Microsoft Excel Objects* section of the Project Explorer window. The Project Explorer window also shows a Forms folder.

Excel and VBA

88

c. Double-click **Forms** in the Project Explorer window, and then double-click **frmData** to display the Expert Financial Services – Residential Loan Application form.

The Borrower Information and Property Information frames are completed. You can select a control, such as the Phone label, and then verify that the property settings match those listed in Table 4 if you want.

> **TROUBLESHOOTING:** If you do not see the Toolbox, click View on the menu and make sure Toolbox is selected. If not, select it. If you still do not see the Toolbox, click the form's title bar.

d. Click **Frame** in the Toolbox, and then click about two dots below the second frame in the form to create a default-sized frame.

e. Select **Frame1** in the **Name property box** in the Properties window, and then type **fmeLoanInfo**.

> **TROUBLESHOOTING:** If you do not see the Properties window, click Properties Window on the toolbar or select View on the menu, and then select Properties Window.

You named the frame fmeLoanInfo to avoid a generic control name.

f. Select the text in the **Caption property box** in the Properties window, and then type **Loan Information:**

g. Scroll down the Properties window if necessary, select the existing value in the **Height property box**, and then type **84**.

You adjusted the height to be the same as the height of the second frame.

h. Scroll down the Properties window, select the existing value in the **Width property box**, and then type **312**. Press **Enter** to accept the new width.

You adjusted the width to be the same as the width of the first two frames.

i. Click **Save** on the toolbar.

STEP 2 ▶ ADD LABEL AND TEXTBOX CONTROLS

You need to add Label and TextBox controls for the loan amount and interest rate in the top-left corner of the Loan Information frame. As you insert the controls, you will set the properties. Refer to Figure 11 as you complete Step 2.

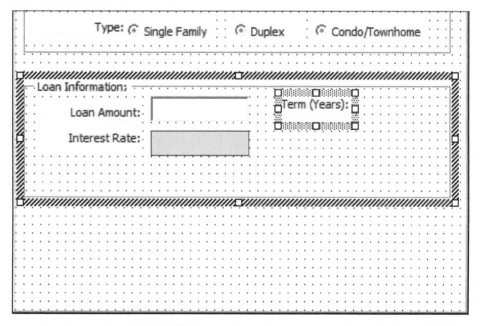

FIGURE 11 Label and TextBox Controls ➤

Excel and VBA

a. Click the border of the Loan Information frame in the form to ensure that it is selected.

> **TIP** Adding Controls to Frames
>
> When you want to group controls on a form, add the Frame control first, and then add the other controls to the frame. You can then reposition all the controls as a group within the frame.

b. Click **Label** in the Toolbox, and then click below the *Loan Information* caption in the frame.

VBA inserts a label within the selected frame.

c. Change the Name property to **lblPrincipal**, change the Caption to **Loan Amount:**, and then change the TextAlign to **3 – fmTextAlignRight**.

You inserted a Label control and set its properties.

d. Press and hold **Ctrl**, select the label you just created, and then drag down to create a copy below the original label.

The copied label shows the same caption and has the same TextAlign value, but you need to change the Name and Caption properties.

e. Change the Name property to **lblRate**, and then change the Caption to **Interest Rate:**

f. Click the Loan Information frame to select it, click **TextBox** in the Toolbox, and then click to the right of the *Loan Amount* label.

g. Change the Name property to **txtPrincipal**, and then set the TabStop, TabIndex, and ControlSource property values as specified in Table 6.

h. Insert a Label control below the TextBox control; change the Name property to **lblRateValue**; and then set the Caption, BackColor, BorderStyle, and TextAlign property values as specified in Table 6.

You inserted two labels for interest rates. The first displays a descriptive label, and the second displays the calculated interest rate, which is determined by the loan amount, loan term, and whether the applicant has opened or will open an investment account.

i. Insert a Label control to the right of the txtPrincipal control, change the Name property to **lblTerm**, change the Caption to **Term (Years):**, and then change the Width to **51**.

j. Click **Save** on the toolbar.

STEP 3 ▶ INSERT LISTBOX, CHECKBOX, AND BUTTON CONTROLS

To finish the Loan Information frame, you need to insert a ListBox control to list the terms, a CheckBox control for customers to verify they have or plan to open another account with EFS, and a CommandButton to close the form. Refer to Figure 12 as you complete Step 3.

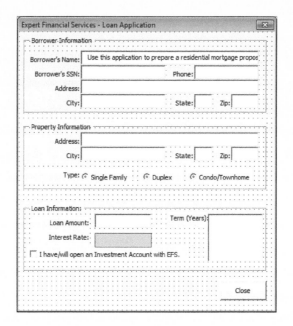

FIGURE 12 Completed
Form ➤

a. Select the outer border of the Loan Information frame in the form.

b. Click **ListBox** in the Toolbox, and then click to the right of the *Term* (*Years*) label. Set the Name property to **lstTerm**, and then set the other six properties as specified in Table 6.

> **TROUBLESHOOTING:** Make sure you type a lowercase l in the Name instead of the number 1.

c. Click **CheckBox** in the Toolbox, and then click below the *Interest Rate* label.

You inserted a CheckBox control in the bottom-left corner of the third frame.

d. Set the Name property to **chkAccount**, and then set the other property values as specified in Table 6. Increase the Width property setting, if necessary, to display the entire caption.

e. Click the form instead of the frame, click **CommandButton** in the Toolbox, and then click in the bottom-right corner of the form.

f. Change the Name property to **cmdClose**, change the Caption property to **Close**, and then change the Width property to **60**. Adjust the location of the button so that the right edge of the button is aligned with the right edge of the frames.

> **TROUBLESHOOTING:** If the window containing the form does not display the entire form, adjust the size of the window so that you can see the entire form. Otherwise, you might change the width of the wrong control.

g. Click the form to select it, and then change the Height property to **369.75**. If necessary, move the controls so that they fit within the form.

h. Save the form. Keep the workbook onscreen if you plan to continue with Hands-On Exercise 2. If not, close the workbook, and then exit Excel.

Functions and Forms

You have used implicit functions in VBA procedures. Implicit functions are predefined VBA functions. For example, the Val function converts a number stored as text into a numeric value for calculations, the Format function formats a value for display, the Input function displays a text box for user input, the MsgBox function displays information in a dialog box, and the IsNumeric function verifies that a value is a number. These are all examples of implicit functions, or functions that are a part of the VBA programming environment. Previously, you created sub procedures to perform actions. For example, you have created sub procedures to display message boxes. Function procedures, on the other hand, perform an action (such as obtaining user input and converting it to values) and return a value (such as calculating the monthly payment).

Microsoft Excel includes hundreds of worksheet functions you can use in your VBA statements. These functions are categorized by topics, such as Logical functions, Text functions, Date and Time functions, Statistical functions, Financial functions, etc. VBA also includes hundreds of implicit functions. By taking advantage of Excel workbook functions, VBA functions, and the custom functions you can create using VBA function procedures, your custom application can perform virtually any task.

> By taking advantage of ... VBA functions, ... your custom application can perform virtually any task.

In this section, you will learn how to use VBA functions and create custom functions. In addition, you will learn how to initialize, display, and close forms.

Using Financial Functions

Excel and VBA include a set of financial functions for performing calculations related to payments, investments, and the depreciation of assets. Excel includes a variety of financial functions. VBA includes 13 implicit financial functions, which are listed in Table 7.

TABLE 7 VBA Financial Functions	
Functions	**Purposes**
DDB, SLN, SYD	Calculates depreciation
FV	Calculates future value
Rate	Calculates an interest rate
IRR, MIRR	Calculates internal rate of return
NPer	Calculates number of periods
IPmt, Pmt, PPmt	Calculates payments
NPV, PV	Calculates present value

All of the VBA functions listed in Table 7 are available as Excel functions as well. The Pmt function calculates the payment for a given period of an annuity, based on periodic, fixed payments and a fixed interest rate. An annuity is a series of constant cash payments made over a continuous period. A residential mortgage is an example of an annuity. Excel and VBA have identical Pmt function syntax. The Rate, Periods, and Present Value arguments are required; the Future Value and Payment Type are optional.

When you add an Excel worksheet function to a cell, the required arguments (values) are typically stored in worksheet cells. The rate is divided by 12 to calculate the annual interest rate on a monthly basis. The term expressed in years is multiplied by 12 to calculate the number of monthly payments. In annuity functions, cash paid out (such as a loan granted to a borrower) is represented by negative numbers, so the cell containing the principal is preceded by a minus sign in the function argument. The Pmt function uses the values supplied by the arguments and returns the result in the cell containing the function. You can create a procedure in VBA to calculate the monthly payment as well (see Code Window 5).

```
Sub Calculate_Payment()
    ' Declare variables for the Principal, Rate, and Term
    Dim curPrincipal As Currency
    Dim sngRate As Single
    Dim intTerm As Integer
    Dim curPayment As Currency

    ' Assign values to the variables
    curPrincipal = 160000
    sngRate = 0.0645
    intTerm = 15

    ' Calculate the loan payment, and display the result
    curPayment = Pmt(sngRate / 12, intTerm * 12, -curPrincipal)

    ' Display the result
    MsgBox (Format(curPayment, "Currency"))

End Sub
```

CODE WINDOW 5 ▲

The Calculate_Payment procedure declares variables to store the principal, rate, term, and calculated payment values. The procedure then assigns values to the principal, rate, and term. The next statement uses the Pmt function and the values stored in the variables to calculate the loan payment (1389.38), which is assigned to the curPayment variable. A message box formats and displays this value as currency.

Creating Function Procedures

You can create function procedures in Excel with VBA. A function procedure begins with the *Function* statement and concludes with the *End Function* statement. They can receive arguments passed to the function by a procedure that calls the function. A procedure that calls a function is called the ***calling procedure***. One advantage of function procedures is that more than one procedure can call the function, so you can streamline your application by creating the procedure once, but calling it from multiple procedures. Code Window 6 illustrates a function procedure (LoanPayment) and the calling procedure (Loan_Payment).

A **calling procedure** is a statement within a procedure that calls or executes a function.

```
' Function to calculate the loan payment
Function LoanPayment(Principal, Rate, Term)

    LoanPayment = Principal * (Rate / (1 - (1 + Rate) ^ -Term))

End Function

' Calling procedure
Sub Loan_Payment()

    ' Declare variables
    Dim curPrincipal As Double
    Dim sngRate As Single
    Dim intTerm As Integer
    Dim curPayment As Currency

    ' Obtain input and assign to variables
    curPrincipal = Val(InputBox("Please enter the loan principal"))
    sngRate = Val(InputBox("Please enter the annual interest rate")) / 12
    intTerm = Val(InputBox("Please enter the term")) * 12

    ' Call the function and pass arguments to it
    curPayment = LoanPayment(curPrincipal, sngRate, intTerm)

    ' Format and display the results
    MsgBox ("The monthly payment is: " & Format(curPayment, "Currency"))

End Sub
```

CODE WINDOW 6 ⋀

The Loan_Payment sub procedure is the main procedure. It declares four variables, displays input boxes to obtain the values from the user, and converts the data to values before storing the values in the declared variables. Within two of the InputBox statements, the APR is divided by 12, and the term is multiplied by 12. The Loan_Payment sub procedure then calls the LoanPayment function and passes curPrincipal, sngRate, and intTerm to the function.

The LoanPayment function procedure receives the three arguments using the alias or similar names Principal, Rate, and Term. Often programmers use similar names for the argument names instead of identical names of the variables being passed to the argument. In this case, the function uses the name Principal instead of the original variable name curPrincipal. The function has one statement to calculate the loan payment. When the term and rate are expressed in monthly payment periods (the years multiplied by 12 months per year for the term and the annual interest divided by 12 months per year), the statement assigns the calculated result to the function name, LoanPayment. The LoanPayment function then returns that value back to the calling procedure in the Loan_Payment sub procedure.

The calling statement must do something with the returned value. In this case, it assigns the returned value to the curPayment variable. The Loan_Payment sub procedure then displays the formatted monthly payment in a message box.

If a user enters 160000 in the input box when prompted, 0.0645 in the input box that prompts for the interest rate, and 15 in the input box that prompts for the term, the resulting message box will display *The monthly payment is: $1,389.38.*

TIP Passing Arguments by Value and by Reference

You can pass arguments to procedures in two ways: by reference and by value. The default is by reference, which means that the value is passed by referencing the variable, and the procedure has access to the variable itself, and can potentially change its value. You can also pass arguments to a procedure by value, meaning that the procedure references a copy of the variable, and its value cannot be changed.

Initializing, Displaying, and Closing Forms

When you add custom forms, you decide how to display the form, when to close it, and how to set the initial values when the form opens. In the EFS loan application, you write code procedures to initialize, display, and close the form for entering borrower, property, and loan information. The form displays when the user clicks a button on the Instructions worksheet. The procedure that displays the form also initializes the application by activating the Customer Information worksheet, disabling the worksheet protection, and setting the initial values: $160,000 for the principal, 30 years for the term, and 5.75% as the interest rate. Changing the principal or the term calls a custom procedure that calculates the interest rate and displays the updated rate in the lblRateValue control. Closing the form enables the worksheet protection and activates the Instructions form.

Insert Controls on a Worksheet

In this project, the data entry form is launched from the Instructions worksheet. Therefore, this worksheet needs a control, such as a command button, so the user can open the form and initialize the application. The first task is to insert a button on the Instructions worksheet that displays and initializes the frmData user form. To insert a control, click the Developer tab, click Insert in the Controls group, and then click the icon for the type of control you want to insert.

When you add a control from the Control Toolbox to an Excel worksheet, the control is in Design mode, which enables you to edit the control. You can also display the Properties window for a control in Design mode. After you create a control, click Design Mode in the Controls group on the Developer tab to disable Design mode. You can then click a control to run its associated procedure.

Show, Hide, and Unload Forms

The command button that displays the data entry form handles a click event that opens the form from the Instructions worksheet. The form displays as a modal form. A modal form disables all other worksheet objects until the form is closed. All data entry and editing must be done while the form is open.

The *Show method* displays the form. The *Hide method* closes the form, but does not remove it from memory. If you use frmForm.Show again, the form will display with its previous values entered. To unload a form from memory, use the statement *Unload frmForm*, substituting the form's actual name.

If you want to initialize controls on the form when it loads into memory, do the following:

1. Display the code window.
2. Click the Object arrow at the top of the form, and then select UserForm. The Object shows the currently selected object for which you are coding. If you are unsure which

arrow is the Object arrow, position the mouse pointer of the arrow to display a ScreenTip, such as Object.

3. Click the Procedures or Methods arrow at the top of the form, and then select Initialize from the Methods list. When you position the mouse pointer over the Methods arrow, the ScreenTip displays *Procedure* or *Method*.

4. Initialize controls. For example, if you want to ensure previously entered data is cleared, you can adapt the following to clear a text box:

```
txtName.Text=""
```

2 Functions and Forms

For the EFS application, your next major tasks involve creating a procedure to calculate and display the interest rate, adding a command button on the Instructions worksheet, writing code procedures for Click events to initialize and display a form, and writing a code procedure for the event that closes the form.

Skills covered: Create a Function Procedure and Calling Procedure • Insert a Command Button on a Worksheet • Add Code Procedure to a Control • Add Code Procedure to Close a Form

---

STEP 1 ▶ CREATE A FUNCTION PROCEDURE AND CALLING PROCEDURE

You need to create a function procedure that calculates the interest rate based on the term or principal. If a term is 10 years or if the principal is greater than or equal to $500,000, the interest rate is 4.75%. If the term is 15 years or if the principal is greater than or equal to $400,000, the interest rate is 5%. If the term is 20 years or if the principal is greater than or equal to $300,000, the interest rate is 5.25%. If the term is 25 years or if the principal is greater than or equal to $200,000, the interest rate is 5.5%. All other terms or principal amounts require a 5.75% interest rate. After you create the function procedure, you will create a calling procedure.

a. Open the macro-enabled *v2h1loan_LastnameFirstname* workbook if you closed it at the end of Hands-On Exercise 1, save it as **v2h2loan_LastnameFirstname**, and then display the VBA window.

b. Right-click the **frmData form** in the Project Explorer, and then select **View Code**.

c. Type **Option Explicit** and then press **Enter** twice.

d. Use Code Window 7 to create the Calculate procedure. Remember to type a lowercase l not the number 1 in *lstTerm.Text*. Also remember to tab in the statements within the If…ElseIf statement block for readability.

```
Sub CalculateRate()
    ' Declare variables
    Dim curPrincipal As Currency
    Dim intTerm As Integer

    ' Obtain values
    curPrincipal = Val(frmData.txtPrincipal.Text)
    intTerm = Val(lstTerm.Text)

    ' Display interest rate
    If intTerm = 10 Or curPrincipal >= 500000 Then
        frmData.lblRateValue.Caption = "4.75%"
    ElseIf intTerm = 15 Or curPrincipal >= 400000 Then
        frmData.lblRateValue.Caption = "5.00%"
    ElseIf intTerm = 20 Or curPrincipal >= 300000 Then
        frmData.lblRateValue.Caption = "5.25%"
    ElseIf intTerm = 25 Or curPrincipal >= 200000 Then
        frmData.lblRateValue.Caption = "5.50%"
    Else
        frmData.lblRateValue.Caption = "5.75%"
    End If

End Sub
```

CODE WINDOW 7 ▶

Excel and VBA

The procedure declares two variables and uses the Text property of the text box and the list box controls to store the current values from the Text properties into the respective variables. You used an If…ElseIf statement block to handle the multiple logical tests. Each If and ElseIf test evaluated to see if either the term was equal to a value or if the principal was greater than or equal to a monetary value.

e. Use Code Window 8 to create the calling procedures.

```
Private Sub lstTerm_Click()

    CalculateRate

End Sub


Private Sub txtPrincipal_AfterUpdate()

    ' Declare string variable
    Dim strMessage As String
    strMessage = "Please enter a value between 100000 and 700000"

    'Validate entry
    If Val(frmData.txtPrincipal.Text) < 100000 Or _
       Val(frmData.txtPrincipal.Text) > 700000 Then
            MsgBox strMessage, vbCritical, "Invalid Loan Principal"
    End If

    CalculateRate

End Sub
```

CODE WINDOW 8 ▲

The procedure declares a string variable and then assigns text to it to avoid having a lot of extra text in the MsgBox statement. The code then checks to determine if the value entered is either too low or too high. If either condition exists, a message box displays an error to the user. The last statement calls the CalculateRate procedure.

> **TROUBLESHOOTING:** Remember to use the line-continuation (space and underscore) for long statements that carry over to a second line. If you forget the line-continuation character, a VBA error message will appear.

f. Click **Save** on the toolbar, and then close the VBA window.

 **TIP** Calling Procedures

A calling procedure can call a function procedure and receive a return value or call a sub procedure and perform an action. Programmers use calling procedures to minimize the amount of code. Creating a sub procedure that can be called by multiple procedures minimizes the amount of code required in your application.

You need to insert a command button on the Instructions worksheet, and then set its control properties. Refer to Figure 13 as you complete Step 2.

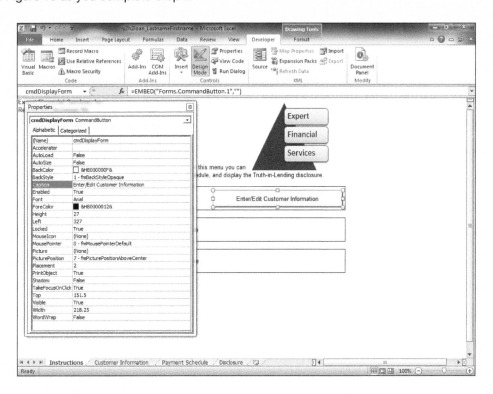

FIGURE 13 Command
Button ▶

a. Right-click the **Instructions sheet tab**, and then select **Unprotect Sheet**.

Excel prevents you from inserting controls on a protected worksheet. You must temporarily unprotect it to insert the control.

b. Click the **Developer tab**, and then click **Insert** in the Controls group.

c. Click **Command Button (ActiveX Control)** on the palette.

The mouse pointer looks like a plus sign.

> **TROUBLESHOOTING:** If you click Button (Form Control) instead of Command Button (ActiveX Control), you will not be able to code it correctly. You must delete the Button control, and then click Command Button (ActiveX Control) on the palette to create the correct type of button control.

d. Drag to create a command button to approximate the size and location shown in Figure 13.

e. Click **Properties** in the Controls group.

The Properties window displays so that you can set the properties for the selected command button. You can widen the Properties window, if needed, to see the property values better.

f. Set the Name property to **cmdDisplayForm**, and then set the Caption property to **Enter/Edit Customer Information**. Notice that the Enabled property is *True* so that the command button can react to a user clicking it.

g. Close the Properties window, and then save the workbook.

Excel and VBA

You need to write code procedure for the cmdDisplayForm command button control. The code will activate and unprotect the Customer Information sheet, populate a list box on the form, set initial values in the form, and then use worksheet data to complete the form. Refer to Figure 14 as you complete Step 3.

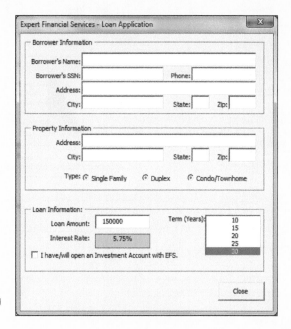

FIGURE 14 Form After Coding the Control ➤

a. Click **Design Mode** in the Controls group, if necessary, to activate Design mode.

b. Right-click the **Enter/Edit Customer Information command button** on the worksheet, and then select **View Code**.

VBA creates a procedure that handles the button's Click event.

c. Type the code shown in Code Window 9.

```vba
Private Sub cmdDisplayForm_Click()

    ' Activate the worksheet
    Worksheets("Customer Information").Activate
    Worksheets("Customer Information").Unprotect

    ' Clear and Populate the List Box
    frmData.lstTerm.Clear
    Dim intItem As Integer
    For intItem = 10 To 30 Step 5
        frmData.lstTerm.AddItem (intItem)
    Next

    ' Set the initial values
    If frmData.txtPrincipal.Text = "" Then
        frmData.txtPrincipal.Text = 150000
        Worksheets("Customer Information").Range("F6") = 150000
    End If

    If Worksheets("Customer Information").Range("F10") <> "" Then
        Dim intTerm As Integer
        intTerm = Val(Worksheets("Customer Information").Range("F10"))
    Else
        intTerm = 30
    End If

    Select Case intTerm
        Case 10
            frmData.lstTerm.Selected(0) = True
        Case 15
            frmData.lstTerm.Selected(1) = True
        Case 20
            frmData.lstTerm.Selected(2) = True
        Case 25
            frmData.lstTerm.Selected(3) = True
        Case 30
            frmData.lstTerm.Selected(4) = True
    End Select

    Worksheets("Customer Information").Range("F10") = intTerm
    frmData.txtName.SetFocus

    'Display the Form
    frmData.Show

End Sub
```

CODE WINDOW 9 ▲

The first two statements activate the Customer Information worksheet and then unprotect it so that the rest of the sub procedure can add data on the worksheet. You can use a repetition structure to add items to a list box at run time. In this case, the procedure for initializing a form uses a repetition structure and a selection structure. The For...Next loop populates the list box with a range of values from 10 to 30, at intervals of 5. The Select Case structure uses the value assigned to the intTerm variable to assign the value of True to the appropriate list box item so that it is selected. The frmData.Show statement displays the form onscreen.

d. Click **Save** on the toolbar, and then close the VBA window.

Excel and VBA

e. Click **Design Mode** in the Controls group on the Developer tab in Excel to deactivate Design mode.

f. Click the **Enter/Edit Customer Information button** to view the form. Click the **Close button** in the top-right corner of the form to close it. Save the workbook.

> TROUBLESHOOTING: If the form does not open when you click the command button, display the VBA window, and then check your code carefully. Make any necessary correction to the code, click Save in VBA, and then repeat step f again.

STEP 4 ▸ ADD CODE PROCEDURE TO CLOSE A FORM

You need to add a procedure to the Close button on the form so that it will close the form. In addition, you need to add a command button on the Customer Information worksheet to return to the Instructions worksheet. Refer to Figure 15 as you complete Step 4.

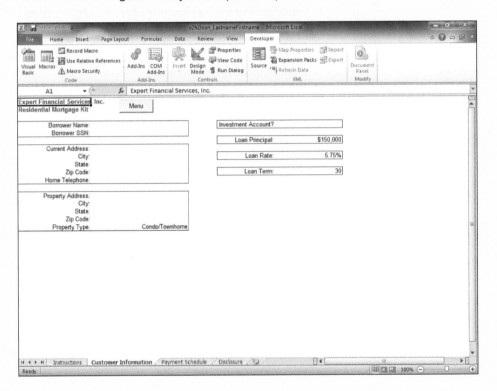

FIGURE 15 Customer Information Worksheet ▸

a. Open the VBA window, and then display the frmData form.

b. Right-click the **Close button**, and then select **View Code**.

c. Type the code shown in Code Window 10 between the Sub and End Sub statements.

```
Private Sub cmdClose_Click()
    ' Determine property type; add to worksheet
    If optSingle.Value = -1 Then
        Worksheets("Customer Information").Range("B17") = "Single Family"
    ElseIf optDuplex.Value = -1 Then
        Worksheets("Customer Information").Range("B17") = "Duplex"
    Else
        Worksheets("Customer Information").Range("B17") = "Condo/Townhome"
    End If

    ' Update interest rate, set protection, hide form
    Worksheets("Customer Information").Range("F8") = frmData.lblRateValue.Caption
    Worksheets("Customer Information").Protect
    frmData.Hide

End Sub
```

CODE WINDOW 10 ▲

The If…ElseIf statement determines which option button is selected. For each logical test, you compare a specific option button's Value property to –1, which is the value assigned by VBA to the selected option button. When a particular option button's Value property equals –1, a text entry will be entered in cell B17 on the Customer Information worksheet.

Next, the caption value in the lblRateValue control is then copied to cell F8 in the Customer Information worksheet. After the data is copied into cell F8, the procedure protects the Customer Information worksheet from further changes. Finally, the frmData.Hide statement hides the form but does not remove it from memory.

d. Save the code, and then minimize the VBA window.

e. Click **Insert** in the Controls group, and then click **Command Button (ActiveX Control)**.

f. Drag to create a command button control to the right side of the Expert Financial Services heading on the left side of the worksheet. Refer to Figure 15 for placement and size.

g. Click **Properties** in the Controls group. Set the Name property to **cmdReturn** and the Caption property to **Menu**.

h. Close the Properties window, right-click the **Menu button**, and then select **View Code**.

VBA creates the Private Sub cmdReturn_Click() and End Sub lines.

i. Press **Enter**, press **Tab**, type **Worksheets ("Instructions"). Activate**, and then press **Enter**. Save and close the VBA window.

j. Click **Design Mode** in the Controls group to deactivate Design mode.

k. Click the **Instructions sheet tab** to make it the active sheet. Click the **Enter/Edit Customer Information button** you created earlier. When the form opens, click **Close** in the bottom-right corner.

The form closes now that you have created a procedure for the Click event.

l. Click the **Menu button** you created at the top of the Customer Information worksheet.

The Click event procedure activates the Instructions worksheet again.

m. Save the workbook. Keep the workbook onscreen if you plan to continue with Hands-On Exercise 3. If not, close the workbook, and then exit Excel.

Excel and VBA

Loan Payment Schedule and Disclosure Worksheets

The loan payment schedule and disclosure worksheets are important to provide additional details about loans to EFS clients. To complete these worksheets, you will incorporate a variety of VBA statements that you have previously learned. For example, you will create procedures that use the object model, declare variables, initialize variables, create a repetition structure, call a custom function procedure, and return a value from a function back to the calling statement.

In this section, you will learn how to create a loan payment schedule using variables, If statements, repetition statements, financial functions, and the Excel object model. Furthermore, you will learn how to complete a loan disclosure worksheet that includes financial and date functions. Finally, you will complete the entire EFS application by setting workbook options to protect the worksheets against unauthorized data entry.

Creating or Searching a List in a Worksheet

Sometimes, it is important to write VBA code that creates a list or search within an existing list in a worksheet. For example, you might want to create an amortization table that lists each monthly payment's details for a particular loan. You can use a repetition structure (i.e., loop) to create a list where through each iteration, data is entered on the next blank line in the list.

A loan payment schedule provides information for each monthly payment until a loan is paid in full. When you make a residential mortgage payment, you pay the same amount each month, but the portion of the payment that applies to the loan principal varies each month. For the initial payments, a greater portion of each payment applies to the interest charged for the loan, but as the payments continue, a greater portion of the monthly payment applies to the outstanding loan principal. A loan repayment schedule is useful for displaying the details of each monthly payment and determining the outstanding balance at any time during the loan.

The EFS workbook includes the Payment Schedule worksheet to display the loan principal, term, rate, monthly payment, and closing costs. It also displays the following details for each monthly payment: the payment number, the amount of the monthly payment that applies to the loan principal, the amount of the monthly payment that applies to the loan interest, the principal paid to date, the interest paid to date, the total principal and interest paid to date, and the outstanding loan balance. Figure 16 displays the structure and sample data in the Payment Schedule worksheet.

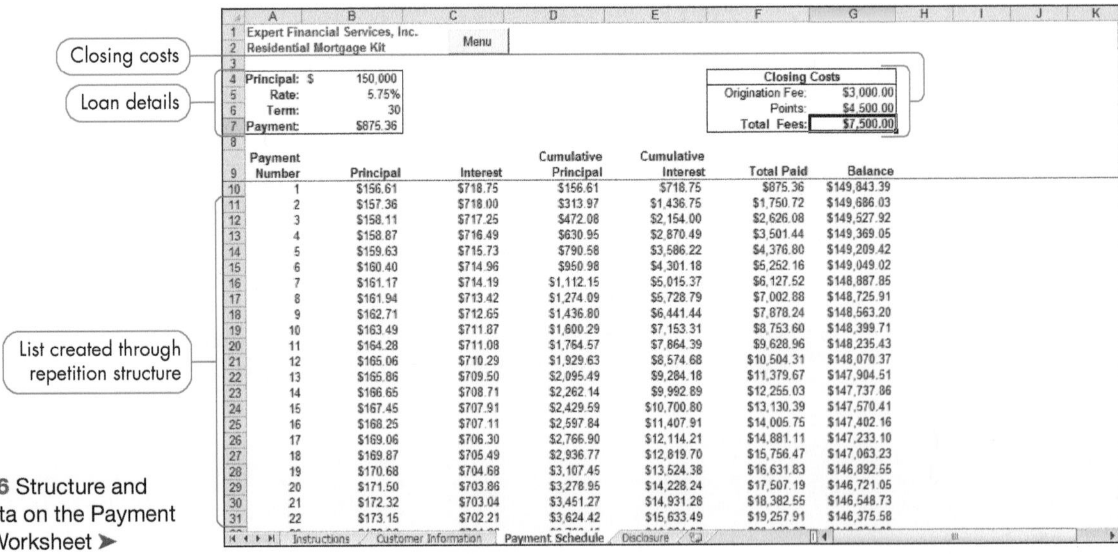

Payment Number	Principal	Interest	Cumulative Principal	Cumulative Interest	Total Paid	Balance
1	$156.61	$718.75	$156.61	$718.75	$875.36	$149,843.39
2	$157.36	$718.00	$313.97	$1,436.75	$1,750.72	$149,686.03
3	$158.11	$717.25	$472.08	$2,154.00	$2,626.08	$149,527.92
4	$158.87	$716.49	$630.95	$2,870.49	$3,501.44	$149,369.05
5	$159.63	$715.73	$790.58	$3,586.22	$4,376.80	$149,209.42
6	$160.40	$714.96	$950.98	$4,301.18	$5,252.16	$149,049.02
7	$161.17	$714.19	$1,112.15	$5,015.37	$6,127.52	$148,887.85
8	$161.94	$713.42	$1,274.09	$5,728.79	$7,002.88	$148,725.91
9	$162.71	$712.65	$1,436.80	$6,441.44	$7,878.24	$148,563.20
10	$163.49	$711.87	$1,600.29	$7,153.31	$8,753.60	$148,399.71
11	$164.28	$711.08	$1,764.57	$7,864.39	$9,628.96	$148,235.43
12	$165.06	$710.29	$1,929.63	$8,574.68	$10,504.31	$148,070.37
13	$165.86	$709.50	$2,095.49	$9,284.18	$11,379.67	$147,904.51
14	$166.65	$708.71	$2,262.14	$9,992.89	$12,255.03	$147,737.86
15	$167.45	$707.91	$2,429.59	$10,700.80	$13,130.39	$147,570.41
16	$168.25	$707.11	$2,597.84	$11,407.91	$14,005.75	$147,402.16
17	$169.06	$706.30	$2,766.90	$12,114.21	$14,881.11	$147,233.10
18	$169.87	$705.49	$2,936.77	$12,819.70	$15,756.47	$147,063.23
19	$170.68	$704.68	$3,107.45	$13,524.38	$16,631.83	$146,892.55
20	$171.50	$703.86	$3,278.95	$14,228.24	$17,507.19	$146,721.05
21	$172.32	$703.04	$3,451.27	$14,931.28	$18,382.55	$146,548.73
22	$173.15	$702.21	$3,624.42	$15,633.49	$19,257.91	$146,375.58

FIGURE 16 Structure and Sample Data on the Payment Schedule Worksheet ➤

The range B4:B7 summarizes the loan details. Because some of this information is already displayed on the Customer Information worksheet, you can use 3-D references to display the same information on this worksheet and the Pmt function to calculate the monthly payment. The range G5:G7 summarizes the closing costs, which include the loan origination fee (2% of the loan principal) and the loan points (which range from 1% to 3% of the loan principal) based upon the loan term. In addition, customers who currently have or plan to open an investment account with EFS receive a 1% discount on the loan points. The total closing cost is the sum of the origination fee and the points. These values can be calculated from the loan information displayed in cells B4 and B6 of the Payment Schedule worksheet, and cell F4 of the Customer Information worksheet, which displays TRUE if the customer has opened or will open an investment account and FALSE if the customer does not have an account.

Financial institutions are required by law to provide loan costs to customers. For residential home loans, the Truth-in-Lending disclosure statement summarizes the loan details so that the customers are aware of what the loan is costing them. The EFS loan application displays this information on the Disclosure worksheet shown in Figure 4 earlier in this chapter.

Preparing an Application for Distribution

When you create a custom application you should test its functionality before you distribute it. However, before testing the application, you should prepare the application for distribution. In the EFS application, the Instructions worksheet provides menu options for opening the data entry form, generating and displaying the payment schedule, and displaying the Truth-in-Lending disclosure. All data entry is through the form, and all the worksheets need to have protection set. In addition, the formula bar and row and column headings can be hidden to improve the user interface and prevent users from trying to make changes directly to worksheet cells.

Users have two methods of navigating the application interface: using the buttons to open and display the various application components or using the sheet tabs. Although the sheet tabs can be hidden, many Excel users prefer the sheet tabs to navigate through a workbook. The sheet tabs display the worksheets; to make changes to the loan scenario or customer information, users need to use the buttons on the Instructions worksheet. After you make the final changes to each worksheet, you can set worksheet protection and then test the worksheet.

TIP Hiding Excel Window Elements

When you create your own applications, you can hide the Formula Bar and row and column headings on an unprotected worksheet. To do this, click the File tab, and then click Options. Click Advanced, and then deselect the *Show formula bar* and the *Show row and column headers* check boxes. Click OK, and then protect the appropriate worksheets.

HANDS-ON EXERCISES

3 Loan Payment Schedule and Disclosure Worksheets

You need to insert command buttons with the respective sub procedures on the Information worksheet to view the loan payment schedule and the loan disclosure information. Finally, you will prepare the application for distribution.

Skills covered: Create Code to View the Loan Payment Schedule • Create Code to Activate the Instructions Worksheet • Add Formulas to the Disclosure Worksheet • Add a Button to Display the Disclosure Worksheet

STEP 1 ▶ CREATE CODE TO VIEW THE LOAN PAYMENT SCHEDULE

You need to insert a command button on the Instructions worksheet, set its control properties, and create a sub procedure to generate the payment schedule. Refer to Figure 17 as you complete Step 1.

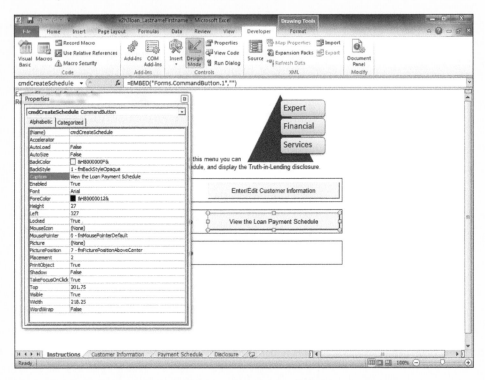

FIGURE 17 Button on Instructions Worksheet ➤

a. Open the *v2h2loan_LastnameFirstname* macro-enabled workbook if you closed it after Hands-On Exercise 2, and then save it as **v2h3loan_LastnameFirstname**.

> **TROUBLESHOOTING:** The Instructions worksheet should still be unprotected. If not, right-click the Instructions sheet tab, and then select Unprotect Sheet.

b. Click the **Instructions sheet tab** if necessary, click the **Developer tab**, and then click **Design Mode** in the Controls group.

c. Click the **Enter/Edit Customer Information command button** to select it, press and hold the left mouse button, press and hold **Ctrl**, and then drag to create a copy of the command button within the second border.

d. Make sure the second command button is selected. Click **Properties** in the Controls group. Type **cmdCreateSchedule** in the **Name property box**, and then type **View the Loan Payment Schedule** in the **Caption property box**. Close the Properties window, and then click **Save** on the toolbar.

Excel and VBA

e. Right-click the **View the Loan Payment Schedule command button**, and then select **View Code**.

> **TROUBLESHOOTING:** If you click View Code in the Controls group on the Developer tab, the VBA window shows existing code. It does not create a sub procedure for the button. If this happens, close the VBA window, right-click the button, and then select View Code.

VBA creates the Private Sub cmdCreateSchedule_Click() and End Sub lines.

f. Type the code shown in Code Window 11.

```
Private Sub cmdCreateSchedule_Click()

    ' Disable worksheet protection
    Worksheets("Payment Schedule").Unprotect

    ' Clear any previous schedules
    Worksheets("Payment Schedule").Range("A10:G369").Clear

    ' Declare variables for calculated values
    Dim intPayments As Integer
    Dim intStartRow As Integer
    Dim intCounter As Integer
    Dim curPrincipal As Currency
    Dim dblRate As Double
    Dim intTerm As Integer
    Dim curPpmt As Currency
    Dim curIpmt As Currency

    ' Obtain worksheet values to calculate and store other values
    intPayments = Worksheets("Payment Schedule").Range("B6") * 12
    curPrincipal = Worksheets("Payment Schedule").Range("B4")
    dblRate = Worksheets("Payment Schedule").Range("B5") / 12
```

CODE WINDOW 11 ▲

When a user clicks the Create Schedule command button, the Payment Schedule worksheet is unprotected so that it can clear a range of data. The procedure declares variables, and uses data on the worksheet to store in variables intPayments, curPrincipal, and dblRate. You will add to the cmdCreateSchedule procedure in the next step.

g. Make sure the insertion point is on the blank line after the *dblRate = Worksheet...* statement that you just typed. Press **Enter**, and then type the code shown in Code Window 12.

Excel and VBA

```
        intTerm = intPayments
        intStartRow = 10

        ' Loop through each monthly payment to calculate & display values
    For intCounter = 1 To intPayments
        Worksheets("Payment Schedule").Range("A" & intStartRow) = intCounter
        curPpmt = PPmt(dblRate, intCounter, intTerm, -curPrincipal)
        Worksheets("Payment Schedule").Range("B" & intStartRow) = curPpmt
        curIpmt = IPmt(dblRate, intCounter, intTerm, -curPrincipal)
        Worksheets("Payment Schedule").Range("C" & intStartRow) = curIpmt

        ' Calculate the cumulative interest and cumulative principal
        Worksheets("Payment Schedule").Range("D" & intStartRow) = curPpmt _
            + Val(Worksheets("Payment Schedule").Range("D" & intStartRow - 1))
        Worksheets("Payment Schedule").Range("E" & intStartRow) = curIpmt _
            + Val(Worksheets("Payment Schedule").Range("E" & intStartRow - 1))

        ' Calculate the total paid to date
        Worksheets("Payment Schedule").Range("F" & intStartRow) = _
        Worksheets("Payment Schedule").Range("D" & intStartRow) + _
        Worksheets("Payment Schedule").Range("E" & intStartRow)

        ' Calculate the outstanding balance
        Worksheets("Payment Schedule").Range("G" & intStartRow) = _
        curPrincipal - Val(Worksheets("Payment Schedule").Range("D" & intStartRow))

        ' Increment the row number
        intStartRow = intStartRow + 1

    Next

    ' Enable worksheet protection
    Worksheets("Payment Schedule").Protect
    Worksheets("Payment Schedule").Activate

End Sub
```

CODE WINDOW 12 ⋀

The procedure sets the intTerm variable equal to the value in the intPayments variable that was obtained from a calculation from cell B6. It then sets the intStartRow value to 10 so that the procedure will start entering data on row 10 of the worksheet.

The repetition statement loops through each monthly payment (based on the intCounter variable's value) to calculate and display values on the respective row. During each iteration, the loop places data on the next available row in the worksheet. Finally, the procedure protects the Payment Schedule worksheet again and then activates it since the Click event occurred on the Instructions worksheet.

h. Save the code, close the VBA window, and then click **Design Mode** in the Controls group to deactivate Design mode.

i. Click the **Create Schedule command button** you just created. Figure 18 shows the results.

> TROUBLESHOOTING: If a Compiler Error message box or a Debugging window displays, review each line of code to determine where the error exists. Fix the error, save the code, and then click the Create Schedule command button again to execute the sub procedure.

Expert Financial Services, Inc.
Residential Mortgage Kit

Principal: $	150,000			Closing Costs		
Rate:	5.75%			Origination Fee:	$3,000.00	
Term:	30			Points:	$4,500.00	
Payment:	$875.36			Total Fees:	$7,500.00	

Payment Number	Principal	Interest	Cumulative Principal	Cumulative Interest	Total Paid	Balance
1	$156.61	$718.75	$156.61	$718.75	$875.36	$149,843.39
2	$157.36	$718.00	$313.97	$1,436.75	$1,750.72	$149,686.03
3	$158.11	$717.25	$472.08	$2,154.00	$2,626.08	$149,527.92
4	$158.87	$716.49	$630.95	$2,870.49	$3,501.44	$149,369.05
5	$159.63	$715.73	$790.58	$3,586.22	$4,376.80	$149,209.42
6	$160.40	$714.96	$950.98	$4,301.18	$5,252.16	$149,049.02
7	$161.17	$714.19	$1,112.15	$5,015.37	$6,127.52	$148,887.86
8	$161.94	$713.42	$1,274.09	$5,728.79	$7,002.88	$148,725.91
9	$162.71	$712.65	$1,436.80	$6,441.44	$7,878.24	$148,563.20
10	$163.49	$711.87	$1,600.29	$7,153.31	$8,753.60	$148,399.71
11	$164.28	$711.08	$1,764.57	$7,864.39	$9,628.96	$148,235.43
12	$165.06	$710.29	$1,929.63	$8,574.68	$10,504.31	$148,070.37
13	$165.86	$709.50	$2,095.49	$9,284.18	$11,379.67	$147,904.51
14	$166.65	$708.71	$2,262.14	$9,992.89	$12,255.03	$147,737.86
15	$167.45	$707.91	$2,429.59	$10,700.80	$13,130.39	$147,570.41
16	$168.25	$707.11	$2,597.84	$11,407.91	$14,005.75	$147,402.16
17	$169.06	$706.30	$2,766.90	$12,114.21	$14,881.11	$147,233.10
18	$169.87	$705.49	$2,936.77	$12,819.70	$15,756.47	$147,063.23
19	$170.68	$704.68	$3,107.45	$13,524.38	$16,631.83	$146,892.55
20	$171.50	$703.86	$3,278.95	$14,228.24	$17,507.19	$146,721.05
21	$172.32	$703.04	$3,451.27	$14,931.28	$18,382.55	$146,548.73
22	$173.15	$702.21	$3,624.42	$15,633.49	$19,257.91	$146,375.58
23	$173.98	$701.38	$3,798.40	$16,334.87	$20,133.27	$146,201.60

Instructions | Customer Information | **Payment Schedule** | Disclosure

FIGURE 18 Payment Schedule Created from VBA Procedure ➤

STEP 2 ▶ CREATE CODE TO ACTIVATE THE INSTRUCTIONS WORKSHEET

You want users to be able to quickly go back to the Instructions worksheet after viewing the results in the Payment Schedule worksheet. Therefore, you need to insert a button with VBA code on the Payment Schedule worksheet to make the Instructions worksheet active again. Refer to Figure 19 as you complete Step 2.

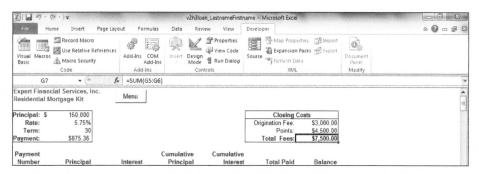

FIGURE 19 Menu Button on Payment Schedule Worksheet ➤

a. Right-click the **Payment Schedule sheet tab**, and then select **Unprotect Sheet**.

b. Click **Insert** in the Controls group, and then click **Command Button** (**ActiveX Control**).

c. Drag to create a command button to the right of the Expert Financial Services heading in the top-left corner.

d. Click **Properties** in the Controls group. Type **cmdReturn** in the **Name property box**, and then type **Menu** in the **Caption property box**. Adjust the height and width to be similar to the button you created on the Customer Information worksheet in Hands-On Exercise 2. Close the Properties window.

e. Right-click the **Menu button**, and then select **View Code**.

VBA creates the Private Sub cmdReturn_Click() and End Sub lines.

f. Press **Enter**, press **Tab**, type **Worksheets("Instructions").Activate** and then press **Enter**.

g. Save and close VBA. Click **Design Mode** in the Controls group to deactivate it.

h. Right-click the **Payment Schedule sheet tab**, select **Protect Sheet**, and then click **OK** in the **Protect Sheet dialog box**.

After inserting the command button and coding it, you protect the worksheet again.

i. Click the **Menu button** you just created on the Payment Schedule worksheet to return to the Instructions worksheet. Save the workbook.

Excel and VBA

The Disclosure worksheet needs formulas that get data from other worksheets and perform calculations, such as the cumulative interest payment and the last payment date. In addition, you need to insert a command button on the Disclosure worksheet to return to the Instructions worksheet again. Refer to Figure 20 as you complete Step 3.

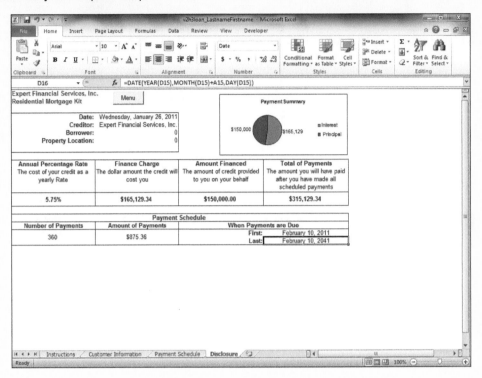

FIGURE 20 Disclosure Worksheet Data ➤

a. Right-click the **Disclosure sheet tab**, and then select **Unprotect Sheet**.

b. Use the Go To feature to go to the respective cells, and then enter the following formulas in the worksheet:

- **Cell B4:** =NOW()
- **Cell B6:** ='Customer Information'!$B$4
- **Cell B7:** ='Customer Information'!$B$13
- **Cell A11:** ='Customer Information'!$F$8
- **Cell A15:** ='Customer Information'!F10*12
- **Cell B11:** =-CUMIPMT(A11/12,A15,C11,1,A15,0)

> **TROUBLESHOOTING:** The cell will display #NUM! error here because cell A11 currently contains 0. The error message will disappear when you enter real values later.

- **Cell B15:** =PMT('Customer Information'!F8/12,'Customer Information'!F10*12, -'Customer Information'!F6)
- **Cell C11:** ='Customer Information'!F6
- **Cell D11:** =B11+C11
- **Cell D15:** =B4+15
- **Cell D16:** =DATE(YEAR(D15),MONTH(D15)+A15,DAY(D15))

Cells B6 and B7 display zeros. This is because the cells referenced by the formulas do not contain any values yet. After you add information about the borrower and the property, these cells display the name of the borrower and the location of the property.

c. Repeat steps 2b–g to insert a command button on the Disclosure worksheet.

Excel and VBA

110

d. Right-click the **Disclosure sheet tab**, select **Protect Sheet**, and then click **OK** in the **Protect Sheet dialog box**.

After inserting the command button and coding it, you need to protect the worksheet again.

e. Click the **Menu button** you just created on the Disclosure worksheet to return to the Instructions worksheet. Save the workbook.

STEP 4 ▶ ADD A BUTTON TO DISPLAY THE DISCLOSURE WORKSHEET

You are ready to add the final button on the Instructions worksheet. When the user clicks this button, the Disclosure worksheet is activated. Refer to Figure 21 as you complete Step 4.

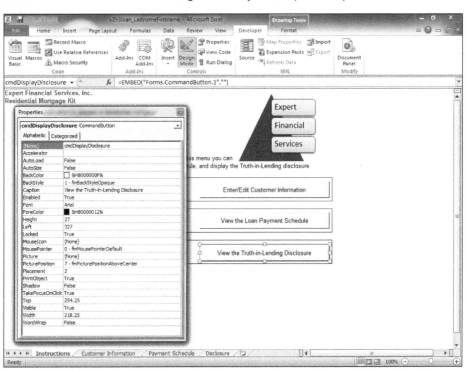

FIGURE 21 Third Button on Instructions Worksheet ▶

a. Click **Design Mode** in the Controls group on the Developer tab. Copy the View the Loan Payment Schedule button, and then paste the duplicate button within the third border directly below the first two command buttons.

b. Click **Properties** in the Controls group. Type **cmdDisplayDisclosure** in the **Name property box**, and then type **View the Truth-in-Lending Disclosure** in the **Caption property box**. Close the Properties window, and then click **Save** on the toolbar.

c. Right-click the **View the Truth-in-Lending Disclosure command button**, and then select **View Code**.

d. Press **Enter**, press **Tab**, type **Worksheets("Disclosure").Activate** and then press **Enter**. Close the VBA window.

e. Click **Design Mode** in the Controls group to deactivate it.

f. Right-click the **Instructions sheet tab**, select **Protect Sheet**, and then click **OK** in the Protect Sheet dialog box. Save the workbook.

g. Click the **View the Truth-in-Lending Disclosure command button** you just created to ensure it works, and then click the **Menu button** in the Disclosure worksheet to return to the Instructions worksheet.

h. Click each button on each worksheet to test the functionality of each button again. If errors exist, view the code, identify the error, save the code, and then click the buttons again.

i. Save and close the workbook. Submit it based on your instructor's directions.

Excel and VBA

CHAPTER OBJECTIVES REVIEW

After reading this chapter, you have accomplished the following objectives:

1. **Complete a software development life cycle.** The software development life cycle (SDLC) is a structured process for planning what inputs, processing, and outputs are needed. Next, the developers design the interface for ease of use. Third, developers write the programming code to execute the program. Finally, developers run the program to test its functionality. If errors exist, programmers identify and fix the errors and run the program again.

2. **Use the Excel Object Model in VBA.** An object is an element, such as a cell. You need to understand how objects are used in order to reference them and use them within their correct hierarchy within VBA code. For example, a worksheet is referred to by the Worksheets object. The specific worksheet name is enclosed in quotation marks and then by parentheses after the Worksheets object name and period. In VBA code, you can set properties of objects, such as the font color of text in a cell, or you can activate a built-in method for an object, such as using the Activate method to activate a particular worksheet object.

3. **Create forms.** The UserForm object is a form on which you can add controls such as labels, text boxes, and list boxes. Forms are usually used to gather information from the user. You can write VBA code for events, such as clicking a command button. Often, the Click event procedure coded for command buttons will capture data entered by the user and store the data in variables and use the data for calculations and output. Each control has a Name property to assign a meaningful name to it. Other useful properties you can set are Width, Height, and Caption. To assist users in navigating through a form, you should set the TabIndex properties of user-interacted controls, such as text boxes and command buttons, so that users can press Tab to go to the next available control.

4. **Use financial functions.** VBA includes implicit or built-in financial functions, similar to financial functions in Excel.

   Some of the common implicit financial functions are FV, Rate, IPmt, Pmt, and PPmt. Like Excel functions, these VBA functions have required arguments that must be passed to the function to calculate the result. Typically, you will use variable names in the argument list.

5. **Create function procedures.** You can create your own function procedures that accept values as arguments, perform specialized tasks, and then return a value through the function name back to the calling statement. The calling statement is a statement that calls a function; that is, it transfers execution to the function to perform its tasks. The calling statement must be written in such a way to do something with the value returned by the function procedure. Often, the calling statement assigns the returned value to a variable.

6. **Initialize, display, and close forms.** You can insert ActiveX controls directly on a worksheet, and then write VBA code to initialize and launch a form you have created. The Controls group on the Developer tab contains options for adding controls. After you name the controls, you can then add procedures to execute code.

7. **Create or search a list in a worksheet.** You can create VBA code with repetition structures (i.e., loops) to perform iterations to add to a list in a worksheet. The loop must be written in such a way to go down to the next blank row to add new data to avoid overwriting an existing row. You can also write code that uses a repetition structure to search through an existing list to find particular data.

8. **Prepare an application for distribution.** After testing a VBA application, you should prepare the file for distribution for the intended users. Often, this means using the Excel Options dialog box to hide the Formula Bar and row and column headings. In addition, you usually protect worksheets from unauthorized data entry.

KEY TERMS

Bound control	Name property	TabIndex property
Calling procedure	Object	TabStop property
Collection	Object model	TextAlign property
ControlSource property	RowSource property	Toolbox
Enabled property	Software development life cycle (SDLC)	Unbound control

MULTIPLE CHOICE

1. You are creating an Excel application that uses a function in a code procedure that performs a calculation and then adds this value to a specific worksheet cell. During which phase of the SDLC do you create the procedure?

   (a) Plan the application.
   (b) Design the interface.
   (c) Write the code.
   (d) Test the application.

2. Which statement makes cell E5 the active cell in the Salary worksheet?

   (a) Worksheet(Salary).Cell(E5)
   (b) Worksheets("Salary").Range("E5")
   (c) Cell("E5").Worksheet("Salary")
   (d) Cell(E5).Worksheet(Salary)

3. What property displays text onscreen for a label control?

   (a) Name
   (b) ControlSource
   (c) TextAlign
   (d) Caption

4. Which control is the least likely to need to have the programmer enter a specific value for the TabIndex property?

   (a) TextBox
   (b) CommandButton
   (c) Label
   (d) OptionButton

5. Which statement is used in a Close button's event procedure to close the current form?

   (a) frmCustomer.Hide
   (b) frmCustomer.Close
   (c) frmCustomer.Exit
   (d) Close.Customer.Form

6. Study the following function that calculates net pay.

```
Function NetPay(GrossPay, FederalTaxes, StateTaxes, LocalTaxes)
   NetPay = GrossPay – (FederalTaxes + StateTaxes + LocalTaxes)
End Function
```

   Given the values curGrossPay = 800, curFedTaxes = 75, curStateTaxes = 20, and curLocalTaxes = 10, what is the value returned by the function?

   (a) 855
   (b) 905
   (c) 705
   (d) 695

7. Which property defines the cell to which a control is bound?

   (a) RowSource
   (b) ControlSource
   (c) Caption
   (d) TabStop

8. Which statement assigns a value from a text box to a variable?

   (a) dblLoan = Val(txtLoan.Text)
   (b) txtLoan = dblLoan
   (c) dblLoan = txtLoan.Name
   (d) txtLoan.Text = dblLoan.Text

9. Which financial function calculates the monthly payment for a mortgage?

   (a) PPMT
   (b) IMPT
   (c) PMT
   (d) CIMPT

10. To finalize a workbook with VBA code for distribution, which one of the following is least important?

    (a) Protect worksheets containing formulas and results.
    (b) Hide all but the first worksheet.
    (c) Save the workbook as a macro-enabled workbook.
    (d) Create command buttons to navigate easily among worksheets.

1 Sports Grill

Matt Claw owns Matt's Sports Grill, a small restaurant in Salt Lake City. The servers have handheld devices that are synchronized to a printer and that use Excel to enter customer orders and calculate totals. Matt wants you to create an application so that the servers can enter the total food and beverage costs and allow customers to enter a tip percentage. The program then will calculate the total taxes, tips, and grand total and display a receipt that can be printed. You started a workbook with two worksheets: Start and Receipt. The Start worksheet will contain a welcome screen and a button to click to display an input form. The input form will enable servers to enter the food and beverage total and the customers to enter a tip percentage. When users click a Calculate button, the VBA code unprotects the Receipts worksheet, calculates and enters values in that worksheet, and then protects the worksheet again. The form needs to have a Clear button and a Close button as well. This exercise follows the same set of skills as used in Hands-On Exercises 1–3 in the chapter. Refer to Figure 22 as you complete this exercise.

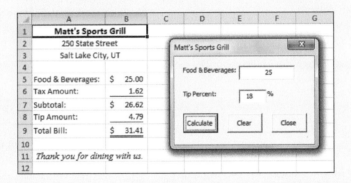

FIGURE 22 Receipt Worksheet and Form ➤

a. Open the macro-enabled *v2p1grill*, and then save it as **v2p1grill_LastnameFirstname**. Click each worksheet tab to see what work has been done and what work you will do. Try typing in the Receipt worksheet, and notice that it is protected.

b. Click the **Developer tab**, and then click **Visual Basic** in the Code group. Click **Insert** on the VBA menu bar, select **UserForm**, and then set these form properties:
   - Name: **frmDataEntry**
   - Caption: **Matt's Sports Grill**
   - Height: **132**
   - Width: **185**

c. Click the form to display the Toolbox, click **Label** in the Toolbox, drag a label to the top-left corner of the form, and then set its properties as the following:
   - Name: **lblFoodBeverage**
   - Caption: **Food & Beverages:**
   - Width: **72**

d. Insert other controls as shown in Figure 22, and then set their properties as indicated in Table 8. Make sure all TabStop values are set to **True**.

TABLE 8	Controls and Properties	
Control	**Property**	**Setting**
TextBox	Name	txtMeal
	TabIndex	0
	TextAlign	2 - fmTextAlignCenter
	Width	72
Label	Name	lblTipPercent
	Caption	Tip Percent:
	Width	72
TextBox	Name	txtTip
	TabIndex	1
	Width	36
Label	Name	lblPercent
	Caption	%
	Width	15
CommandButton	Name	cmdCalculate
	Caption	Calculate
	Height	24
	TabIndex	2
	Width	45
CommandButton	Name	cmdClear
	Caption	Clear
CommandButton	Name	cmdClose
	Caption	Close

e. Press and hold **Ctrl** as you click all three buttons to select them, click **Format** on the menu bar, point to **Make Same Size**, and then select **Both** to make all three buttons the same height and width. Select **Format** on the menu bar, point to **Horizontal Spacing**, and then select **Make Equal** to equalize the space between buttons.

f. Right-click the **Calculate button**, select **View Code**, and then enter the code shown in Code Window 13.

```
Private Sub cmdCalculate_Click()

    ' Declare variables
    Dim dblMeal As Double
    Dim dblTip As Double
    Dim dblTotal As Double
    Dim dblTaxAmount As Double
    Dim dblAmountDue As Double

    ' Get cost of meal from text box
    dblMeal = txtMeal.Text

    ' Function call to perform calculations
    dblAmountDue = TotalBill(dblMeal, dblTip, dblTotal, dblTaxAmount)

    ' Complete the receipt
    Worksheets("Receipt").Unprotect
    Worksheets("Receipt").Range("B5") = dblMeal
    Worksheets("Receipt").Range("B6") = dblTaxAmount
    Worksheets("Receipt").Range("B7") = dblTotal
    Worksheets("Receipt").Range("B8") = dblTip
    Worksheets("Receipt").Range("B9") = dblAmountDue

    Worksheets("Receipt").Protect
    Worksheets("Receipt").Activate

End Sub
```

CODE WINDOW 13 ⋏

The code declares variables, obtains text entered in the txtMeal text box and assigns it to a variable, calls the TotalBill function and assigns the returned value to a variable. Then, the sub procedure unprotects the Receipt worksheet and then uses the values stored in the variables to enter into five cells in the Receipt worksheet. Finally, the procedure protects and activates the Receipt worksheet.

g. Press **Enter** twice after the End Sub statement, and then create the function that will accept variables, perform calculations, and then return the total amount due shown in Code Window 14.

```
Function TotalBill(dblMeal, dblTip, dblTotal, dblTax)

    ' Declare constant and variable
    Const dblTaxRate As Double = 0.065
    Dim dblTipRate As Double

    ' Calculate the tax and subtotal
    dblTax = Round(dblMeal * dblTaxRate, 2)
    dblTotal = dblMeal + dblTax

    ' Calculate the tip and grand total
    dblTipRate = Val(txtTip.Text) / 100
    dblTip = Round(dblTotal * dblTipRate, 2)
    TotalBill = dblTotal + dblTip

End Function
```

CODE WINDOW 14 ⋏

The function uses the Round function to round taxes and tips to the nearest cent. Because the user types the tip percent as a whole number, such as 18, the code must convert that to a decimal equivalent, such as .18.

The code declares a constant and variables. Then, it calculates the tax, subtotal, tip, and total bill. It returns the value of the total bill to the calling statement.

h. Create the event procedures for the Clear and Close buttons as shown in Code Window 15.

```
Private Sub cmdClear_Click()

    ' Clear data entry form
    txtMeal.Text = ""
    txtTip.Text = ""
    txtMeal.SetFocus

End Sub

Private Sub cmdClose_Click()

    ' Close the form
    frmDataEntry.Hide
    Worksheets("Start").Activate

End Sub
```

CODE WINDOW 15 ⋏

The cmdClear procedure clears the data entry form and sets the focus to the txtMeal box. The cmdClose procedure hides the data entry form and then activates the Start worksheet.

i. Save and close the VBA window, and then click the **Start sheet tab**.

j. Click the **Developer tab** if necessary, click **Insert** in the Controls group, select **Command Button** (**ActiveX Control**), and then drag to create a button below the server information. Then, do the following:
   • Click **Properties** in the Controls group, select the existing text in the **Name property box**, and then type **cmdStart**.
   • Select the existing text in the **Caption property box**, and then type **Click to Start**.

k. Close the Properties window, right-click the **Click to Start button**, and then select **View Code**. Press **Enter**, press **Tab**, type **frmDataEntry.Show**, and then press **Enter**. This line of code will display the form you created when a user clicks the button. Save and close the VBA window. Click **Design Mode** in the Controls group on the Developer tab.

l. Click the **File tab**, click **Options**, click **Advanced**, scroll down to the *Display options for this worksheet* section, deselect the **Show row and column headers check box**. Click the **Start arrow**, select **Receipt**, deselect the **Show row and column headers check box**, and then click **OK**.

m. Click **Design Mode** to deselect it. Click the **Click to Start button** on the Start worksheet, enter **25** in the **Food & Beverages box**, press **Tab**, type **18**, and then click **Calculate**. Refer to Figure 22.

n. Click **Clear**, and then click **Close**.

o. Save and close the workbook, and then submit based on your instructor's directions.

2 Monthly Investment Schedule

Janelle Mayer is a financial consultant. She works with people who are considering investment opportunities. Because of your extensive work with Excel and interest in VBA coding, you volunteered to help create an application in which Janelle can enter data for a potential investment, click a button, and then display a summary of results and a list of month-by-month data to show how much interest is made. This exercise follows the same set of skills as used in Hands-On Exercises 1–3 in the chapter. Refer to Figure 23 as you complete this exercise.

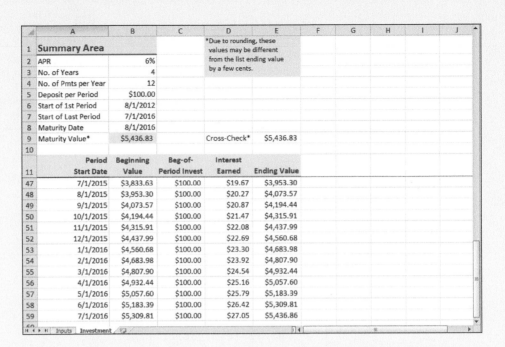

FIGURE 23 Monthly Investment Schedule ➤

a. Open the macro-enabled *v2p2invest*, and then save it as **v2p2invest_LastnameFirstname**.

b. Click the **Developer tab**, click **Insert** in the Controls group, click **Command Button (ActiveX Control)**, and then draw a command button in the **range A10:A11**. Click **Properties** in the Controls group, type **cmdDisplayResults** in the **Name property box**, type **Display the Results** in the **Caption property box**, and then close the Properties window.

c. Right-click the **Display the Results command button**, and then select **View Code**. Type the variable declarations shown in Code Window 16.

These variables will store data the user enters in the Inputs worksheet, calculations to display in the Investment worksheet, and variables needed for the VBA code. You will continue adding to the procedure in the next step.

```vba
Private Sub cmdDisplayResults_Click()

    ' Declare variables for input from worksheet cells
    Dim dblAPR As Double
    Dim intYears As Integer
    Dim dblAmountInvest As Double
    Dim dteStartDate As Date

    ' Declare variables for calculated output
    Dim dteLastPeriod As Date
    Dim dteMaturityDate As Date
    Dim dblFutureValue As Double

    ' Declare variables for calculations and loop
    Dim intCounter As Integer
    Dim dteCurrentDate As Date
    Dim dblBegBalance As Double
    Dim dblBalance As Double
    Dim dblInterest As Double
    Dim intPrevRow As Integer
    Dim intStartRow As Integer
```

CODE WINDOW 16 ▲

d. Position the insertion point two blank lines below the code you just typed, and then type the code shown in Code Window 17. You will continue adding to the procedure in the next step.

```
' Clear any previous schedules
Worksheets("Investment").Unprotect
Worksheets("Investment").Range("A12:E373").Clear

' Get inputs from worksheets
dblAPR = Worksheets("Inputs").Range("B4")
intYears = Worksheets("Inputs").Range("B5")
dblAmountInvest = Worksheets("Inputs").Range("B6")
dteStartDate = Worksheets("Inputs").Range("B7")
dteLastPeriod = Worksheets("Investment").Range("B7")

' Calculate and verify maturity date (should be equal to B8 in Investments)
dteMaturityDate = Application.WorksheetFunction.EDate(dteStartDate, intYears * 12)

' Calculate and display first period's interest and balance
dblInterest = dblAmountInvest * dblAPR / 12
dblBalance = dblAmountInvest + dblInterest
Worksheets("Investment").Range("A12") = Format(dteStartDate, "Short Date")
Worksheets("Investment").Range("C12") = Format(dblAmountInvest, "$##,##0.00")
Worksheets("Investment").Range("D12") = Format(dblInterest, "$##,##0.00")
Worksheets("Investment").Range("E12") = Format(dblBalance, "$#,##0.00")
```

CODE WINDOW 17 ▲

This code unprotects the Investment worksheet so that the VBA procedure can clear existing data in the month-by-month list and enter new data in the worksheet.

The second block of code obtains values from the Inputs and Investment worksheets and stores the values in the variables you declared.

The third block of code uses the Excel EDate function to determine the ending or maturity date of the investment. Its arguments are the starting investment date and the total number of investment periods (months). Because monthly payments are made, the argument must multiply the number of investment years by 12 months in a year.

The final block of code calculates the interest and balance for the first investment period and then displays formatted results in the first row (row 12) of the month-by-month list. That block of code uses the Format function to display the contents of a variable in a specific way. The date format *Short Date* and the monetary values *$##,##0.00* are enclosed in quotation marks.

e. Position the insertion point two blank lines below the code you just typed, and then type the code shown in Code Window 18.

Excel and VBA

119

```
        ' Initialize row to start the loop
        intStartRow = 13

        ' Loop through each monthly period to calculate and display values
        For intCounter = 1 To (intYears * 12 - 1)
            intPrevRow = intStartRow - 1

            ' Calculate beginning balance, balance after deposit, and interest
            dteCurrentDate = Application.WorksheetFunction.EDate(dteStartDate, intCounter)
            dblBegBalance = Val(Worksheets("Investment").Range("E" & intPrevRow))
            dblBalance = dblBegBalance + dblAmountInvest
            dblInterest = dblBalance * dblAPR / 12

            ' Display formatted values in the list
            Worksheets("Investment").Range("A" & intStartRow) = _
                        Format(dteCurrentDate, "Short Date")
            Worksheets("Investment").Range("B" & intStartRow) = _
                        Format(dblBegBalance, "$##,##0.00")
            Worksheets("Investment").Range("C" & intStartRow) = _
                        Format(dblAmountInvest, "$##,##0.00")
            Worksheets("Investment").Range("D" & intStartRow) = _
                        Format(dblInterest, "$##,##0.00")
            Worksheets("Investment").Range("E" & intStartRow) = _
                        Format(dblBalance + dblInterest, "$##,##0.00")

            ' Increment the row number
             intStartRow = intStartRow + 1
        Next

        ' Calculate and display a cross check to compare with last cell in list
        dblFutureValue = FV(dblAPR / 12, intYears * 12, -dblAmountInvest, , 1)
        Worksheets("Investment").Range("E9") = Format(dblFutureValue, "$##,##0.00")

        ' Finalize worksheet
        Worksheets("Investment").Protect
        Worksheets("Investment").Activate

End Sub
```

CODE WINDOW 18 ▲

This code uses the intStartRow variable to designate row 13 as the row to start the rest of the table. Prior to the loop, the code populated the first month's data. The loop takes over starting with the second investment period since it must identify the previous month's balance and add this month's investment in order to calculate the interest earned.

The code then formats and displays output for the current month during each iteration of the loop and then increments the intStartRow variable so that the next iteration of the loop places data on the next available row in the worksheet.

After the loop terminates, the code provides a cross-check to determine if the future value is almost identical (excluding a little rounding in cents) with what is produced by the Excel FV function and with the final ending investment value produced by the loop.

Finally, the procedure protects the Investment worksheet and then displays it to the user.

f. Save and close the VBA window. Turn off the **Design Mode** on the Developer tab.

g. Click the **Inputs sheet tab** if necessary, select the **range B4:B7**, display the **Format Cells dialog box**, click the **Protection tab**, deselect the **Locked check box**, and then click **OK**.

h. Right-click the **Inputs sheet tab**, select **Protect Sheet**, and then click **OK** in the Protect Sheet dialog box.

Steps g and h ensure that the user can enter values only in the input cells on the Inputs worksheet.

i.   Type **6**, **4**, **100**, and **8/1/2012** in the respective input cells in the Inputs worksheet. Click the **Display the Results button**. After the VBA code executes, the Investment worksheet is active and displays the data. Scroll through the list to review the monthly start date, beginning balance, investment, interest earned, and ending balance.

The Start of Last Period date stored in cell B7 matches the last date in the list. The Maturity Date value stored in cell B8 is one month after that. Note the final ending value may be a few cents different from the FV function results stored in cell B9 and the VBA FV function results stored in cell E9 due to rounding.

j.   Save and close the workbook, and then submit based on your instructor's directions.

Excel and VBA

1 Test Scores

You are a teaching assistant for one of your professors, Dr. Patti Blakesley. You created a small grade-book with student IDs, first names, and three test scores to create a prototype application that you can modify for larger classes. Dr. Blakesley would like a program that prompts her for a student's ID and test number and then displays the student's name, test score, and letter grade. You will use VBA to create an easy-to-use form within Excel. In addition, you need to create a command button that Dr. Blakesley can click to open the form. Refer to Figure 24 as you complete this exercise.

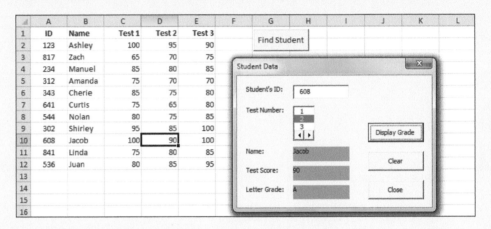

FIGURE 24 Test Scores and Form ➤

a. Open the macro-enabled *v2m1grades* workbook, and then save it as **v2m1grades_LastnameFirstname**.

b. Use VBA to create a form named **frmStudent** with the labels, text boxes, list box, and command buttons shown in Figure 24. Set these properties for the controls:
   - Name: Use standard prefixes and descriptive names.
   - Caption: Use captions as shown in the Figure.
   - Left: Align common controls on the left side.
   - BackColor: Use a light blue background color for the output labels as shown.

c. Adjust the widths, heights, and vertical spacing as needed to ensure balance and consistency.

d. Write the VBA procedure for the Clear button to clear the input text box, set the list box value to –1 (to avoid selecting a test number by default), and then clear the output labels. The procedure should set the focus back to the input text box.

e. Write the VBA procedure for the Close button to close the form.

f. Write the VBA procedure for the Display Grade button:
   - Declare integer variables for the ID, test number, and test score. Declare a string variable for the student's name.
   - Assign the values in the form's text box and list box to appropriate variables. Convert the list box selected test number to a value before assigning it to a variable.
   - Create a function call to a GetName function in which you pass the ID variable. The returned value should be the student's name stored in a string variable.
   - Use a Select Case statement that uses the selected test number to move the active cell to the right on the same row by the correct number of columns. Each Case statement uses the ActiveCell.Offset method to offset the active cell on the same row and over the appropriate number of columns (1 through 3, respectively).
   - Store the active cell's content (the respective test score) in a variable using **ActiveCell.Value**.
   - Display the string variable and test score variable contents in respective output labels within the form.
   - Create a function call to a GetGrade function in which you pass the test score variable and then display the respective letter grade in an output label on the form.

g. Create a GetName function that does the following:
   - Use **Application.Goto** to go to **cell A1**.

DISCOVER

- Use the **Cells.Find statement** to find the ID, and then make that cell the active cell. (Hint: If needed, record a temporary macro to record displaying the Find dialog box, searching down a column for an exact match. Copy and modify that code within your GetName function.)
- Use the **ActiveCell.Offset statement** to make the respective name the active cell, and then use **ActiveCell.Value** to assign it to the function name.

h. Create a GetGrade function that uses a Select Case block to do the following:
- If the score is greater than or equal to 90, assign an **A** to the function name.
- If the score is greater than or equal to 80, assign a **B** to the function name.
- If the score is greater than or equal to 70, assign a **C** to the function name.
- If the score is greater than or equal to 60, assign a **D** to the function name.
- For all other scores, assign an **F** to the function name.

DISCOVER

i. Change the Object to **UserForm** at the top of the code window, and then select the **Initialize procedure**. Delete any other empty procedures that might be created as you get to this one. Enter three lines of code to populate the list box with 1, 2, and 3. Set the focus to the first text box in the form. This procedure will populate the list box and set the focus when the form first loads each time.

j. Save and close the VBA window. Create a **Find Student button**, and then write the code so that when a user clicks it, the Student Data form displays. Click the **Find Student button**, type **608** in the **text box**, select **2** in the list box, and then click the **Display Grade button** on the form. See Figure 24. Clear the form, and then try out several other combinations to ensure the program selects the right data.

k. Test the Close button to make sure it works.

l. Save and close the workbook, and then submit based on your instructor's directions.

2 Financial Functions

You want to compare the results of Excel financial functions with the results of VBA financial functions. You will use a workbook that contains two worksheets. You will write the code for three command buttons on the Inputs worksheet that, when clicked, will execute respective procedures. Each procedure will call functions that can be used by multiple procedures that get user input via input boxes. The results will display on the Output worksheet, along with the results from direct financial functions in that worksheet. Refer to Figures 25 and 26 as you complete this exercise.

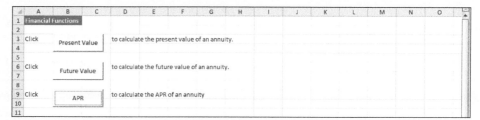

FIGURE 25 Input Sheet with Command Buttons ➤

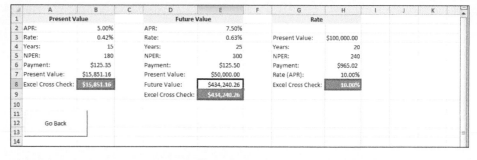

FIGURE 26 Output Sheet with Results ➤

a. Open the macro-enabled *v2m2financefunctions* workbook, and then save it as **v2m2financefunctions_LastnameFirstname**.

b. Enter the following finance functions on the Output worksheet:
- PV function in **cell B8**. Use cell references in column B as the three arguments.
- FV function in **cell E9**. Use cell references in column E as the four arguments. Make sure the result is a positive value.
- RATE function with formula to convert to APR in **cell H8**. Use cell references in column H as the three arguments.

c. Display the VBA window, change the Object to (**General**), and change the Procedure to (**Declarations**). Type **Option Explicit**, and then declare the following variables: **dblPV**, **dblAPR**, **dblYears**, **dblRate**, **dblNPER**, **dblPMT**, and **dblFV**. You declare these at this level so that they are available throughout all procedures.

d. Create these four functions with each function displaying an input box asking for the appropriate data and storing it in the function name. Make sure the functions are Public not Private so that the functions can be accessed from any given module or procedure.

- **GetAPR function.** Display the prompt **Enter the annual rate, such as 0.06 instead of 6%:**. The input box title bar should display **Rate**. The data entered by the user should be converted to a value and then saved to the function name so that the value gets returned back to the calling statement in the main procedure.
- **GetYears function.** Display the prompt **Enter the number of years for the annuity:**. The input box title bar should display **Term in Years**. The data entered by the user should be converted to a value and then saved to the function name so that the value gets returned back to the calling statement in the main procedure.
- **GetPMT function.** Request the monthly payment with an appropriate prompt and title for the input box. Convert the value, and then save it to the function name.
- **GetPV function.** Request the present value of the annuity with an appropriate prompt and title for the input box. Convert the value, and then save it to the function name.

e. Create the procedure for the cmdPresentValue button with these requirements:

- Include function calls for the APR, years, and monthly payment, and then store each returning value in the appropriate variable. The calling statements do not pass any variables to the functions you created.
- Calculate the periodic rate, the NPER, and the present value. Store each calculated result in the respective variable.
- Unprotect the Output worksheet. Display the results in **cells B2 through B7** for the APR, rate, years, NPER, payment, and present value. Format the percentages and monetary values appropriately within the VBA code.
- Protect the Output worksheet again, and then activate the Output worksheet.

f. Create the procedure for the cmdFutureValue button with these requirements:

- Include function calls for the APR, years, monthly payment, and present value, and then store each returning value in the appropriate variable. The calling statements do not pass any variables to the functions you created.
- Calculate the periodic rate, the NPER, and the future value. Store each calculated result in the respective variable.
- Unprotect the Output worksheet. Display the results in **cells E2 through E8** for the APR, rate, years, NPER, payment, present value, and future value. Format the percentages and monetary values appropriately within the VBA code.
- Protect the Output worksheet again, and then activate the Output worksheet.

g. Create the procedure for the cmdAPR button with these requirements:

- Include function calls for the years, monthly payment, and present value, and then store each returning value in the appropriate variable. The calling statements do not pass any variables to the functions you created.
- Calculate the NPER, the periodic rate, and the APR. Store each calculated result in the respective variable.
- Unprotect the Output worksheet. Display the results in **cells H3 through H7** for the present value, years, NPER, payment, and APR. Format the percentages and monetary values appropriately within the VBA code.
- Protect the Output worksheet again, and then activate the Output worksheet.

h. Protect the Input worksheet in Excel (not VBA code).

i. Click the **Present Value button** on the Input worksheet, and then type these values when prompted: **0.05** (APR), **15** (years), and **125.35** (payment). Compare your answers with Figure 26, and then click the **Go Back button** on the Output worksheet.

j. Click the **Future Value button** on the Input worksheet, and then type these values when prompted: **0.075** (APR), **25** (years), **125.50** (payment), and **50000** (present value). Compare your answers with Figure 26, and then click the **Go Back button** on the Output worksheet.

k. Click the **APR button** on the Input worksheet, and then type these values when prompted: **20** (years), **965.02** (payment), and **100000** (present value). Compare your answers with Figure 26, and then click the **Go Back button** on the Output worksheet.

l. Save and close the workbook, and then submit based on your instructor's directions.

CAPSTONE EXERCISE

You manage a small temp agency in your town. You hire up to 25 college students to perform a variety of jobs. Instead of investing in a payroll system, you started an Excel workbook that contains two worksheets: StartPage and Payroll. You will create forms and write VBA code to obtain information and calculate gross pay.

Get the Number of Employees

You want to click the *# of Employees* button on the StartPage worksheet to display an input box to enter that week's number of employees. The result should store the value in a publicly declared variable that is accessible from all procedures. The sub procedure should then disable the *# of Employees* button until the user clicks the Reset button.

a. Open the macro-enabled *v2c1payroll*, and then save it as **v2c1payroll_LastnameFirstname**.

b. Type the **Option Explicit statement** at the top of the *General Declarations* section of the code window for the StartPage worksheet. Create a public integer variable to store the number of employees.

c. Create a sub procedure for the *# of Employees* button's Click event.
   - Display an input box to ask the user how many employees worked that week. Include an appropriate title for the input box title bar.
   - Assign the value entered by the user to the appropriate public variable you declared in step b.
   - Change the *# of Employees* button's Enabled property to **False**.

d. Save the VBA code.

Display the Payroll Worksheet

Although users will click the Display Payroll button third, you want to program it now because it will be easier to code. When users click the Display Payroll button, the sub procedure should activate the Payroll worksheet and then change the Display Payroll button's Enabled property to False.

a. Create a sub procedure for the Display Payroll button's Click event.
   - Activate the Payroll worksheet.
   - Change the Display Payroll button's Enabled property to **False**.

b. Save the VBA code.

Reset the Command Buttons

As users click each button, the respective button is disabled so that users will not accidentally click a button and empty the Payroll worksheet too soon. You now need to code the Reset button so that it will enable the first three buttons when clicked.

a. Create a sub procedure for the Reset button's Click event.

b. Type three statements, one to change each of the first three buttons' Enabled property to **True**.

c. Save the VBA code.

Design Employee Input Form

You want an easy-to-use interface to enter each employee's name, pay rate, and hours worked each weekday.

a. Create a user form named **frmEmployee**, type **Employee Data** for the Caption property, set **285** for the Height, and set **171** for the Width.

b. Create and format eight labels for **Last Name, First Name, Pay Rate, Monday Hours, Tuesday Hours, Wednesday Hours, Thursday Hours**, and **Friday Hours**. Align these labels on the left side, and then ensure consistent heights, widths, and vertical spacing.

c. Insert eight text boxes to the right of the eight labels. Assign descriptive names for the text boxes, such as txtLast and txtFirst. Align the text boxes on the left side, and then ensure consistent height, consistent vertical spacing.

d. Insert a command button in the bottom-right corner named **cmdSave**. Set its Caption property to **Save**.

e. Set the TabIndex property for the text boxes and command button in proper sequence with the txtLast control with a value of **0** and the cmdSave control with a value of **8**.

f. Make any necessary adjustments to the properties for the labels, text boxes, or command button.

Code the Form's Initialize Method

The form will display several times during execution, once for each employee. To ensure the form is cleared of previously entered data, you need to create an Initialize method for the UserForm.

a. Select the form, display the code window for the UserForm, and then select the **UserForm object** and the **Initialize method**.

b. Type statements to clear each text box on the form, such as *txtLast.Text = ""*, substituting the actual text box names you assigned.

c. Type a statement to set the focus back to the txtLast box on the form.

d. Save the VBA code.

Write a GetHours Function

You need to write a public function that you can call from the Save button's sub procedure. You will create the function before creating the button's sub procedure. The GetHours function will not accept any arguments. It declares a variable to hold the cumulative hours worked. It should obtain the hours worked from the respective text boxes, convert the data to values, and then add to the cumulative weekly hours. For example, the Monday hours are added to 0 hours to start. The Tuesday hours are added to the Monday hours, etc. For example, if an employee worked 8 hours on Monday, 8 is added to the initial cumulative variable value of 0 for a total of 8 hours so far.

If the employee worked 7 hours on Tuesday, those 7 hours are added to the cumulative 8 hours previously for a total of 15 hours. The function returns the total hours to the calling statement.

a. Type the function header **Public Function GetHours()** outside any other sub procedure, and then press **Enter** twice.

b. Declare a local variable named **dblHours** to store the cumulative hours worked for the current employee.

c. Write five statements, one for each weekday's text box (such as txtMonday.Text) to obtain the value in the respective text box, and convert it to a value and add it to the dblHours variable. The last statement should store the result in the GetHours function name, which will return the total hours worked to the calling statement you will create later.

d. Save the VBA code.

Write a GetPay Function

You need to write a *public* function that you can call from the Save button's sub procedure. You will create the function before creating the button's sub procedure. The GetPay function will accept six arguments. Use alias names for the received argument variables. The function does not declare any other variables. The function should determine how many of the total hours are regular and overtime hours. It should then calculate the regular pay (pay rate * regular hours), overtime pay (pay rate * 1.5 * overtime hours), and gross pay, which will be returned to the calling statement.

a. Type the function header **Public Function GetPay(Hours, RegHours, OTHours, PayRate, RegPay, OTPay)** outside any other sub procedure, and then press **Enter** twice.

b. Create an If…Else statement to determine how many hours are regular hours. Regular hours are up to 40 hours worked. For example, if a person works 36 hours, the total regular hours are 36. If a person works 45 hours, the regular hours are 40. Assign the correct number of hours to the RegHours variable.

c. Calculate the number of overtime hours (any hours over 40). For example, if a person worked 45 hours, the number of overtime hours is 5. You do not need an If statement for this calculation. Assign the correct number of overtime hours to the OTHours variable.

d. Calculate the regular pay as a product of the regular hours worked and the pay rate.

e. Calculate the overtime pay as a product of the overtime hours, pay rate, and 1.5.

f. Calculate the gross pay, and then assign its value to the GetPay function name, which will then return that value to the calling statement.

g. Save the VBA code.

Code the Form's Save Button

When the form displays, the user enters data into the text boxes and then clicks the Save button. You need to write the sub procedure to obtain the data in the text boxes, call functions, and then display formatted output into the Payroll worksheet.

a. Create a sub procedure for the Save button.

b. Declare nine variables of appropriate data types: last name, first name, pay rate, hours, regular hours, overtime hours, regular pay, overtime pay, and gross pay.

c. Assign the value 0 to the hours, regular hours, and overtime hours variables.

d. Write statements to obtain the last name, first name, and pay rate from the respective text boxes on the form and assign the data to the appropriate variables.

e. Call the GetHours function, and then return its accumulated total hours to the hours variable.

f. Type the statement **ActiveCell.FormulaR1C1 = strLast**, substituting the name of the last name variable you declared. This statement will enter the last name in the active cell in the Payroll worksheet (which is cell A2 for the first person).

g. Type the statement **ActiveCell.Offset(0, 1).Select** to move the active cell one cell to the right on the same row.

h. Type the statement to assign the first name variable contents to the active cell, similar to step f.

i. Type another statement with the Offset method statements to move over one cell for total hours worked. Use the Format function to format hours in this format "#0.0".

j. Type a function call statement for the GetPay function. Pass the hours, regular hours, overtime hours, pay rate, regular pay, and overtime pay variables to the function (which you created earlier). The function will assign values to these variables and calculate the gross pay, which gets returned through the GetPay function name. Assign the result to the gross pay variable.

k. Continue typing the ActiveCell.Offset statements with each of those statements followed by the ActiveCell.FormulaR1C1 statements. Format the regular hours and overtime hours in the "#0.0" format. Format the pay rate, regular pay, overtime pay, and gross pay with the "Currency" format.

l. Type the statement **ActiveCell.Offset(1, -8).Select** to go down one row and to the left by eight cells so that the active cell in the next blank row is ready to enter data for the next employee.

m. Type the statement **Unload frmEmployee** to unload the form from memory. You do not want to simply hide the form or it will preserve the previously entered data.

n. Save the VBA code.

Code the Employee Data Button

You need to code the third button on the StartPage worksheet, the Employee Data button. When the user clicks this button, the sub procedure should unprotect the Payroll worksheet, clear existing payroll data, make cell A2 the active cell, and then loop through to display the Employee Data form once for each employee. After the data is gathered and displayed using the form's Save button and the two functions you previously created, the Employee Data button's sub procedure should then protect the Payroll worksheet, activate the StartPage worksheet, and then display the Employee Data button.

a. Create a sub procedure for the Employee Data button.

b. Declare **intCount** as a counter variable for a loop. Assign the value of **1** to the variable.

c. Write statements that do the following tasks. Type the bold statements exactly as shown below:
- Unprotect the Payroll worksheet.
- **Worksheets("Payroll").Select**
- Select the **range A2:I26**.
- **Selection.ClearContents**
- **Worksheets("Payroll").Application.Goto Reference:="R2C1"**

d. Write a For...Next loop to iterate as many times as the number of employees. The first statement in the body of the loop should load the frmEmployee form, and the second statement should show the form. No other statements should be in the body of the loop. The form's Save button's sub procedure takes over when the user clicks Save each time.

e. Write statements to protect the Payroll worksheet, activate the StartPage worksheet, and then change the Employee Data button's Enabled property to **False**.

f. Save the VBA code.

Test the Buttons

You need to test the buttons to ensure the application works.

a. Click the **Payroll sheet tab**, and try to type in an empty cell. The worksheet should be protected.

b. Click the **StartPage sheet tab**.

c. Click the **# of Employees button** to display the input box. Type **3**, and then click **OK** in the input box. The *# of Employees* button should now be disabled so that you cannot click it.

d. Click the **Employee Data button** to display the form. Enter your name, a pay rate without the $, and **10** hours each day. Click the **Save button**, and the data is entered on row 2 of the Payroll worksheet. An empty form displays.

e. Enter data for a second employee. Enter **7** hours each day. Click the **Save button**, and data is entered on row 3 of the Payroll worksheet. An empty form displays.

f. Enter data for a third employee. Enter **8** hours each day. Click the **Save button**, and data is entered on row 4 of the Payroll worksheet. No more forms display because you specified 3 employees in the input box earlier. The Payroll worksheet should be protected again, the StartPage worksheet is activated, and the Employee Data button should now be disabled so that you cannot click it.

g. Click the **Display Payroll button** to display the Payroll form. Try typing in the Payroll worksheet and notice it is disabled.

h. Click the **StartPage sheet tab**, and then click the **Reset button**. The first three buttons are now enabled again.

i. Save and close the workbook, and then submit based on your instructor's directions.

BEYOND THE CLASSROOM

Valentine's Day Dance

GENERAL CASE

Victoria Johnson is a party organizer for a student organization that is sponsoring a Valentine's Day Ball at your university. She has identified sources of income and expenses and started an Excel workbook. However, she does not want people to directly enter data in the worksheet. As the IT developer for the student organization, you volunteer to create forms and write VBA code that provide prompts for users to enter information and store it in the protected worksheet. Open the macro-enabled *v2b1dance* workbook, and then save it as **v2b1dance_LastnameFirstname**. Open *v2b1dance.docx* in Word to read more details about the program, what buttons are needed, what event procedures are needed, etc. Use this document to guide you as you design the form and create VBA procedures in the workbook.

The Instructions worksheet should have four buttons. The first button displays an input box to ask the user for the number of attendees, the second button displays a form to enter income sources, the third button displays a form to enter expenses, and the fourth button displays the results on the protected worksheet. The Budget worksheet contains some formulas, but clicking the OK button on the Expenses form performs two calculations.

Save and close the workbook, and then submit based on your instructor's directions.

Apartment Rentals

RESEARCH CASE

You want to create an Excel application for apartment managers. The program should prompt the manager to enter the number of complexes managed. A repetition statement should ask the user to enter the name of each complex, how many one-bedroom apartments are located there, how many one-bedroom apartments are rented, how many two-bedroom apartments are located there, and how many two-bedroom apartments are rented. The procedure calculates the occupancy rate of each apartment type. For example, if 10 one-bedroom apartments are located in a complex and nine are rented, the occupancy rate is 90%. Open the macro-enabled v2b2apartments workbook, and then save it as v2b2apartments_LastnameFirstname. Open v2b2apartments.docx in Word to read more details about the program, what functions are needed, and see screenshots to help you code the program. Use this document to guide you as you design the form and create VBA procedures in the workbook.

The workbook contains variable declarations. Research in Help how to convert an integer to a double within an expression. If you do not convert the integers to doubles, the resulting percentages will not be stored. In the chapter, you learned how to create a function calling statement and assign the returned value to a variable. Use Help to research how to create another procedure with a calling statement to the procedure without having a return value. Review the use of loops, input boxes, and message boxes.

Save and close the workbook, and then submit based on your instructor's directions.

Studio Equipment Loan

DISASTER RECOVERY

You work for a company that sells studio equipment. Most customers make a down payment and obtain a short-term loan to pay off the balance for the equipment they purchase. To help them determine how much their monthly payment will be and to see how much each payment consists of principal and interest, you developed a workbook that contains a list of inputs and a place for the monthly payment information. Open the macro-enabled *v2b3equipment* workbook, and then save it as **v2b3equipment_LastnameFirstname**.

You created a VBA form for input and then to store the values obtained in the top-left corner of the worksheet. However, the form does not populate the list box correctly, and several financial functions are producing incorrect results. Furthermore, the output is often incorrect or not formatted correctly. Review the VBA code carefully and make all necessary corrections. Save and close the workbook, and then submit based on your instructor's directions.

VBA
CUSTOMIZING ACCESS WITH VBA
Enhancing a Database

CASE STUDY | Technology Seminars Offered in Major Cities

KRH Seminars, Inc. has been providing Technology Seminars to customers of all ages and skill levels for 20 years. Its most popular training courses are Microsoft Office 2010, Intro to Microsoft Windows 7, and How to Build a Web Site. Seminars are held in many major cities, and the company expects to expand in the next several years. Seminar sizes range from a minimum of 50 students to a maximum of 250. In most cases, attendees are provided with access to a PC in order to practice newly acquired skills.

The company is using a Microsoft Access database to record registration information, send confirmations, and determine logistical needs such as classroom size, number of computers given out, and instructor assignments. The database has been working well, but the office manager, Kathryn Rose, would like to add additional features to improve the accuracy of the database. Some of the new features include data validation, data entry shortcuts, and the ability to search all records easily based on multiple search criteria.

Your job is to add VBA code to the database to improve the accuracy of the data entry process and to add the additional features that she would like.

OBJECTIVES AFTER YOU READ THIS CHAPTER, YOU WILL BE ABLE TO:

1. Write code in modules
2. Write code for forms and reports
3. Work with objects
4. Create functions
5. Use DAO to access data
6. Use ADO to access data
7. Add VBA to forms
8. Add VBA to reports
9. Handle errors in VBA

From Chapter 3 of *Exploring Getting Started with VBA for Microsoft® Office 2010*, First Edition, Robert T. Grauer, Keith Mulbery, Keith Mast, Mary Anne Poatsy. Copyright © 2012 by Pearson Education, Inc. Published by Pearson Prentice Hall. All rights reserved.

Introduction to VBA and Access

Visual Basic for Applications (VBA) is a programming language that you can use to customize Access as well as the other Office applications in order to enhance its functionality. Within Access, you can create standard VBA modules that will run whenever you execute them. You can also create form and report modules that contain procedures that run whenever an event occurs—such as clicking a control, opening a report, or closing a form—during the normal use of Access. You can also create functions using the same VBA programming code you use for other modules. A function is a special type of procedure that performs an action and returns a value when called from within a module. Another type of module, a class module, is used by experienced VBA programmers to create a special type of program that creates a custom object.

As you work with VBA in Access, you will need to open the Visual Basic Editor (VB Editor), and then determine which type of module to create. Because the VB Editor is a separate program from Access, the program will always open in a new window. Once the VB Editor is open, you may be unsure about which type of module to create. This section will explore a variety of methods for creating code and modules so that you can determine how to create the correct procedure in the correct module.

In this section, you will use the VB Editor to learn how to create procedures in modules, write code for forms and reports, work with objects, and create functions.

Writing Code in Modules

When you create VBA code in Access, you can create the code using one of three modules: a standard module, a class module, or an Access object module. A standard module stores procedures that are available to any event in the application and an Access object module stores procedures that are available to a specific form or report. Class modules are advanced programs that are used to create custom objects. To specify the module type, follow one of the steps listed below.

> When you create VBA code in Access, you can create the code using one of three modules: a standard module, a class module, or an Access object module.

Insert a Standard Module: Open the VB Editor, as shown in Figure 1. In this figure, no code is showing because no procedures have been created. You can create a procedure by inserting a module and then creating the VBA code. To insert a module, click Insert on the menu bar, and then select Module. The VB Editor appears with the statement Option Compare Database at the top of the Code window; Module1 appears in the Project Explorer on the left. Begin the procedure by typing Sub followed by the Name of the procedure, such as Sub YearsOfService (). The editor will add End Sub automatically after you press Enter, as shown in Figure 2. Continue typing the rest of the code until the procedure is completed.

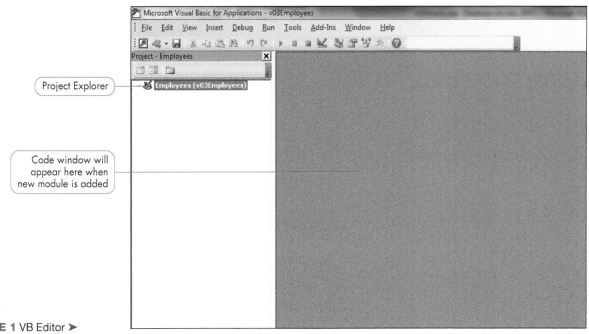

FIGURE 1 VB Editor ➤

Project Explorer

Code window will appear here when new module is added

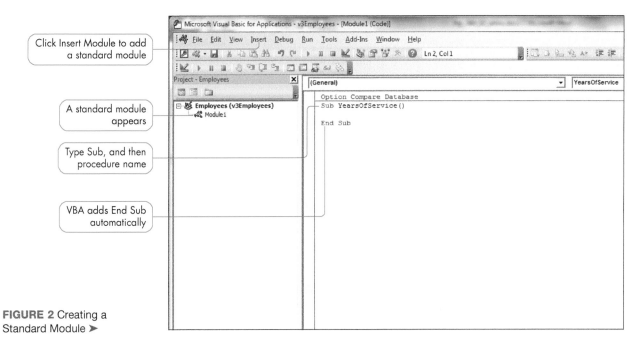

Click Insert Module to add a standard module

A standard module appears

Type Sub, and then procedure name

VBA adds End Sub automatically

FIGURE 2 Creating a Standard Module ➤

Insert a Class Module: The VB Editor opens with no code showing if no procedures have been created. You can create a procedure by inserting a class module and then creating the VBA code. To insert a class module, click Insert on the menu bar, and then select Class Module. The code window appears with the statement Option Compare Database at the top; Class1 appears in the Project Explorer on the left. Begin the procedure by typing Public Sub followed by the Name of the procedure, such as Public Sub AddEmployee(). The editor will add End Sub automatically after you press Enter, as shown in Figure 3. Continue typing the rest of the code until the procedure is completed.

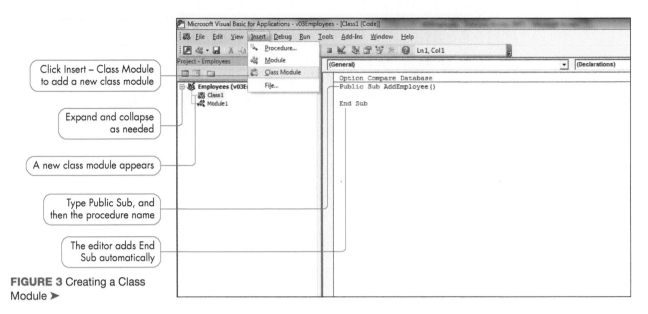

Click Insert – Class Module to add a new class module

Expand and collapse as needed

A new class module appears

Type Public Sub, and then the procedure name

The editor adds End Sub automatically

FIGURE 3 Creating a Class Module ➤

Create an Access object module: Open an Access form or report in Design view, and then insert an event procedure into an event property. Access will automatically open the VB Editor and insert the respective object module. VBA begins the procedure by adding Private Sub followed by the name of the procedure based on the event, such as Private Sub Form_Current(). The editor will add End Sub automatically. Type the rest of the code between the Sub and End Sub statements until the procedure is completed.

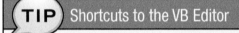

TIP Shortcuts to the VB Editor

You can open the VB Editor by pressing Alt + F11. Another way to open the VB Editor is to double-click a module or class module in the Navigation Pane. When you double-click a module in the Navigation Pane, the VB Editor opens that module so you can view or edit the code immediately.

Writing Code for Forms and Reports

To create VBA code for a form or a report, first open the object in Design view, and then click Property Sheet in the Tools group. Next, select an event (e.g., On Current), and then click Build on the right side of the property cell. The Choose Builder dialog box appears with three options—Macro Builder, Expression Builder, and Code Builder on the Event tab. Select the Code Builder, and then click OK to open the VB Editor, as shown in Figure 4.

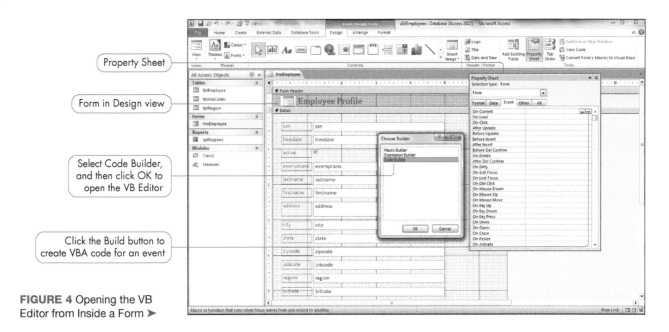

Property Sheet

Form in Design view

Select Code Builder, and then click OK to open the VB Editor

Click the Build button to create VBA code for an event

FIGURE 4 Opening the VB Editor from Inside a Form ➤

When the VB Editor opens, a new form module is created to store the VBA code for the selected form. Notice the Private Sub Form_Current() statement is automatically inserted into the code window by the editor along with the End Sub statement. The Option Compare Database and Option Explicit declarations also appear at the top of the code by default. The *Option Compare Database* statement is used in a module to declare that string comparisons are not case sensitive when data is compared. The *Option Explicit* statement is used in a module to require that all variables be declared before they are used. At this point, you (the programmer) probably have a reason for wanting to add a procedure to the On Current event of the form. For example, you may want to remind the user how long the employee has worked for the company. Add the remaining code to your procedure, as shown in Figure 5, and then save the code. When you close the VB Editor, the original Access form is available.

The **Option Compare Database** statement is used in a module to declare the default comparison method to use when string data is compared.

The **Option Explicit** statement is used in a module to require that all variables be declared before they are used.

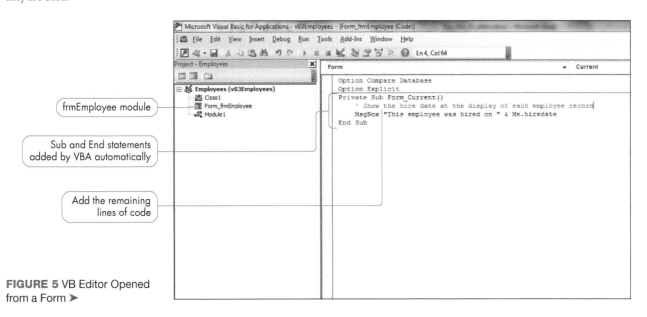

frmEmployee module

Sub and End statements added by VBA automatically

Add the remaining lines of code

FIGURE 5 VB Editor Opened from a Form ➤

Customizing Access with VBA

133

TIP Require Variable Declaration

The Option Explicit statement at the top of a procedure requires that all variables be declared before they are introduced. Because this is the best practice used by most programmers, you should set this feature as the default. In the VB Editor, click Tools on the menu bar, and then select Options. Click the Require Variable Declaration check box to set the option, as shown in Figure 6, and then click OK to close the dialog box.

Verify this item is selected

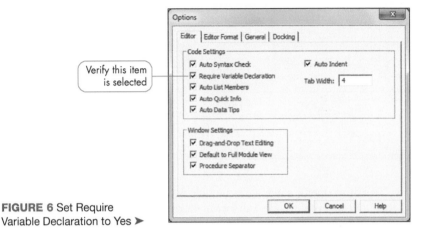

FIGURE 6 Set Require Variable Declaration to Yes ➤

Working with Objects

To create VBA code for a form or a report, first open the object in Design view....

Object libraries contain the objects that are available in the applications that support VBA.

VBA works with the objects in the various *object libraries* that are available in the applications that support VBA. You can use objects in the object libraries along with their resources in order to accomplish the programming tasks. These object libraries include Access and Excel, which are the two most popular applications that support VBA. Word, PowerPoint, and Outlook can also be automated using VBA.

In addition to the Office applications, you can also set references to other object libraries such as Fax Service, Adobe Acrobat, and Yahoo Messenger. All of these libraries require you to set a reference in the VB Editor. Click Tools on the menu bar, click References, and then select the check boxes for the references (or libraries) that you need in the References dialog box, as shown in Figure 7. By default, some of the references you need may already be selected. Knowing which references to select will take practice and some trial and error.

Select the references you require

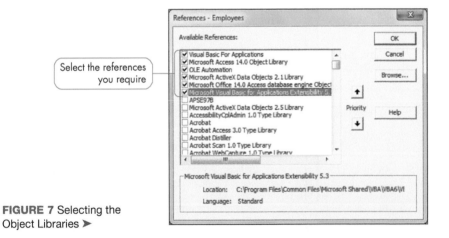

FIGURE 7 Selecting the Object Libraries ➤

Understand Properties

A property is a physical attribute of an object. When working with forms, you will notice they each have a size, a type of border, a back color, and various bound and unbound controls. All of these represent properties of the form except for the bound and unbound controls, which are objects themselves. As a rule, any form property you can change in Design view can also be changed using VBA code. If you can change the back color property of a form to Text 2, Lighter 80%, you can also change the same property using VBA. When using VBA to designate the back color, you must use the numerical equivalent. For example, if you create a form based on the Office Theme, you can set the back color to Text 2, Lighter 80% in VBA using the number 14347005 (see Figure 8).

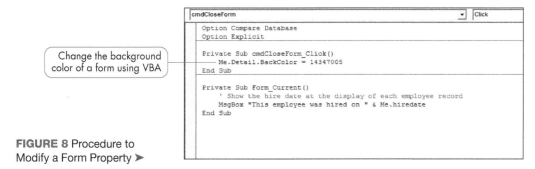

Change the background color of a form using VBA

FIGURE 8 Procedure to Modify a Form Property ➤

If you are a VBA programmer, you have to ask yourself the question, "Why would I want to change the background color of a form?" Programmers usually think of the reason first and the action second. For example, you might want to convey a message to the user, as he or she is entering the data into the fields. When the user successfully fills in the required fields, the form could change color to notify the user the required fields have been filled in. Another technique is to simply display a message to tell the user whether or not they are successful when the record is saved.

Understand Methods

A method is an action that is performed by an object. A few examples of form methods are open, close, refresh, go to new record, and filter for certain criteria. You can accomplish all of these actions manually in Form view by using the Ribbon and the Record Navigation bar. Many actions that you can perform in Form view can also be performed automatically using VBA code. For example, to refresh the form in order to give the user the most up-to-date information, you could create a command button and attach a procedure, as shown in Figure 9. The VBA code to refresh a form is Me.Refresh.

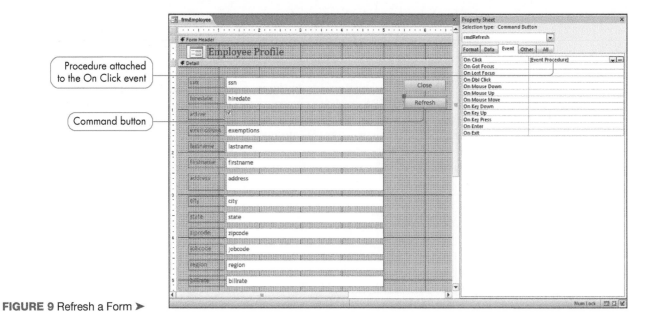

Procedure attached to the On Click event

Command button

FIGURE 9 Refresh a Form ➤

At first, you may find it difficult to differentiate between methods and properties. You may want to change a property or use a method only to discover that VBA reports an error. VBA provides some visual help when adding code to a procedure using the Me prefix. Me refers to the current instance of the object you are in. When you type the Me keyword and then type a period, the editor will provide a list of available items and indicate which items are properties and which are methods using a unique icon. This list is helpful because you do not have to memorize all the properties and methods on a form or report. If you are still unsure and use a property or method improperly, VBA will correct you. As a rule, methods are more difficult to use and master.

Understand Events

An event is what happens when a user takes an action. For example, users can take the following actions when working in a form—change a record, open a form, close a form, and filter the records in a form. The corresponding events that are triggered are shown in Table 1, Event Examples.

TABLE 1 Event Examples		
User Action	**How Access Responds**	**Event Triggered**
Change and save a record in a form	Saves the record	Before Update
Click a button to open a form	Opens the form	On Open
Click the Close button to close a form	Closes the form	On Close
Find records in a form with certain criteria	Filters the record source	On Filter

Events are extremely useful to programmers because they can interrupt user actions and verify that the user really wants to take the action they requested. The first example in the table above, change and save a record in a form, may need confirmation from the user. Did the user intentionally change the data? Adding a message that asks, "Do you want to save your changes?" helps to eliminate inadvertent changes. You can intercept the save process with the Before Update event and then ask the user to confirm; this gives the user a chance to discard the changes. The message would appear to the user, as shown in Figure 10.

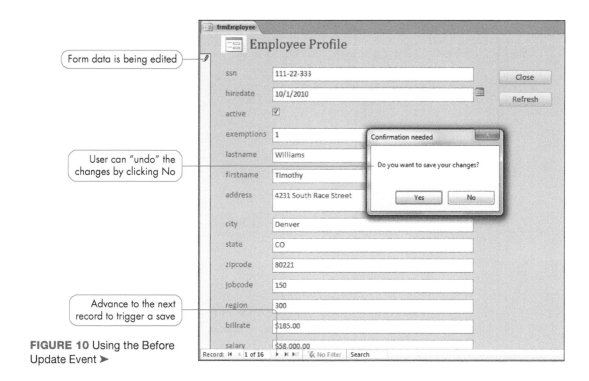

Form data is being edited

User can "undo" the changes by clicking No

Advance to the next record to trigger a save

FIGURE 10 Using the Before Update Event ➤

Creating Functions

As discussed earlier, a function is a procedure that performs an action and returns a value. Many functions are predefined in VBA and ready to use. To use a predefined function, simply add the function to your procedure and insert the required arguments; when the procedure runs, the function will assign the value to the function name.

To create a custom function, open a module, and then type a statement into the Code window with the format:

Function NameOfFunction (Argument As Data Type) As Data Type

End Function

The VB Editor automatically adds the statement End Function after you press Enter. An argument is the value that the procedure passes to the function; arguments can be assigned a specific data type. The data type at the end of the first statement refers to the type of data the function returns to the procedure. Add the remaining lines of code to complete the function, save, and then test the function. When a procedure encounters a function, the procedure takes the following steps:

1. A procedure contains a function.
2. The procedure runs and encounters the function.
3. The procedure calls the function and passes one or more values to it.
4. The function receives the values and processes them according to the function code.
5. The function returns a different value (with possibly a different data type) to the calling procedure by assigning the result to the function name.

If a user could enter a 50-character message into a field, and you wanted to display the number of characters that remained to the user, you could create your own function. The function would contain the lines of code, as shown in Figure 11. In this example, the number of characters remaining could be displayed to the user in a text box, as shown in Figure 12.

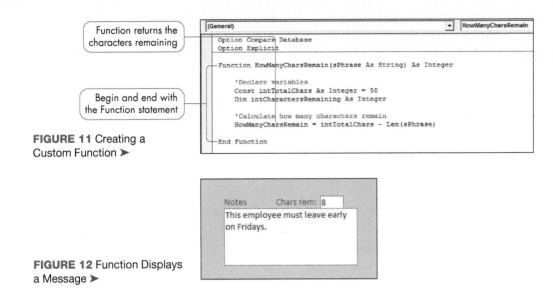

Function returns the characters remaining

Begin and end with the Function statement

FIGURE 11 Creating a Custom Function ➤

```
(General)                                                    ▼   HowManyCharsRemain

Option Compare Database
Option Explicit

Function HowManyCharsRemain(sPhrase As String) As Integer

    'Declare variables
    Const intTotalChars As Integer = 50
    Dim intCharactersRemaining As Integer

    'Calculate how many characters remain
    HowManyCharsRemain = intTotalChars - Len(sPhrase)

End Function
```

Notes   Chars rem: 8
This employee must leave early on Fridays.

FIGURE 12 Function Displays a Message ➤

In Hands-On Exercise 1, you will write code in modules, write code for forms and reports, work with objects, and create a custom function.

HANDS-ON EXERCISES

1 Introduction to VBA and Access

KRH Seminars needs to improve their data entry efficiency. You create a new form to test a few improvements that you will show to Kathryn. Your goal is to remind users when data is missing from the data entry form. This will give the users a chance to ask the attendees for the information while they are still on the phone.

Skills covered: Write Code in Modules • Write Code to Test for Key Data in a Form • Add Validation to a Form • Work with Objects • Create a Function That Checks Elapsed Time

---

STEP 1 ▶ WRITE CODE IN MODULES

You open the VB Editor, and then verify that the Require Variable Declaration check box is set to Yes. You write a simple procedure to practice creating and running a procedure. Refer to Figure 13 as you complete Step 1.

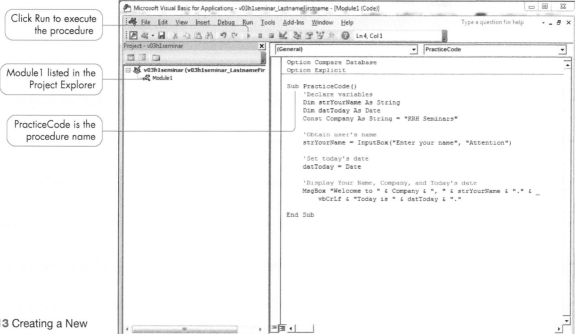

Click Run to execute the procedure

Module1 listed in the Project Explorer

PracticeCode is the procedure name

FIGURE 13 Creating a New Module ▶

a. Open the *v3h1seminar* database, and then save it as **v3h1seminar_LastnameFirstname**.

> **TROUBLESHOOTING:** If you make any major mistakes in this exercise, you can close the file, repeat step a above, and then start over. Throughout the remainder of this chapter, click Enable Content whenever you are working with student files.

b. Click the **Database Tools tab**, and then click **Visual Basic** in the Macro group.

The VB Editor opens.

c. Click **Tools** on the menu bar, and then select **Options**.

The Options dialog box opens.

d. Click the **Require Variable Declaration check box** if necessary to select it.

This option requires that all variables be declared prior to being introduced.

e. Click **OK** to close the Options dialog box.

f. Click **Insert** on the menu bar, and then select **Module**.

The Option Compare Database and Option Explicit statements appear at the top of the code window.

g. Create a new procedure by typing the code shown in Code Window 1.

```
Sub PracticeCode()
    'Declare variables
    Dim strYourName As String
    Dim datToday As Date
    Const Company As String = "KRH Seminars"

    'Obtain user's name
    strYourName = InputBox("Enter your name", "Attention")

    'Set today's date
    datToday = Date

    'Display Your Name, Company, and Today's date
    MsgBox "Welcome to " & Company & ", " & strYourName & "." & _
        vbCrLf & "Today is " & datToday & "."

End Sub
```

CODE WINDOW 1 ⌃

h. Click **Run Sub/Userform** on the toolbar with the insertion point inside the PracticeCode procedure. Enter your name, and then click **OK**.

The procedure runs and asks you for your name. After you type your name, a message box displays KRH Seminars, your name, and today's date.

> **TROUBLESHOOTING:** If the VB Editor reports an error, check the highlighted line for errors, correct the error, and then try again.

i. Click **OK** to close the dialog box. Click **Save** on the toolbar, and then click **OK** in the Save dialog box to save the new module as **Module1**. Close the VB Editor.

STEP 2 ▶ WRITE CODE TO TEST FOR KEY DATA IN A FORM

You will create a new form based on the Attendees table. You need to create a procedure that will check for missing zip code on each record. Refer to Figure 14 as you complete Step 2.

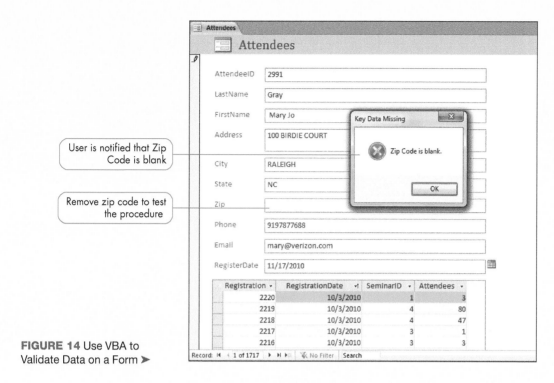

User is notified that Zip Code is blank

Remove zip code to test the procedure

FIGURE 14 Use VBA to Validate Data on a Form ➤

a. Click the **Attendees table** in the Navigation Pane, click the **Create tab**, and then click **Form** in the Forms group.

   A new Attendees form is created with a registration subform.

b. Save the form as **Attendees**. Switch to Design view.

c. Click **Property Sheet** in the Tools group to open the Property Sheet if necessary. Select the form using the Selection type box at the top of the Property Sheet. Click the **Before Update event** on the Event tab.

d. Click **Build**, select **Code Builder** in the Choose Builder dialog box, and then click **OK**.

   The VB Editor opens with an icon for Form_Attendees added to the Project Explorer. A new procedure is started in the Code window.

e. Add the code to the procedure, as shown in Code Window 2.

```
Private Sub Form_BeforeUpdate(Cancel As Integer)
    'Verify that Zip code, Phone, and Email are not blank
    If IsNull(Me.Zip) Then
        MsgBox "Zip Code is blank.", vbCritical, "Key Data Missing"
        Cancel = True
        Exit Sub
    End If

End Sub
```

CODE WINDOW 2 ▲

This section of code verifies that the zip code is not blank. If it is, the user is notified and the record cannot be saved, because the statement Cancel = True cancels the update. Exit Sub stops the procedure from executing the rest of the code.

f. Save the procedure, and then minimize the VB Editor. Display the Attendees form in Form view.

Customizing Access with VBA

141

g. Delete the Zip in the first record of the Attendees form. Press **Tab** until the focus reaches the RegisterDate. Press **Tab** once more. When the message appears, click **OK**, and then press **Esc** to restore the zip code.

The message appeared alerting you that zip code is blank; the record cannot be saved.

STEP 3 ▶ ADD VALIDATION TO A FORM

You also need to validate that phone and e-mail exist for each attendee. You will add additional code to verify that these fields are not blank. Refer to Figure 15 as you complete Step 3.

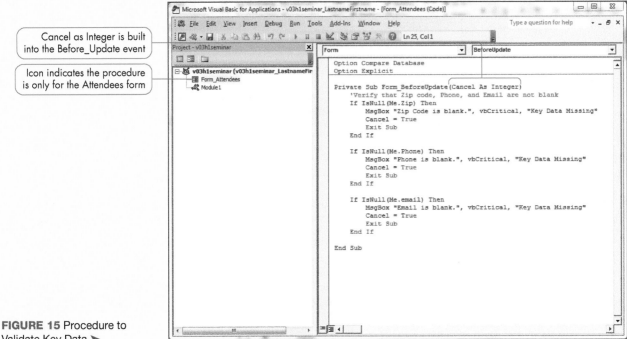

Cancel as Integer is built into the Before_Update event

Icon indicates the procedure is only for the Attendees form

FIGURE 15 Procedure to Validate Key Data ➤

a. Return to the VB Editor. Add additional code to the Form_BeforeUpdate procedure, as shown in Code Window 3.

```
Private Sub Form_BeforeUpdate(Cancel As Integer)
    'Verify that Zip code, Phone, and Email are not blank
    If IsNull(Me.Zip) Then
        MsgBox "Zip Code is blank.", vbCritical, "Key Data Missing"
        Cancel = True
        Exit Sub
    End If

    If IsNull(Me.Phone) Then
        MsgBox "Phone is blank.", vbCritical, "Key Data Missing"
        Cancel = True
        Exit Sub
    End If

    If IsNull(Me.email) Then
        MsgBox "Email is blank.", vbCritical, "Key Data Missing"
        Cancel = True
        Exit Sub
    End If

End Sub
```

CODE WINDOW 3 ⬆

Customizing Access with VBA

This section of code verifies that the phone and e-mail are not blank. If either is, the user is notified and the record cannot be saved, because the statement Cancel = True cancels the update.

b. Save the procedure, and then minimize the VB Editor.

c. Delete the phone number in the first record of the Attendees form. Press **Tab** until the focus reaches the RegisterDate. Press **Tab** once more. When the message appears, click **OK**, and then press **Esc** to restore the phone number.

The message appeared alerting you that phone is blank; the record cannot be saved.

d. Delete the e-mail address in the first record of the Attendees form. Press **Tab** until the focus reaches the RegisterDate. Press **Tab** again. When the message appears, click **OK**, and then press **Esc** to restore the e-mail.

The message appeared alerting you that e-mail is blank; again, the record cannot be saved.

e. Save the changes to the Attendees form.

STEP 4 ▶ WORK WITH OBJECTS

You decide to try another validation method—highlighting key fields with missing data. You will add a command button to the form to accomplish this. Refer to Figure 16 as you complete Step 4.

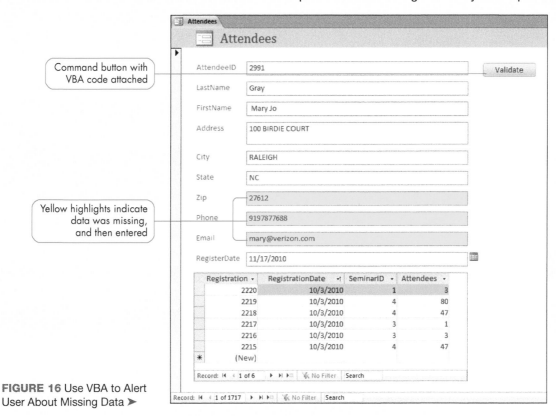

FIGURE 16 Use VBA to Alert User About Missing Data ➤

a. Display the Attendees form in Design view.

b. Reduce the width of all the form fields to make room for the new command button, as shown in Figure 16.

c. Click the **Form Design Tools Design tab**, and then click the **Button control** in the Controls group. Click to the right of the AttendeeID field to add a command button.

The Command Button wizard opens.

d. Click **Cancel** to close the wizard.

You want to add your own code rather than choose from the predefined procedures.

e. Click the **All tab** in the Property Sheet, scroll to the top, and then modify the following properties of the command button:

Name:	cmdValidate
Caption:	Validate

f. Click the **Event tab** in the Property Sheet, and then click the **On Click event**. Click **Build**, click **Code Builder** in the Choose Builder dialog box, and then click **OK**.

The VB Editor opens and a new procedure, Sub cmdValidate_Click(), is added to the Code window above the Form_BeforeUpdate procedure.

g. Type the code shown in Code Window 4 into the Sub cmdValidate_Click() procedure.

```
Private Sub cmdValidate_Click()
    'Validate key data by highlighting fields with missing data
    If IsNull(Me.Zip) Then
        Me.Zip.BackColor = 62207
    End If

End Sub
```

CODE WINDOW 4

This section of code verifies that the zip code is not blank. If it is, the field is highlighted in yellow to alert the user.

h. Save the procedure, and then minimize the VB Editor. Display the Attendees form in Form view.

i. Delete the zip code in the first record of the Attendees form. Click the **Validate button**.

The background color of zip is highlighted in yellow, alerting you that zip code is blank.

j. Press **Esc** to restore the deleted zip code. Return to the VB Editor, and then add additional code to the cmdValidate_Click() procedure, as shown in Code Window 5.

```
Private Sub cmdValidate_Click()
    'Validate key data by highlighting fields with missing data
    If IsNull(Me.Zip) Then
        Me.Zip.BackColor = 62207
    End If

    If IsNull(Me.Phone) Then
        Me.Phone.BackColor = 62207
    End If

    If IsNull(Me.email) Then
        Me.email.BackColor = 62207
    End If

End Sub
```

CODE WINDOW 5

This section of code verifies that the phone and e-mail are not blank. If either is, the user is alerted with a yellow background, the same as the zip field.

k. Save the procedure, and then minimize the VB Editor.

l. Delete the phone number in the first record of the Attendees form. Click the **Validate button**.

The phone field is highlighted with a yellow background.

m. Press **Esc** to restore the deleted phone number. Delete the e-mail address in the first record of the Attendees form. Click the **Validate button**.

The e-mail field is highlighted with a yellow background.

n. Press **Esc** to restore the deleted e-mail. Close the VB Editor, and then save the changes to the Attendees form. Close the form.

STEP 5 ▸ CREATE A FUNCTION THAT CHECKS ELAPSED TIME

Emily, one of the sales reps, would like to know which attendees have not taken a class in over a year so that she can contact them to see if they are in need of any training. You decide to create a function to handle this request. Refer to Figure 17 as you complete Step 5.

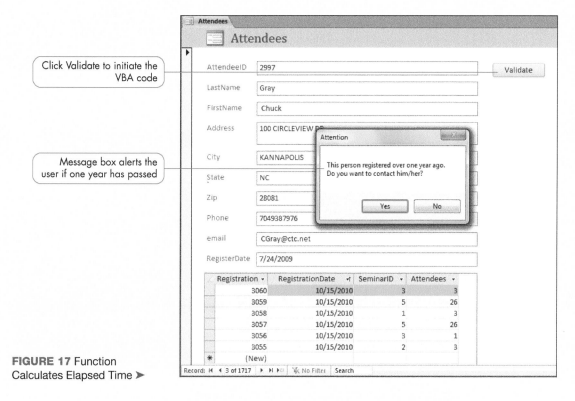

FIGURE 17 Function Calculates Elapsed Time ➤

a. Click the **Database Tools tab**, and then click **Visual Basic** in the Macro group to open the VB Editor.

b. Click **Insert** on the menu bar, and then select **Module**.

The Module2 icon appears in the Project Explorer.

c. Type the following code into the code window:

```
Function MakeContact(sRegisterDate As Date) As Boolean
    'Declare variables
    Dim datRegisterDate As Date

    'Check to see if attendee registered over a year ago
    datRegisterDate = sRegisterDate
    If Date - datRegisterDate > 365 Then
        MakeContact = True
    End If

End Function
```

CODE WINDOW 6 ➤

If the RegisteredDate is more than one year away from today's date, this function will return true by assigning the value to the function name.

d. Save the Module with the name **Functions**.

Now, you will add additional code to the Validate button in order to call the MakeContact function.

e. Double-click the **Form_Attendees icon** in the Project Explorer. Add the code shown in Code Window 7 to the bottom of the cmdValidate_Click() procedure.

```
Private Sub cmdValidate_Click()
    'Validate key data by highlighting fields with missing data
    If IsNull(Me.Zip) Then
        Me.Zip.BackColor = 62207
    End If

    If IsNull(Me.Phone) Then
        Me.Phone.BackColor = 62207
    End If

    If IsNull(Me.email) Then
        Me.email.BackColor = 62207
    End If

    'Check the register date to see if the company should make contact
    If MakeContact(Me.RegisterDate) Then
        MsgBox "This person registered over one year ago." & _
            vbCrLf & "Do you want to contact him/her?", vbYesNo, _
            "Attention"
    End If

End Sub
```

CODE WINDOW 7 ⋀

The above code calls the MakeContact function while passing the RegisteredDate argument.

f. Save the procedure, and then minimize the VB Editor.

g. Return to the Attendees form, and then switch to Form view. Click **Next Record** in the Navigation bar twice until you get to the third record of the Attendees form, and then click the **Validate button**.

Because the person registered over one year ago, the message appears asking if you want to contact this person.

h. Click **No** to close the dialog box. Close the Attendees form. Save the form if necessary.

i. Save the database. Keep the database onscreen if you plan to continue with Hands-On Exercise 2. If not, close the database, and then exit Access.

Customizing Access with VBA

Working with Recordsets

A **recordset** is a set of records in memory selected from a table or query.

A *recordset* is a set of records in memory selected from a table or query. A recordset is similar to a table or a query; the same data source would be represented in all three cases. For example, if you were working with a database that contained employee data, the same results would be achieved with any of the three methods shown in Table 2.

TABLE 2	Table Data Achieved with Three Methods
Method	**Results**
Open Employee table	All columns and all records are displayed
Create a query based on the Employee table	All columns and all records are displayed (as long as all columns are added to the design grid)
Create a Recordset using VBA based on the Employee table	All columns and all records are stored in memory (as long as all columns are selected in the OpenRecordset statement)

The Employee table would display all the columns and all the records in Datasheet view, but could then be filtered into groups and sorted based on multiple criteria. A query based on the Employee table could limit the number of columns (by selecting a subset of fields); the query could also limit the number of records by entering criteria in one or more fields. A recordset could limit the number of columns and fields, evaluate each record in the recordset individually, and then take action based on the logic of the procedure.

The benefit of the recordset is the versatility of working with records and data programmatically. Although you can manipulate records and data using an action query, only recordsets enable you to update records using decision structures.

In this section, you will learn how to manipulate recordsets using DAO (Data Access Objects) and ADO (ActiveX Data Objects).

Using DAO to Access Data

DAO (Data Access Objects) refers to an object library specifically created to work with Access databases.

... only recordsets enable you to update records using decision structures.

DAO (Data Access Objects) refers to an object library specifically created to work with Access databases. The DAO object library was first released in 1992 along with Access 1.0. Needless to say, it has evolved and improved with all the versions of Access released since, including Access 2010. Although newer database object libraries have been created, DAO remains the object library of choice for many Access developers.

Create Recordsets

As stated earlier, a recordset is a set of records in memory. To create the recordset, you first write a procedure using VBA that extracts data from one or more tables in an Access database and then places the results in memory. Once the recordset has been placed in memory, you can then logically examine the records and make decisions and changes based on your own criteria.

To create a recordset in DAO, you must first explicitly connect to a database, usually the database that is currently opened. Next, you create a recordset object based on a table, a query, or an SQL statement. Then, you can loop through the records in the recordset and count the total number of records, count only the records that meet a certain criteria, or modify field data of all records that meet a certain criteria.

An outline for a procedure that creates a DAO recordset is shown in Figure 18.

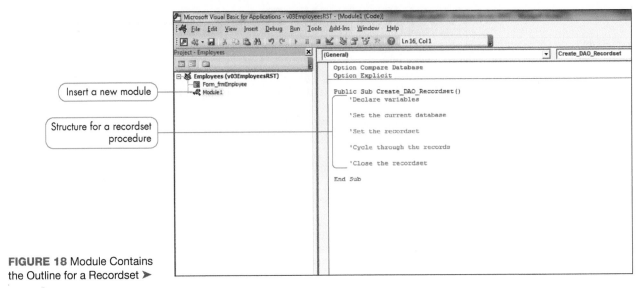

FIGURE 18 Module Contains the Outline for a Recordset ➤

Insert a new module

Structure for a recordset procedure

Find Records in a Recordset

To create a recordset and then look for records that meet certain criteria, you must first identify the table or query that contains the initial recordset. For example, if you need to find all the employees who live in Colorado, you could create a recordset based on the Employee table. After the recordset has been set, you could use the *MoveNext* method to advance through the records of the recordset. Stopping at each record, you could test the employee's State to see if it equals CO. If an employee resides in CO, the procedure would then take the appropriate action to update one or more field values in the matching records.

The **MoveNext** method is used to advance through the records of a recordset.

Figure 19 shows a sample procedure that creates a DAO recordset and then advances through the records looking for employees who live in CO.

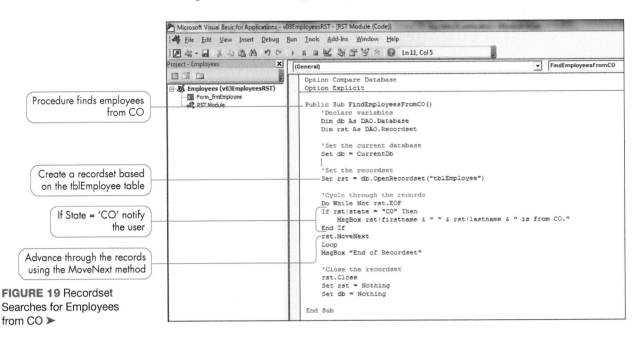

Procedure finds employees from CO

Create a recordset based on the tblEmployee table

If State = 'CO' notify the user

Advance through the records using the MoveNext method

FIGURE 19 Recordset Searches for Employees from CO ➤

In the FindEmployeesFromCO procedure shown in Figure 19, the Database and Recordset variables are first declared using the DAO object prefix. The DAO prefix is used to distinguish from any other database libraries that might be referenced in this database. Next, the database object is set to the Current Database using the CurrentDb method. The statement is abbreviated in our sample procedure; the full statement reads Application.CurrentDb. In most cases, the abbreviated CurrentDb method is sufficient.

In the next line of code, the recordset is established using the OpenRecordset method of the db object. Our example opens the tblEmployee table and sets the rst object equal to it. At this point, the recordset object (rst) exists in memory. The procedure can now cycle through the records looking for a match to the code's criteria.

The Do Loop is used in combination with the MoveNext method to cycle through the employee records. The While clause is used to end the loop when the End of File (EOF) is reached. As each new record is visited, the state value is compared to CO. If it matches, then a predefined action is performed. In our example, the user is notified that an employee lives in CO. This sequence of statements, shown in Code Window 8, is very common when working with recordsets; you will repeat these statements for almost every recordset you create:

CODE WINDOW 8 ➤

```
'Cycle through the records
Do While Not rst.EOF
If rst!state = "CO" Then
    MsgBox rst!firstname & " " & rst!lastname & " is from CO."
End If
rst.MoveNext
Loop
```

Finally, the recordset object rst is closed and then set to nothing. The database object db is also set to nothing. Closing the recordset and setting it to nothing frees the computer memory being used by VBA so that it can be used for other procedures and applications. Your computer could become sluggish if you open several large recordsets without closing them because they tie up memory resources.

 TIP Working with Recordset Fields

When you create a recordset procedure in VBA, you refer to the fields in the recordset using the rst! prefix. When you create a recordset object, refer to the field names as rst!EmployeeName, rst!EmployeePhone, and rst!EmployeeSalary. If you omit the object rst or the ! delimiter, the fields will not be recognized by VBA.

Update Records in a Recordset

The **edit** method enables you to change the data in a recordset.

The **update** method enables you to save the changes in a recordset.

To update the field values in a recordset, you must first open the recordset for edits, make the change, and then close the recordset to further edits. This process repeats for each record you need to edit. The two methods you need to accomplish a recordset edit are *edit* and *update*. Edit enables the edit to happen and update saves the changes and closes the edit process. See Figure 20 for a sample procedure that updates the employee bill rate for employees who live in Colorado.

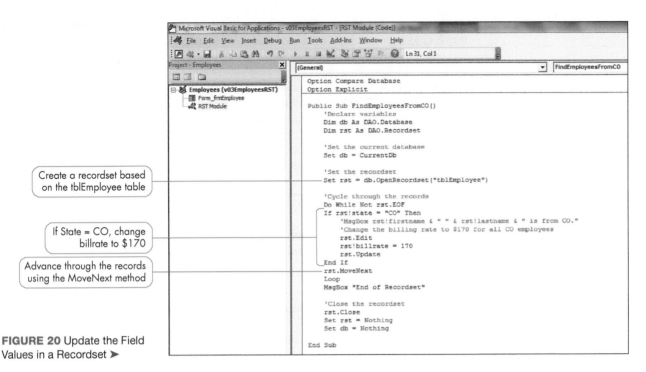

Create a recordset based on the tblEmployee table

If State = CO, change billrate to $170

Advance through the records using the MoveNext method

FIGURE 20 Update the Field Values in a Recordset ➤

```
Microsoft Visual Basic for Applications - v03EmployeesRST - [RST Module (Code)]
File  Edit  View  Insert  Debug  Run  Tools  Add-Ins  Window  Help
                                                              Ln 31, Col 1
Project - Employees                    (General)                        FindEmployeesFromCO

Employees (v03EmployeesRST)
    Form_frmEmployee
    RST Module
```

```
Option Compare Database
Option Explicit

Public Sub FindEmployeesFromCO()
    'Declare variables
    Dim db As DAO.Database
    Dim rst As DAO.Recordset

    'Set the current database
    Set db = CurrentDb

    'Set the recordset
    Set rst = db.OpenRecordset("tblEmployee")

    'Cycle through the records
    Do While Not rst.EOF
    If rst!state = "CO" Then
        'MsgBox rst!firstname & " " & rst!lastname & " is from CO."
        'Change the billing rate to $170 for all CO employees
        rst.Edit
        rst!billrate = 170
        rst.Update
    End If
    rst.MoveNext
    Loop
    MsgBox "End of Recordset"

    'Close the recordset
    rst.Close
    Set rst = Nothing
    Set db = Nothing

End Sub
```

Because VBA updates to a recordset are not easily reversible, it would be a good idea to back up your database before you run an update procedure. The first time you create an update procedure, you must be prepared for errors and unexpected results. Always check the results by opening the affected table(s); if there are problems, revert back to the backup version of the database.

Delete Records in a Recordset

Sometimes, you may need to delete records from a recordset, the same way you need to delete records from a table. The difference is that you can create a VBA procedure to cycle through the records and delete only the records that meet your predefined criteria. This is much more efficient than scanning the records in the table and then pausing to delete the records that you want to remove. See Figure 21 for a sample procedure that deletes all employees from the tblEmployees2 table who are inactive.

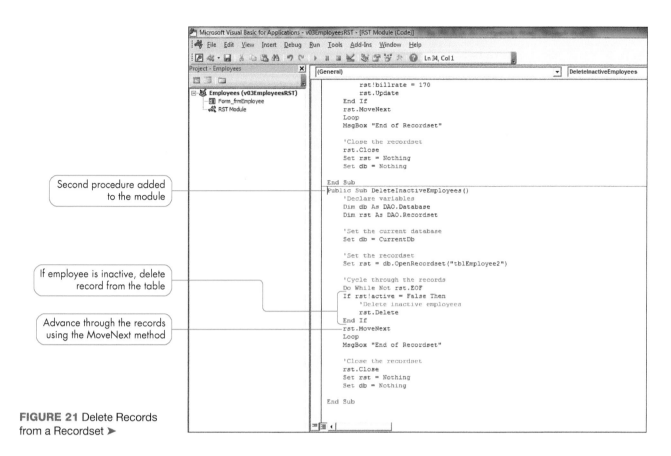

Second procedure added to the module

If employee is inactive, delete record from the table

Advance through the records using the MoveNext method

FIGURE 21 Delete Records from a Recordset ➤

The key lines of code that enable you to delete records from a recordset are shown in Code Window 9. The Delete method actually provides the delete as the Do Loop cycles through the records in the table.

```
'Cycle through the records
Do While Not rst.EOF
If rst!active = False Then
     'Delete inactive employees
     rst.Delete
End If
rst.MoveNext
Loop
```

CODE WINDOW 9 ➤

Insert Records in a Recordset

Sometimes, you may want to insert records into a recordset, the same way you need to insert records into a table. The difference is that you can create a VBA procedure to insert a record when a certain event takes place in your database. For example, if a customer enters data into an application form for processing, you may want to insert the data into another table only after the application is approved. See Figure 22 for a sample procedure that inserts a record into the tblEmployee table.

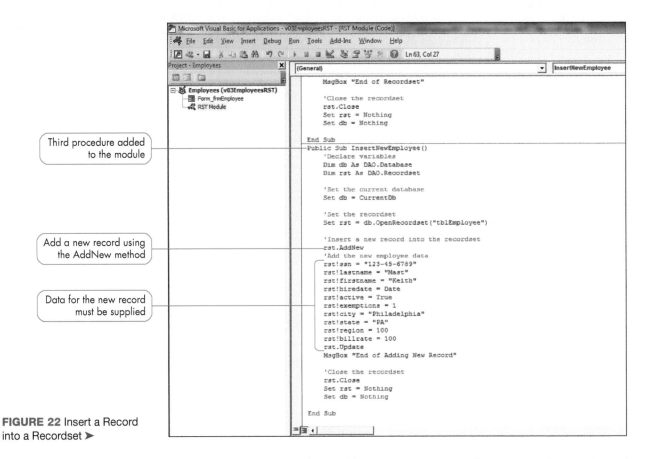

FIGURE 22 Insert a Record into a Recordset ➤

Third procedure added to the module

Add a new record using the AddNew method

Data for the new record must be supplied

The key lines of code that enable you to insert a record into a recordset are shown in Code Window 10. The AddNew method actually provides the permission for the procedure to insert a new record into the recordset. The Update method completes the insertion of the new data into the recordset.

```
'Insert a new record into the recordset
rst.AddNew
'Add the new employee data
rst!ssn = "123-45-6789"
rst!lastname = "Mast"
rst!firstname = "Keith"
rst!hiredate = Date
rst!active = True
rst!exemptions = 1
rst!city = "Philadelphia"
rst!state = "PA"
rst!region = 100
rst!billrate = 100
rst.Update
```

CODE WINDOW 10 ➤

Using ADO to Access Data

ADO (ActiveX Data Objects) was designed for connecting to a wide range of external data sources.

Starting with Access 2000, Microsoft introduced ADO, another object library for accessing data. *ADO (ActiveX Data Objects)* was designed for connecting to a wide range of external data sources. Although DAO was designed to work with your local Access database, ADO was designed to connect to relational databases, ISAM data sources, disk files, and so on. Whereas DAO uses the db = CurrentDb statement to connect to the current database, ADO uses the CurrentProject.Connection argument, as shown in Figure 23.

Customizing Access with VBA

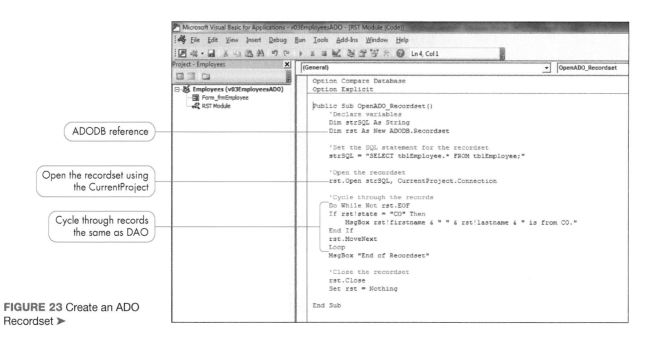

FIGURE 23 Create an ADO
Recordset ➤

In ADO (as in DAO), it is important to declare database variables with the object library prefix. For example, when declaring the rst variable, use *Dim rst As ADODB.Recordset*. After the variable is declared, you can open the recordset using the rst.Open statement. Cycle through the records in the recordset using the Do Loop (the same as the DAO recordset).

Before you can use the ADO object library, you must create a link to the library by clicking Tools on the menu bar, and then selecting References. Figure 24 shows the references dialog box for a typical Access database, including a link to the ADO library.

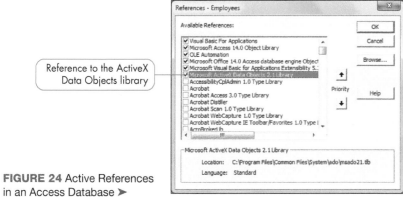

FIGURE 24 Active References
in an Access Database ➤

TIP Make a Copy Before Changing References

Changing the references in a database can cause serious problems. Always make a copy of your database before changing references. If anything goes wrong, you can revert back to the original database. Even if your database contains no VBA code, the built-in functions that are probably in use in various places will stop working if you disconnect one of the references.

In Hands-On Exercise 2, you will create recordsets, find records in a recordset, update records in a recordset, delete records from a recordset, and insert records in a recordset.

HANDS-ON EXERCISES

2 Working with Recordsets

Sometimes, KRH Seminars needs to quickly update their attendee records. You create a new procedure to help Kathryn update their records based on certain criteria. While you are creating the new recordset, you may want to delete and insert records at the same time. Keep this in mind as you develop the procedure.

Skills covered: Create a Recordset Using DAO • Find Records in a Recordset • Update Records in a Recordset • Delete Records in a Recordset • Insert Records in a Recordset

---

STEP 1 ▶ CREATE A RECORDSET USING DAO

You need to create a recordset using the Attendees table in the Seminar database. You will make sure to add comments for each section so you can easily diagnose problems or make changes later. You will add additional lines of code as you complete the remaining steps in this activity. Refer to Figure 25 as you complete Step 1.

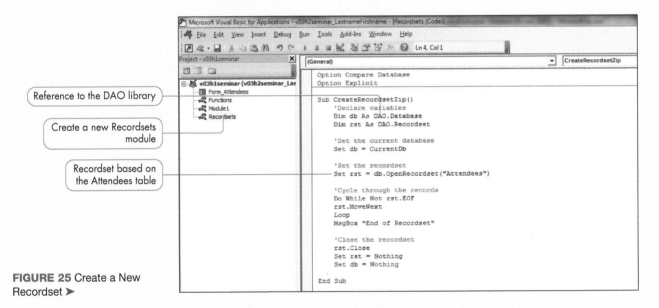

FIGURE 25 Create a New Recordset ➤

a. Open the *v3h1seminar_LastnameFirstname* database if you closed it at the end of Hands-On Exercise 1, and then save it as **v3h2seminar_LastnameFirstname**.

b. Click the **Database Tools tab**, and then click **Visual Basic** in the Macro group.

The VB Editor opens.

c. Click **Insert** on the menu bar, and then select **Module**.

The Option Compare Database and Option Explicit statements appear at the top of the code window.

d. Click **Save** on the toolbar, type **Recordsets** in the **Save dialog box** as the module name, and then click **OK**.

The Recordsets module appears in the Project Explorer.

e. Type the lines of code shown in Code Window 11.

```
Sub CreateRecordsetZip()
    'Declare variables
    Dim db As DAO.Database
    Dim rst As DAO.Recordset

    'Set the current database
    Set db = CurrentDb

    'Set the recordset
    Set rst = db.OpenRecordset("Attendees")

    'Cycle through the records
    Do While Not rst.EOF
    rst.MoveNext
    Loop
    MsgBox "End of Recordset"

    'Close the recordset
    rst.Close
    Set rst = Nothing
    Set db = Nothing

End Sub
```

CODE WINDOW 11 ➤

f. Click **Run Sub/Userform** on the toolbar, with the insertion point inside the CreateRecordsetZip procedure. Click **OK** when the message appears.

The procedure runs, and then displays the End of Recordset message.

> TROUBLESHOOTING: If the VB Editor reports an error, check the highlighted line in the Code window for errors, correct the error, and then try again.

g. Save the Recordsets module.

STEP 2 ➤ FIND RECORDS IN A RECORDSET

You need to revise the Attendees recordset in order to find records with a certain zip code. Because this step does not alter the data, you do not have to save a backup of the database. You will display the matching records using the message box function. Refer to Figure 26 as you complete Step 2.

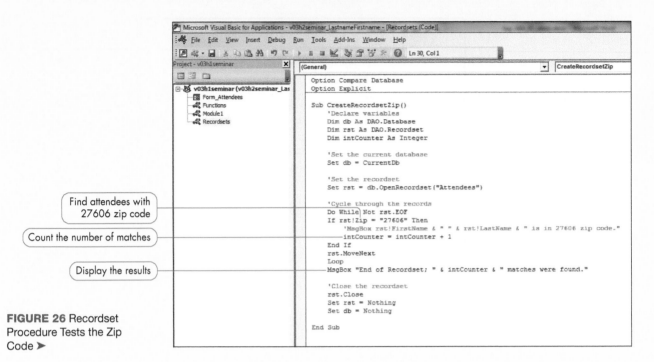

FIGURE 26 Recordset
Procedure Tests the Zip
Code ➤

Labels pointing to code:
- Find attendees with 27606 zip code
- Count the number of matches
- Display the results

a. Insert the three lines of code shown in Code Window 12 into the procedure.

```
'Cycle through the records
Do While Not rst.EOF
If rst!Zip = "27606" Then
    MsgBox rst!FirstName & " " & rst!LastName & " is in 27606 zip code."
End If
rst.MoveNext
Loop
MsgBox "End of Recordset"
```

CODE WINDOW 12 ⋀

b. Place the insertion point inside the CreateRecordsetZip procedure, and then click **Run Sub/Userform** on the toolbar. Click **OK** as needed, and then count the number of matches.

The procedure runs and then displays the names of all attendees that match the zip code.

> TROUBLESHOOTING: If the VB Editor reports an error, check the highlighted line in the Code window for errors, correct the error, and then try again.

c. Minimize the VB Editor. Open the Attendees table, and then filter the table for zip code 27606. Verify the table contains the same number of matches as step b. Close the table without saving.

You decide to add a counter so the procedure counts the records for you.

d. Return to the VB Editor, and then revise the procedure by adding two lines of code and modifying two lines, as shown in Code Window 13.

```
Sub CreateRecordsetZip()
    'Declare variables
    Dim db As DAO.Database
    Dim rst As DAO.Recordset
    Dim intCounter As Integer

    'Set the current database
    Set db = CurrentDb

    'Set the recordset
    Set rst = db.OpenRecordset("Attendees")

    'Cycle through the records
    Do While Not rst.EOF
    If rst!Zip = "27606" Then
        'MsgBox rst!FirstName & " " & rst!LastName & " is in 27606 zip code."
        intCounter = intCounter + 1
    End If
    rst.MoveNext
    Loop
    MsgBox "End of Recordset; " & intCounter & " matches were found."

    'Close the recordset
    rst.Close
    Set rst = Nothing
    Set db = Nothing

End Sub
```

CODE WINDOW 13 ▲

> e. Run the procedure.
>
> There should be 22 matches reported at the end of the procedure.

> TROUBLESHOOTING: If the individual matches are displayed, verify that the apostrophe appears before the MsgBox statement.

> f. Click **OK** to close the message box, and then save the module.

STEP 3 **UPDATE RECORDS IN A RECORDSET**

You need to revise the Attendees recordset in order to modify records with a certain zip code. You will enter code to add −9999 to each matching zip code in order to conform to the post office's more specific ZIP+4 notation, and then you display the matching records using the message box function. Because this step alters the data, you save a backup copy of the database. Refer to Figure 27 as you complete Step 3.

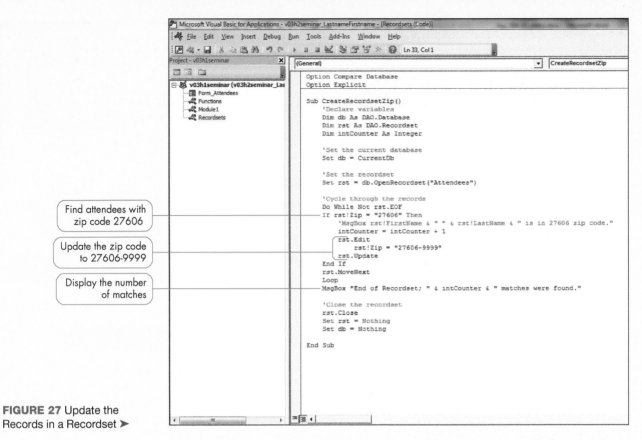

Find attendees with zip code 27606

Update the zip code to 27606-9999

Display the number of matches

FIGURE 27 Update the Records in a Recordset ➤

a. Return to Access, click the **File tab**, click **Save & Publish**, click **Back Up Database**, and then click **Save As**. Accept the default file name (e.g., *v3h2seminar_LastnameFirstname_2011-03-07*), and then click **Save**.

You created a backup of the database. Verify the original *v3h2seminar_LastnameFirstname* database is still open.

b. Open the VB Editor, and then revise the procedure by adding three lines of code into the Code window, as shown in Code Window 14.

```
'Cycle through the records
Do While Not rst.EOF
If rst!Zip = "27606" Then
    'MsgBox rst!FirstName & " " & rst!LastName & " is in 27606 zip code."
    intCounter = intCounter + 1
    rst.Edit
        rst!Zip = "27606-9999"
    rst.Update
End If
rst.MoveNext
Loop
MsgBox "End of Recordset; " & intCounter & " matches were found."
```

CODE WINDOW 14 ▲

c. Run the procedure.

The procedure runs and then displays the number of attendees that match the zip code.

d. Minimize the VB Editor. Open the Attendees table, and then filter the table for zip code 27606-9999. Verify the table contains the correct number of records with the new zip code. Close the table without saving.

e. Maximize the VB Editor, and then save the module.

Customizing Access with VBA

158

You need to create a new procedure that identifies attendees without a zip code. You will first display the matching records using the message box function. Next, you will delete the records with the missing zip code. Refer to Figure 28 as you complete Step 4.

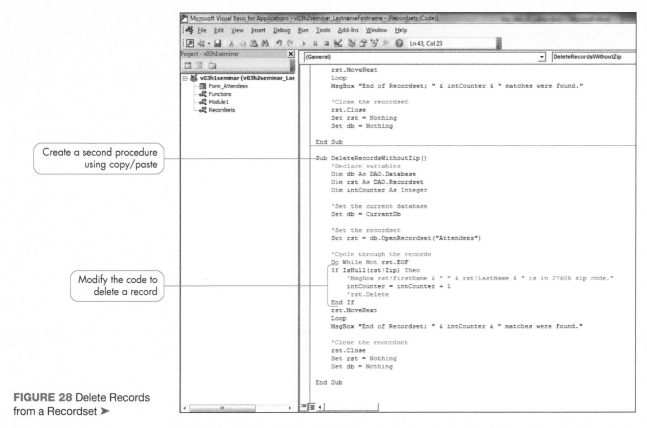

FIGURE 28 Delete Records from a Recordset ▶

a. Copy the entire CreateRecordsetZip procedure, and then paste it below the End Sub statement.

b. Change the name of the second procedure to **DeleteRecordsWithoutZip**.

c. Modify the procedure by changing the *Do While* section of the code, as noted in Code Window 15. (Note that some lines will need to be deleted.)

```
'Cycle through the records
Do While Not rst.EOF
If IsNull(rst!Zip) Then
    'MsgBox rst!FirstName & " " & rst!LastName & " is in 27606 zip code."
    intCounter = intCounter + 1
    'rst.Delete
End If
rst.MoveNext
Loop
MsgBox "End of Recordset; " & intCounter & " matches were found."
```

CODE WINDOW 15 ▲

d. Run the procedure.

The procedure runs, and then displays the End of Recordset message box with the number of matches found.

> **TROUBLESHOOTING:** If the procedure does not find two records, diagnose the problem, and then run the procedure again until there are only two records found.

Customizing Access with VBA

e. Remove the comment (') in front of the rst.Delete statement. Run the procedure again.

VBA deletes the two attendees without a zip code.

f. Minimize the VB Editor. Open the Attendees table, and then sort the table by ascending zip code. Verify the table contains no records with a blank zip code. Close the Attendees table.

g. Return to the VB Editor, and then save the module.

STEP 5 INSERT RECORDS IN A RECORDSET

You need to create a new procedure that inserts a new record into the Attendees table. You will supply the key field data in the procedure, and then insert the data into the table. You will verify the record was added by opening the table. Refer to Figure 29 as you complete Step 5.

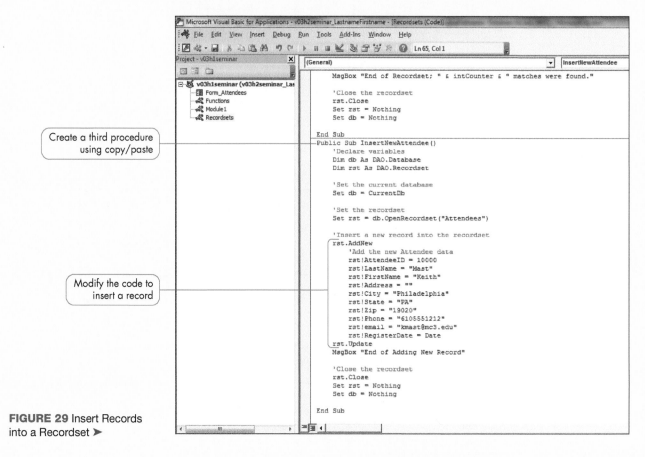

FIGURE 29 Insert Records into a Recordset ➤

a. Open the VB Editor, copy the entire CreateRecordsetZip procedure, and then paste it below the last End Sub statement in the Code window.

b. Change the name of the new procedure to **InsertNewAttendee**.

c. Modify the procedure by removing the *Do While* section of the code and adding the insert section as noted below. (Note that some lines will need to be deleted.)

```
'Insert a new record into the recordset
rst.AddNew
    'Add the new Attendee data
    rst!AttendeeID = 10000
    rst!LastName = "Mast"
    rst!FirstName = "Keith"
    rst!Address = ""
    rst!City = "Philadelphia"
    rst!State = "PA"
    rst!Zip = "19020"
    rst!Phone = "6105551212"
    rst!email = "kmast@mc3.edu"
    rst!RegisterDate = Date
rst.Update
MsgBox "End of Adding New Record"
```

CODE WINDOW 16 ➤

d. Run the procedure.

The procedure runs and then inserts the new person into the Attendees table.

e. Minimize the VB Editor. Open the Attendees table, and then sort the table by descending AttendeeID. Verify the table contains the new record. Close the Attendees table.

f. Return to the VB Editor, save the module, and then close the VB Editor.

g. Save the database. Keep the database onscreen if you plan to continue with Hands-On Exercise 3. If not, close the database, and then exit Access.

Forms, Reports, and Errors in VBA

Enhancing the functionality of forms and reports is one of the most common uses of VBA. By themselves, Access forms and reports work well most of the time. However, sometimes, you may need the programming power of VBA to add functionality to a form or report. When a user opens a form and begins to enter data, VBA can monitor the data entry process and warn the user when invalid data is entered. VBA can also increase the versatility of a report by allowing the user to choose from a list of parameters. For example, a user may want to see a report based on the previous fiscal year as opposed to the current fiscal year. VBA can help accomplish this.

When you add VBA code to your application, you should include error trapping in your procedures. Errors are a common occurrence whenever you add VBA code to a database; *error trapping* is the process of intercepting and handling errors at run time. Errors are part of any software application and it is important to account for them. As a VBA programmer, your job is to test and find the logical and syntax errors before the code runs; once the code runs, you must also account for run time errors. These run time errors can be addressed with VBA's error trapping techniques. The VB Editor also enables error debugging as part of the built-in tools; these tools enable you to pinpoint the cause of an error and hopefully help you find a solution.

Error trapping is the process of intercepting and handling errors at run time.

... sometimes, you may need the programming power of VBA to add functionality to a form or report.

In this section, you will learn how to enhance forms and reports using VBA. You will also learn how to handle run time errors that appear in VBA code.

Adding VBA to Forms

Almost all of the VBA code added to a form is triggered by an event. Common events include On Open, On Click, On Enter, On Exit, Before Update, and After Update. As you learned earlier, events are what happen when a user takes action. In order for the On Open event to occur, the user must open a form (see Table 1 for more examples). All of the available events are found on the Event tab on the Property Sheet, as shown in Figure 30.

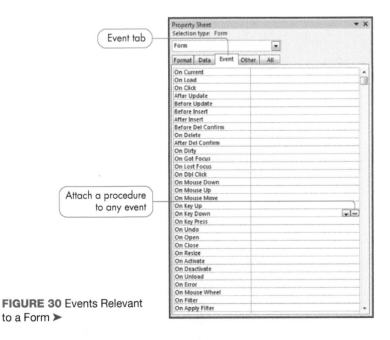

FIGURE 30 Events Relevant to a Form ➤

A form has one set of events and each object on a form has another set of events. Many events overlap between a form and the objects on a form. For example, a form and a text box on a form both have the On Click event. They also both contain the Before Update and After Update events. However, although a form contains the On Current event, a text box does not. *On Current* is the event that is triggered by a record being loaded into a form. A text box is needed to display the data in a record, but it is not responsible for loading the data.

A text box can trigger the On Enter event, a form does not. *On Enter* refers to the act of placing the insertion point in a text box (using the mouse or pressing Tab or Enter). However, a form is opened rather than entered.

On Current is the event that is triggered by a record being loaded into a form.

On Enter refers to the act of placing the insertion point in a text box.

Add an Event Procedure to a Form

While you are editing a record in a form, the pencil appears in the record selector on the left. When the pencil disappears, the record has been saved. A user may miss the pencil (or the pencil may be missing if the record selector is turned off). To notify the user when a record is being changed, you could add a hidden message to the top of the form and then make the message visible while a user is changing a record (see Figure 31). After the record is saved, the message could be hidden again.

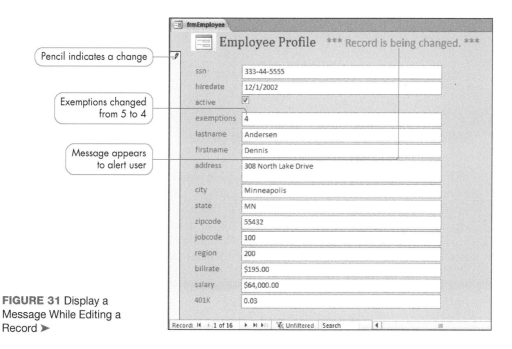

FIGURE 31 Display a Message While Editing a Record ➤

On Dirty is triggered when a record is being edited.
After Update is triggered after a record is saved.

To add the additional message, you need to add a label control to the form header and then create two event procedures that control when the label is visible. The first event, *On Dirty*, is triggered when a record is being edited. When the event is triggered, the event procedure will display the label. The second event, *After Update*, is triggered after a record is saved. When the event is triggered, the event procedure will hide the label again.

In Design view, add a label control to the form header, and then type an appropriate message. The two event procedures will then control whether or not the label is visible in Form view. The procedures would only contain one line of code each (in addition to the Sub and End Sub statements). The two procedures are shown in Figure 32.

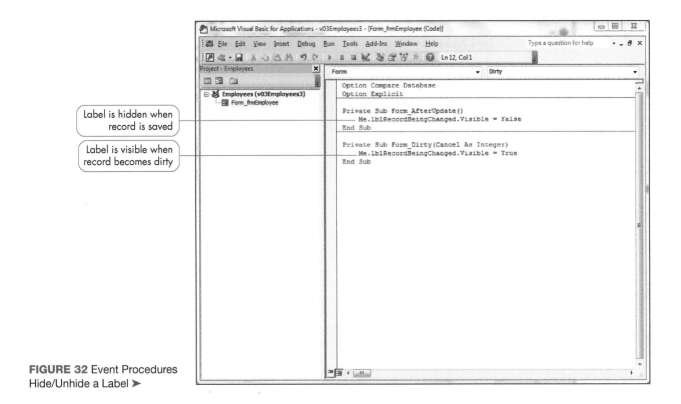

Label is hidden when record is saved

Label is visible when record becomes dirty

FIGURE 32 Event Procedures Hide/Unhide a Label ➤

Validate Data Before an Update

Before Update is triggered before a record is saved.

The Before Update event is used to intercept the saving of a record if any key fields are blank or if any fields contain data outside the acceptable boundaries. *Before Update* is triggered before a record is saved. Notifying a user that fields are blank or that data is outside normal boundaries can greatly improve the reliability of the data. Retrieving the data later, running reports, and analyzing data with queries will be much more effective if the data is reliable.

To create a procedure that will validate a record before saving it, start an event procedure attached to the Before Update event. When the VB Editor opens, add a comment in the Code window that explains what each statement is validating, and then add the appropriate conditional statements. For example, if you were working with the Employee form, you could verify that the following conditions were not violated:

- Hire date must be 10 days before or after today
- Exemptions must be between 0 and 9
- Bill rate must be between 0 and $250
- Salary must be between 0 and $125,000
- 401k contribution must be between 0 and 15%

Open the Employee form in Design view, open the Property Sheet, and then click the Before Update procedure. Click Build, select the Code Builder from the Choose Builder dialog box, and then click OK. The Visual Basic window opens and the Sub BeforeUpdate() procedure has been started. Add one section for each type of validation; each section should contain a comment, a conditional statement (If...then), and a message to the user if the condition is violated. If a condition is violated, exit from the procedure; this will give the user a chance to correct the first problem before notifying him or her of the next issue. See Figure 33 for a sample Before Update procedure that checks the five conditions mentioned earlier. The alert message when data is entered outside of the acceptable range is shown in Figure 34.

TIP Shortcut: Add a Procedure to an Event

To quickly add a procedure to an event, double-click the event name or inside the event property box. [Event Procedure] appears in the event property box. Next, click Build and you are immediately taken to the VB Editor.

Validation of hire date

Validation of exemptions

Validation of bill rate, salary, and 401k

```
Private Sub Form_BeforeUpdate(Cancel As Integer)
    'Hiredate must be 10 days before or after today
    If Not (Me.hiredate >= (Date - 10) And Me.hiredate <= (Date + 10))
        'stop the save
        Cancel = True
        MsgBox "Hire date must fall within 10 days from today."
        Exit Sub
    End If

    'Exemptions must be between 0 and 9
    If Not (Me.Exemptions >= 0 And Me.Exemptions <= 9) Then
        'stop the save
        Cancel = True
        MsgBox "Exemptions must fall within 0 and 10."
        Exit Sub
    End If

    'Billrate must be between 0 and $250
    If Not (Me.billrate >= 0 And Me.billrate <= 250) Then
        'stop the save
        Cancel = True
        MsgBox "Bill rate must fall within 0 and $250."
        Exit Sub
    End If

    'Salary must be between 0 and $125,000
    If Not (Me.salary >= 0 And Me.salary <= 125000) Then
        'stop the save
        Cancel = True
        MsgBox "Bill rate must fall within 0 and $125,000."
        Exit Sub
    End If

    '401K contribution must be between 0 and 15%
    If Not (Me.Ctl401K >= 0 And Me.Ctl401K <= 0.15) Then
        'stop the save
        Cancel = True
        MsgBox "401K rate must fall within 0 and 15%."
        Exit Sub
    End If
End Sub
```

FIGURE 33 Before Update
Procedure to Validate Data ➤

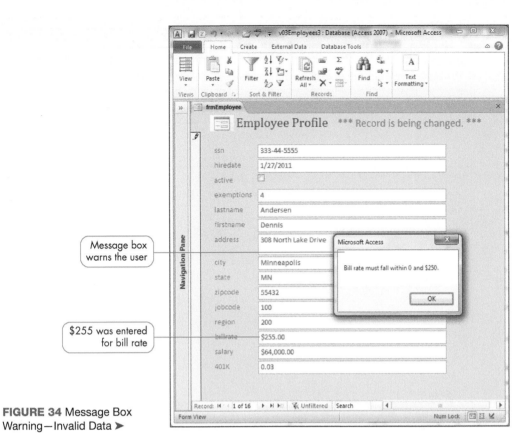

Message box
warns the user

$255 was entered
for bill rate

FIGURE 34 Message Box
Warning—Invalid Data ➤

Adding VBA to Reports

Sometimes, you may want to modify the layout of a report before the report prints. For example, a report that contains multiple sections may have one or more sections that you want to hide, even though they contain data. Access does not have an option for hiding a section at run time. You can use VBA to test if a section matches a certain criteria and then tell Access how to respond when the condition is met. One option is to simply tell Access to hide the matching sections and show all other sections. The procedure would be similar to the code in Figure 35.

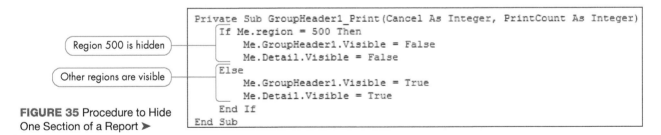

Region 500 is hidden

Other regions are visible

FIGURE 35 Procedure to Hide
One Section of a Report ➤

```
Private Sub GroupHeader1_Print(Cancel As Integer, PrintCount As Integer)
    If Me.region = 500 Then
        Me.GroupHeader1.Visible = False
        Me.Detail.Visible = False
    Else
        Me.GroupHeader1.Visible = True
        Me.Detail.Visible = True
    End If
End Sub
```

Understand Report Events

Report events are similar to form events; however, once a report runs, most of the events happen in succession with very little intervention by the user. When you run a report, the On Open, On Load, and On Activate events fire in succession. A user cannot change the order of events; the order is predefined by Access. An explanation of these three events is listed in Table 3.

TABLE 3	Explanation of Common Report Events
Event	**Explanation**
On Open	This event is triggered when the report is open but before the first record is displayed. If there are no records, you can add Cancel = True to the procedure to cancel the opening of the report.
On Load	This event occurs when the report is open and its record(s) are displayed. Here, you can set the values of controls or do calculations with records displayed on the report.
On Activate	This occurs when the window of your report becomes the active window.

Set the Record Source Based on Form Properties

A report is more versatile if you let the user set one or more parameters before you open it. Setting parameters can be done using a blank form that contains no record source. The form would contain all the parameters that affect the report and a method for selecting the parameters. For example, if an employee report contained a list of regions, a combo box containing all the available regions could be created. The user could select a region prior to running the employee report. Figure 36 shows a sample parameter form with a region combo box and a button to preview the report for region 300.

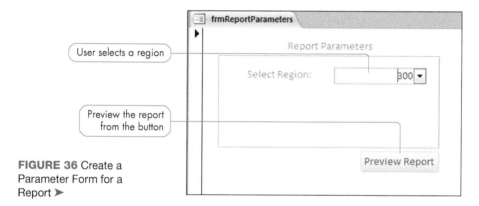

FIGURE 36 Create a Parameter Form for a Report ➤

When the report opens, a procedure (triggered by the On Open event) looks at the selected parameter (for example, region 300) and then creates the record source, as shown in Figure 37. Because the On Open event is triggered before the report contains any records, the record source can be created using the selected region. Next, the On Load event is triggered and the record source has been set. The report is displayed for region 300 employees only, as shown in Figure 38.

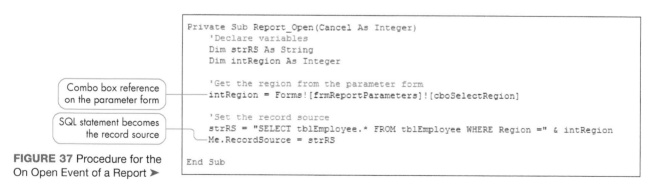

FIGURE 37 Procedure for the On Open Event of a Report ➤

```
Private Sub Report_Open(Cancel As Integer)
    'Declare variables
    Dim strRS As String
    Dim intRegion As Integer

    'Get the region from the parameter form
    intRegion = Forms![frmReportParameters]![cboSelectRegion]

    'Set the record source
    strRS = "SELECT tblEmployee.* FROM tblEmployee WHERE Region =" & intRegion
    Me.RecordSource = strRS

End Sub
```

Employees by Region

Region	Jobcode	Hiredate	Active	Exempts	Lastname	Firstname	City	State	Billrate	Salary
300										
	100	2/1/2001	☑	4	Smith	Amanda	Denver	CO	$175.00	$55,000.00
	200	7/1/2002	☑	3	Keating	Brian	Boulder	CO	$210.00	$89,500.00
	150	10/1/2010	☑	1	Williams	Timothy	Denver	CO	$185.00	$58,000.00

FIGURE 38 Employee Report for Region 300 ➤

Handling Errors in VBA

Two types of errors exist in VBA—handled and unhandled. If you create procedures and functions without error handling, when VBA reports an error message, the code will stop working and the user will be presented with a confusing list of options. On the other hand, if you create a procedure with a built-in error handling routine, you can intercept errors and tell VBA to display a friendly message to the user, with options that make sense.

As an example, the procedure in Figure 37 illustrates how to assign the record source to a report after the user selects a region. If the user did not choose a region—and the combo box was left blank on the parameter form—the report would produce an error, as shown in Figure 39. Some users might understand the problem immediately and know how to fix it; but, the message contains perplexing choices: Continue, End, Debug, and Help. Continue is unavailable, and clicking Debug or Help may cause additional confusion. Clicking End would be the only choice that would enable the user to select another region, and then try again.

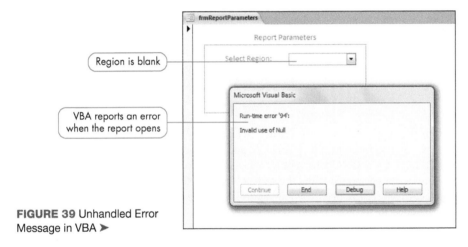

FIGURE 39 Unhandled Error Message in VBA ➤

Add an Error Handling Routine

The **On Error statement** directs the code to skip to a particular line in the procedure.

To produce a more user-friendly error message than the one shown in Figure 39, an error routine can be added to the code in Figure 37. A typical error routine has been added to the procedure shown in Figure 40. In this procedure, when an error occurs, the *On Error statement* directs the code to skip to a particular line in the procedure (usually at the bottom) where the appropriate message is displayed and any corrective action can be taken.

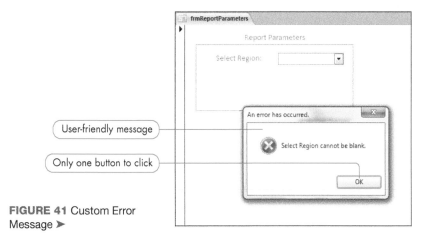

On Error statement added

Exit routine added

Error routine added

```
Private Sub Report_Open(Cancel As Integer)
On Error GoTo Error_Routine

    'Declare variables
    Dim strRS As String
    Dim intRegion As Integer

    'Get the region from the parameter form
    intRegion = Forms![frmReportParameters]![cboSelectRegion]

    'Set the record source
    strRS = "SELECT tblEmployee.* FROM tblEmployee WHERE Region =" & intRegion
    Me.RecordSource = strRS

Exit_Routine:
    Exit Sub

Error_Routine:
    If Err.Number = 94 Then
        MsgBox "Select Region cannot be blank.", vbCritical, "An error has occurred."
    Else
        MsgBox Err.Number & " " & Err.Description & vbCrLf & _
            "Contact your  technical support staff.", vbCritical, "An error has occurred."
    End If
    Resume Exit_Routine

End Sub
```

FIGURE 40 Procedure with an Error Routine ➤

In the new procedure, when error number 94 occurs, a custom message is displayed and the user only has the option to click OK. See Figure 41. This message replaces the confusing message shown previously in Figure 39. If another occurs (i.e., not 94), the procedure will still display a revised message, but not a custom message. If another error appears, a second custom error message could be added using the ElseIf statement.

TIP Where Do Error Numbers Come From?

Error numbers, such as 94, are generated by Microsoft Access. Error numbers range from 3 to 746 with gaps between some numbers. Errors can also fall between 31001 and 31037. Once an error number is known, you can use VBA's error handling techniques to trap the error and give the user a helpful message.

User-friendly message

Only one button to click

FIGURE 41 Custom Error Message ➤

Customizing Access with VBA

**Resume Exit_Routine state-
ment** directs the code to jump to
the exit line.

The **Resume Exit_Routine statement** directs the code to jump to the exit routine. The exit routine will then exit the procedure. If the Resume Exit_Routine statement did not exist, then the error routine would exit at the End Sub statement. The reason why the resume statement is used is to enable the procedure to execute a number of cleanup statements.

Test and Debug Code

In addition to error handling, programmers also need to debug code that is not working. Errors indicate that an obvious change is needed; but, the lack of an error does not mean a procedure is working correctly. A VBA procedure must be tested thoroughly to verify it is working as expected. The more options and the more complex a procedure, the more difficult it will be to test the logic.

In addition to error messages, VBA also provides a tool to debug a procedure that is not working properly. When an error appears and it is not evident what is causing the error, you can use the debugger. The **VBA debugger** enables the programmer to momentarily suspend the execution of VBA code so that the following debug tasks can be done:

The **VBA debugger** enables the
programmer to momentarily
suspend the execution of VBA
code.

- Check the value of a variable in its current state.
- Enter VBA code in the Immediate window to view the results.
- Execute each line of code one at a time.
- Continue execution of the code.
- Halt execution of the code.

To use the debugger, set a breakpoint by clicking in the left margin next to any line of executable code, as shown in Figure 42. When the procedure is triggered (for example, when a report is opened in Print Preview), the debugger pauses at the breakpoint and waits for the user to take action. The current line appears highlighted in yellow, as shown in Figure 43. To watch the procedure run one line at a time, press F8 or click Step Over in the Debug toolbar. To open the Debug toolbar, right-click any toolbar, and then select Debug from the list.

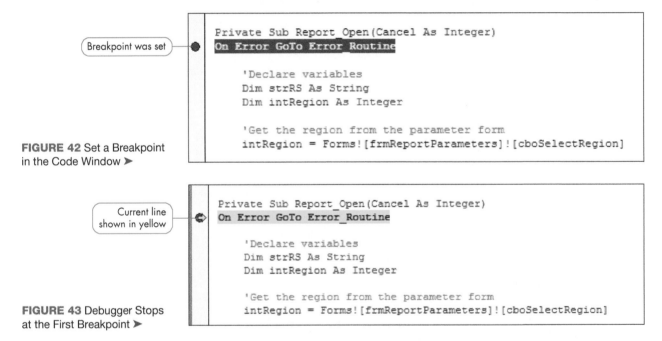

FIGURE 42 Set a Breakpoint in the Code Window ➤

FIGURE 43 Debugger Stops at the First Breakpoint ➤

As the debugger steps through each line of code, you can determine where the error(s) occur. Once you determine where the errors occur, you can stop the debugger and correct the code. To stop the debugger, click Reset on the Debug toolbar. After the code is fixed, remove the breakpoint by clicking the dot in the margin, and then run the procedure again.

In Hands-On Exercise 3, you will add VBA code to forms and reports, and practice handling errors, testing, and debugging.

3 Forms, Reports, and Errors in VBA

Kathryn would like to add a survey form to her database. To accomplish this, you will use the existing Survey Questions table to create a new Survey Questions form. You need to add code to the form to verify that the responses fall within predefined boundaries. You also decide to add a new Survey Results report to print the average of all responses. You will add an error routine so Kathryn does not have to deal with any unexpected errors later.

Skills covered: Create a New Survey Questions Form • Add a Data Validation Procedure to the Survey Questions Form • Create a New Survey Results Report and a Select Seminar Form • Add VBA Code to the New Form and the New Report • Add Error Handling to the Survey Results On Open Event

---

STEP 1 ▶ CREATE A NEW SURVEY QUESTIONS FORM

You need to create a new survey question form to collect data from each attendee about each seminar. You decide to use the Multiple Items tool to create the form. Refer to Figure 44 as you complete Step 1.

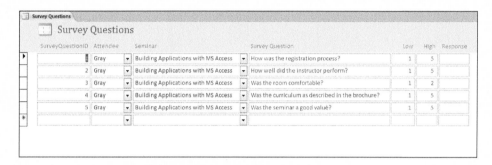

FIGURE 44 Multiple Items Form ➤

a. Open the *v3h2seminar_LastnameFirstname* database if you closed it at the end of Hands-On Exercise 2, and then save it as **v3h3seminar_LastnameFirstname**.

b. Click the **Survey Questions table**, click the **Create tab**, click **More Forms** in the Forms group, and then select **Multiple Items**.

   Access creates a new Multiple Items form based on the Survey Questions table.

c. Modify the three right column headings using Figure 44 as a guide.

   The column heading text can be shortened to help reduce the overall width of the form.

d. Modify the height and width of the columns using Figure 44 as a guide.

   The goal is to reduce the overall width of the form.

e. Switch to Form view, and then type the following responses into the first five Response fields:

   Question 1 = 4
   Question 2 = 3
   Question 3 = 4
   Question 4 = 1
   Question 5 = 0

f. Save the form as **Survey Questions**.

   You will add validation code next.

ADD A DATA VALIDATION PROCEDURE TO THE SURVEY QUESTIONS FORM

You notice that the responses for Questions 3 and 5 are outside the low and high boundaries but are still accepted by the form. You need to add a Before Update procedure to validate the response values. Refer to Figure 45 as you complete Step 2.

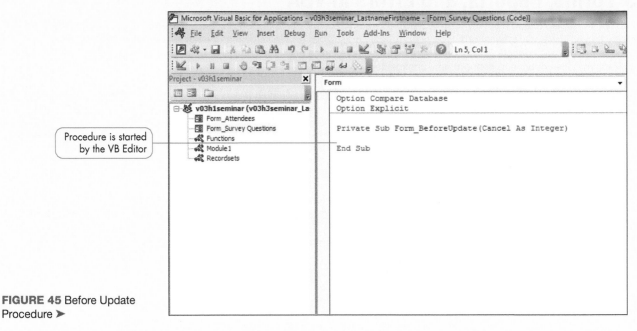

Procedure is started by the VB Editor

FIGURE 45 Before Update Procedure ➤

a. Switch to Design view, and then open the Property Sheet.

You will open the VB Editor from the Before Update event.

b. Select **Form** from the combo box at the top of the Property Sheet, if necessary. Click the **Event tab**, and then double-click the **Before Update event**.

c. Click **Build** to open the VB Editor.

The VB Editor opens and a new subroutine is started in the code window, as shown in Figure 45.

d. Add the following code to the Form_BeforeUpdate procedure:

```
Private Sub Form_BeforeUpdate(Cancel As Integer)
    'Verify that each response falls within the 'low' and 'high' boundaries
    If Not IsNull(Me.SurveyResponse) Then
        If Me.SurveyResponse >= Me.SurveyLowRank And Me.SurveyResponse <= Me.SurveyHighRank Then
            'do nothing
        Else
            'Response outside boundaries
            MsgBox "Response is outside the boundaries.", vbCritical, "Invalid entry"
            Cancel = True
            Exit Sub
        End If
    End If

End Sub
```

CODE WINDOW 17 ▲

This section of code verifies that the response is within the low and high ranking. If it falls outside the boundaries, the user is notified and the record cannot be saved because of the statement Cancel = True.

e. Minimize the VB Editor, switch to Form view of the Survey Questions form, and then retype the responses from Step 1 to trigger the Before Update event. Take note how the code responds.

Questions 3 and 5 contain invalid values; the form will not allow the data to be saved.

f. Enter a **2** for Question 3 and a **3** for Question 5.

g. Maximize the VB Editor, and then save the procedure. Close the editor.

STEP 3 **CREATE A NEW SURVEY RESULTS REPORT AND A SELECT SEMINAR FORM**

Now that you are collecting the survey responses, Kathryn would like to know the average response for each seminar. You create a Survey Results report using the Report Wizard tool. You also create a Select Seminar form to make it easy for Kathryn to isolate one seminar. Refer to Figure 46 as you complete Step 3.

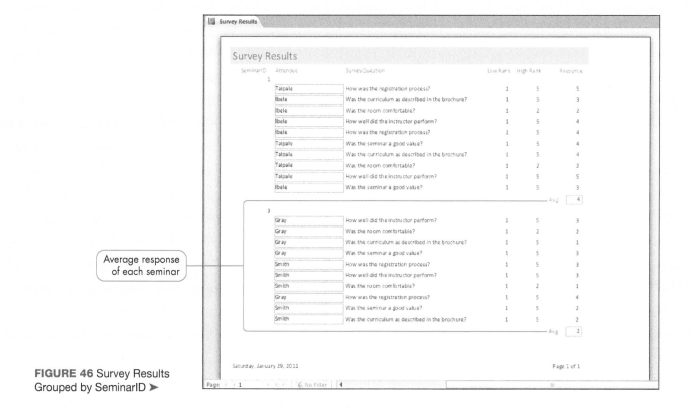

FIGURE 46 Survey Results Grouped by SeminarID ➤

Customizing Access with VBA

173

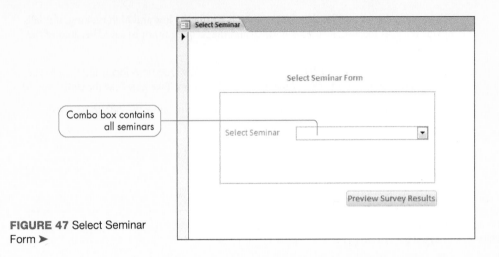

Combo box contains
all seminars

FIGURE 47 Select Seminar
Form ➤

a. Click the **Survey Questions form tab**, and then enter the remaining responses using any response that falls within the acceptable range.

You need to enter sample survey data in order to test the new report.

b. Close the Survey Questions form.

c. Click the **Survey Questions table**, click the **Create tab**, and then click **Report Wizard** in the Reports group. Provide the wizard with the following answers, and then click **Finish**:

Which fields do you want on your report?

• Select **All** (except SurveyQuestionID).

Do you want to add any grouping levels?

• Select **SeminarID**.

What sort order and summary information do you want…?

• Click **Summary Options**, and then click the **Avg check box** for the SurveyResponse field.
• Select **Detail** and **Summary**.
• Skip sort order.

How would you like to lay out your report?

• Select **Landscape**.

What title do you want for your report?

• Type **Survey Results**.

d. Modify the report so it looks like the report shown in Figure 46.

Your average will be different than the figure; the format of the report does not need to be exact.

e. Save the report as **Survey Results**. Close the report.

Next, you will create a Select Seminar form to make it easy to launch the Survey Results report.

f. Click the **Create tab**, and then click **Form Design** in the Forms group.

A blank form is displayed.

g. Click the **Combo Box control** in the Controls group, and then click in the middle of the form. Provide the Combo Box wizard with the following answers, and then click **Finish**:

How do you want your combo box to get its values?

• Select **Option 1** (from another table).

Which table or query should provide the values for your combo box?

- Select **Seminars**.

Which fields contain the values you want included in your combo box?

- Select **SeminarID** and **SeminarName**.

What sort order do you want for the items in your list box?

- Skip.

How wide would you like the columns in your combo box?

- Double-click the right edge of the column heading box to accommodate the longest entry.

What label would you like for your combo box?

- Type **Select Seminar**.

h. Add the following controls to the form, as shown in Figure 47. When the Command Button Wizard opens, click **Cancel**.

- Use the Rectangle control to add a rectangle surrounding the combo box and label.
- Use the Label control to add a label above the rectangle.
- Use the Button control to add a button below the rectangle.

i. Save the form as **Select Seminar**.

STEP 4 ▶ **ADD VBA CODE TO THE NEW FORM AND THE NEW REPORT**

Using the new Select Seminar form, you will open the Survey Results report based on the seminar selected from the combo box. You need to create two additional VBA procedures in order to accomplish this. Refer to Figure 48 as you complete Step 4.

Procedure sets the record source

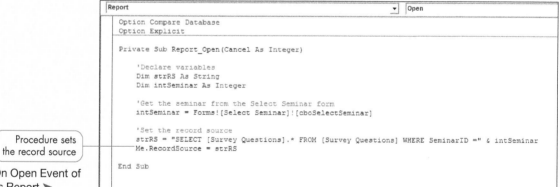

FIGURE 48 On Open Event of Survey Results Report ▶

```
Report                                              ▼   Open

    Option Compare Database
    Option Explicit

    Private Sub Report_Open(Cancel As Integer)

        'Declare variables
        Dim strRS As String
        Dim intSeminar As Integer

        'Get the seminar from the Select Seminar form
        intSeminar = Forms![Select Seminar]![cboSelectSeminar]

        'Set the record source
        strRS = "SELECT [Survey Questions].* FROM [Survey Questions] WHERE SeminarID =" & intSeminar
        Me.RecordSource = strRS

    End Sub
```

a. Display the Select Seminar form in Design view if necessary. Click the **combo box**, and then open the Property Sheet. Click the **All tab**, and then change the Name property to **cboSelectSeminar**.

b. Click **Preview Survey Results**. Change the Name property to **cmdPreviewSurveyResults**.

c. Click the **Event tab**, and then double-click the **On Click event**.

d. Click **Build** to open the VB Editor.

The VB Editor opens and a new procedure is started in the Code window.

e. Type the following code into the procedure, and then save the code.

DoCmd.OpenReport "Survey Results", acViewPreview

f. Minimize the VB Editor, display the form in Form view, and then click the **Preview Survey Results button.**

The Survey Results report opens in Print Preview.

g. Click **Close Print Preview**, and then display the Survey Results report in Design view. Open the Property Sheet if necessary.

h. Click the **Event tab**, and then double-click the **On Open event**.

You will modify the record source of the report when the On Open event is triggered based on which seminar was selected in the Select Seminar form.

i. Click **Build** to open the VB Editor.

The VB Editor opens and a new procedure is started in the Code window.

j. Type the code from Figure 48 into the procedure, and then save the code.

k. Minimize the VB Editor, and then open the Select Seminar form if necessary. Click the **Select Seminar arrow** in the Select Seminar form, click **Microsoft Office 2010**, and then click **Preview Survey Results**.

> **TROUBLESHOOTING:** If the report produces an error, end the error, open the VB Editor, and then see if you can debug the code.

l. If the report appears with the correct seminar, keep the VB Editor, the Survey Results report, and the Select Seminar form open.

STEP 5 ▶ **ADD ERROR HANDLING TO THE SURVEY RESULTS ON OPEN EVENT**

You will add error handling to the VBA procedure in order to trap run time errors. Refer to Figure 49 as you complete Step 5.

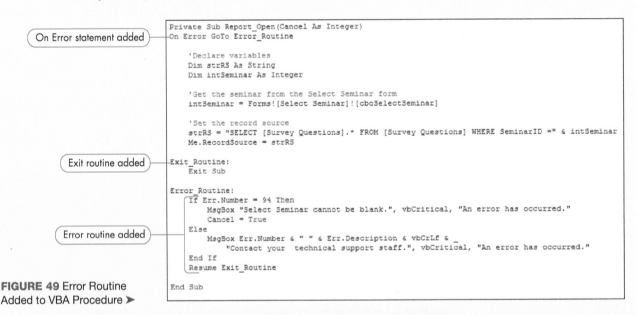

```
Private Sub Report_Open(Cancel As Integer)
On Error GoTo Error_Routine

    'Declare variables
    Dim strRS As String
    Dim intSeminar As Integer

    'Get the seminar from the Select Seminar form
    intSeminar = Forms![Select Seminar]![cboSelectSeminar]

    'Set the record source
    strRS = "SELECT [Survey Questions].* FROM [Survey Questions] WHERE SeminarID =" & intSeminar
    Me.RecordSource = strRS

Exit_Routine:
    Exit Sub

Error_Routine:
    If Err.Number = 94 Then
        MsgBox "Select Seminar cannot be blank.", vbCritical, "An error has occurred."
        Cancel = True
    Else
        MsgBox Err.Number & " " & Err.Description & vbCrLf & _
            "Contact your  technical support staff.", vbCritical, "An error has occurred."
    End If
    Resume Exit_Routine

End Sub
```

On Error statement added ⟶

Exit routine added ⟶

Error routine added ⟶

FIGURE 49 Error Routine Added to VBA Procedure ➤

a. Return to the VB Editor, and then locate the Report_Open procedure for the Survey Results report.

b. Add the *On Error GoTo*, *Exit_Routine*, and the *Error_Routine* sections, as shown in Figure 49.

One line of code is added above the existing procedure; the rest of the code is added below the existing procedure.

c. Save the code, and then minimize the VB Editor.

Customizing Access with VBA

d. Delete the contents of the Select Seminar combo box, and then click the **Preview Survey Results button**.

A message box appears that says *Select Seminar cannot be blank.*

e. Click **OK** in the message box to open the second message box, and then click **End**.

To clear the second message, an error routine must be added to the cmdPreviewSurveyResults_Click() procedure in the Select Seminar form.

f. Revise the cmdPreviewSurveyResults_Click() procedure by adding the code shown in Code Window 18.

```
Private Sub cmdPreviewSurveyResults_Click()
On Error GoTo Error_Routine

    DoCmd.OpenReport "Survey Results", acViewPreview

Exit_Routine:
    Exit Sub

Error_Routine:
    If Err.Number = 2501 Then
        'do nothing
    Else
        MsgBox Err.Number & " " & Err.Description & vbCrLf & _
            "Contact your  technical support staff.", vbCritical, "An error has occurred."
    End If
    Resume Exit_Routine

End Sub
```

CODE WINDOW 18 ⋀

g. Save the code, and then minimize the VB Editor. Click the **Preview Survey Results button**.

Only the first message appears. The second message was intercepted by the error routine.

h. Close the VB Editor, and then close the form and report.

i. Save and close the database. Submit it based on your instructor's directions, and then exit Access.

After reading this chapter, you have accomplished the following objectives:

1. **Write code in modules.** When you create VBA code in Access, you can create the code in three ways: a standard module, a class module, or an Access object module. A standard module stores procedures that are available to any event in the application and an Access object module stores procedures that are available to a specific form or report. Class modules are advanced programs that are used to create custom objects.

2. **Write code for forms and reports.** To create VBA code in a form or report, first open the object in Design view, and then click Property Sheet in the Tools group. Next, select an event (e.g., On Current), and then click Build on the right side of the property cell. Then, Choose Builder dialog box appears with three options—Macro Builder, Expression Builder, and Code Builder—enabling you to build a procedure with any of these tools. Select the Code Builder, and then click OK to open the VB Editor. Add the remaining code to your procedure in the Code window, and then save the code; close the VB Editor and Access will return you to the original form.

3. **Work with objects.** VBA is an object-oriented programming language. That means VBA can work with the objects in the various object libraries that are available in the applications that support VBA. You can use objects in the object libraries along with their resources in order to accomplish the programming tasks. These object libraries include Access and Excel, which are the two most popular applications that support VBA. Word, PowerPoint, and Outlook can also be automated using VBA. A property is a physical attribute of an object. A method is an action that is performed by an object. An event is what happens when a user takes an action.

4. **Create functions.** A function is a procedure that performs an action and returns a value. Many functions are predefined in VBA and ready to use. To use these predefined functions, simply add the function to your procedure and insert the required arguments; when the procedure runs, the function will return the correct value. To create your own custom function, open a module, and then type the statement with the format Function NameOfFunction (Argument As Data Type) As Data Type, press Enter, and then the VB Editor adds the statement End Function. Argument refers to the value or values that the procedure passes to the function; the argument can be a specific data type. As Data Type at the end refers to the type of data the function returns to the procedure. Add the remaining lines of code to complete the function, save, and then test the function.

5. **Use DAO to access data.** DAO (Data Access Objects) refers to an object library specifically created to work with Access databases. A recordset is a set of records in memory. To create the recordset, you first write a procedure using VBA that extracts data from one or more tables in an Access database and then places the results in memory. Once the recordset has been placed in memory, you can then logically examine the records and make decisions and changes based on your own criteria. Because VBA updates can have unexpected results, it would be a good idea to back up your database before you run an update procedure. The first time you create an update procedure, you must be prepared for errors and unexpected results. Always check the results by opening the affected table(s); if there are problems, revert back to the backup version of the database.

6. **Use ADO to access data.** ADO (ActiveX Data Objects) was designed for connecting to a wide range of external data sources. Although DAO was designed to work with your local Access database, ADO was designed to connect to relational databases, ISAM data sources, disk files, and so on. Before you can use the ADO object library, you must create a link to the library by clicking the Tools menu, and then selecting References.

7. **Add VBA to forms.** Almost all of the VBA code added to a form is triggered by an event. Common events include On Open, On Click, On Enter, On Exit, Before Update, and After Update. Events are what happen when a user takes action and Access performs a method behind the scenes. A form has one set of events and each object on a form has another set of events. Events link to event procedures which contain the VBA code that executes when the event is triggered.

8. **Add VBA to reports.** There may be times when you may want to modify the layout of a report before the report prints. For example, a report that contains multiple sections may have one or more sections that you want to hide, even though they contain data. Access does not have an option for hiding a section at run time. You can use VBA to test if a section matches a certain criteria and then tell Access how to respond when the condition is met. One option is to simply tell Access to hide the section when the section is found and show all other sections. When you run a report in Print Preview, the On Open, On Load, and On Activate events fire in succession.

9. **Handle errors in VBA.** You need to find and fix syntax and logical errors before you run the code; while the code is running, you need to set a trap for run time errors. If you create procedures and functions without error handling, when VBA reports an error message, the code will stop working and the user will be presented with an unclear list of options. On the other hand, if you create a procedure with a built-in error handling routine, you can intercept errors and tell VBA to display a friendly message to the user, with options that make sense. In addition to error handling, programmers also need to debug code that is not working. The VB Editor also provides a tool to debug a procedure that is not working properly. When an error appears and it is not evident what is causing the error, you can use the debugger. The VBA debugger enables the programmer to momentarily suspend the execution of VBA code so that you can execute each line of code one at a time and observe which line is causing the error.

KEY TERMS

ADO (ActiveX Data Objects)
After Update
Before Update
DAO (Data Access Objects)
Edit
Error trapping

MoveNext
Object libraries
On Current
On Dirty
On Enter
On Error statement

Option Compare Database
Option Explicit
Recordset
Resume Exit_Routine statement
Update
VBA debugger

1. All of these types of modules are found in VBA except:

    (a) Debug module.

    (b) Class module.

    (c) Standard module.

    (d) Access object module.

2. Which event would be used to modify a report before it prints?

    (a) Before Load

    (b) On Activate

    (c) On Open

    (d) On Load

3. Which definition is incorrect?

    (a) Object libraries are only used by Access and Excel.

    (b) A property is an attribute of an object.

    (c) A method executes an action on an object.

    (d) An event is triggered by a user action.

4. Functions are created in:

    (a) The Object Explorer.

    (b) Procedures.

    (c) Class modules.

    (d) Standard modules.

5. DAO can be used to accomplish all of these except:

    (a) Modify database objects.

    (b) Connect to Excel spreadsheets.

    (c) Create tables and queries.

    (d) Add procedures to form events.

6. ADO is similar to DAO in which way?

    (a) One is simply a newer version of the other.

    (b) Both can easily access external data sources.

    (c) Both can access database objects.

    (d) Both were originally created by IBM.

7. A common reason to add VBA to a form is to:

    (a) Display a different background color for different data entry tasks.

    (b) Remind users which field comes next during data entry.

    (c) Time a user as he or she enters data.

    (d) Validate data as it is entered.

8. Which is not a common reason to add VBA to a report?

    (a) Allow users to change the font size of the data being printed.

    (b) Modify the content of the report.

    (c) Highlight one section to emphasize it.

    (d) Display an error message when no data exists.

9. The On Error GoTo statement is used to:

    (a) Go to the line immediately after an error.

    (b) Redirect the procedure to skip over code and execute the error routine.

    (c) Start the debugger.

    (d) Start over after the user clicks OK.

10. To update a record in a recordset, you use which VBA statement?

    (a) Edit only.

    (b) Update only.

    (c) Both Edit and Update.

    (d) Do Loop.

1 Wholesale Food Business

T&F Wholesalers exports its food products to customers in Germany, France, Brazil, the United Kingdom, and the United States. The owners of T&F would like to improve the efficiency of their data entry forms by adding a validation process. They would also like to add automatic entry for fields that are calculated based on other fields. This exercise follows the same set of skills as used in Hands-On Exercises 1 and 3 in the chapter. Refer to Figure 50 as you complete this exercise.

```
Form                                                    ▼   BeforeUpdate
    Option Compare Database
    Option Explicit

    Private Sub OrderDate_Enter()
        'Set the order date = today
        If IsNull(Me.OrderDate) Then
            Me.OrderDate = Date
        End If
    End Sub

    Private Sub OrderDate_Exit(Cancel As Integer)
        'Set the expected ship date = order date plus 2 days
        If IsNull(Me.ExpectedShipDate) Then
            Me.ExpectedShipDate = Me.OrderDate + 2
        End If
    End Sub

    Private Sub Form_BeforeUpdate(Cancel As Integer)
        'Validate freight amount. Must be between 0 and 199.
        If Me.Freight >= 0 And Me.Freight <= 199 Then
            'do nothing
        Else
            MsgBox "Freight must be between 0 and $199", vbOKOnly, _
                "Invalid freight amount"
            Cancel = True
        End If
    End Sub
```

FIGURE 50 Form Module with Three Procedures ➤

a. Open *v3p1wholesale*. Save the database as **v3p1wholesale_LastnameFirstname**, and then enable the content.

b. Open the Orders form in Design view. Click the **Order Date box**.

c. Open the Property Sheet if necessary, and then click the **Event tab**. Double-click the **On Enter event**.

d. Click **Build** to open the VB Editor. Type the code from the *Sub OrderDate_Enter* section inside the procedure, as shown in Code Window 19.

```
Private Sub OrderDate_Enter()
    'Set the order date = today
    If IsNull(Me.OrderDate) Then
        Me.OrderDate = Date
    End If
End Sub
```

CODE WINDOW 19 ➤

e. Minimize the VB Editor, and then display the Orders form in Form view. Save the form.

f. Test the code using the first record. Press **Tab** until you reach the OrderDate, and then verify the code does nothing because an order date already exists. Then, delete the order date and test the code again by tabbing into the field to verify today's date appears.

g. Switch to Design view. Verify that the OrderDate box is still selected. Double-click the **On Exit event**. Click **Build** to open the VB Editor. Type the code from the *Private Sub OrderDate_Exit* section inside the procedure, as shown in Code Window 20. Save the code.

```
Private Sub OrderDate_Exit(Cancel As Integer)
    'Set the expected ship date = order date plus 2 days
    If IsNull(Me.ExpectedShipDate) Then
        Me.ExpectedShipDate = Me.OrderDate + 2
    End If
End Sub
```

h. Minimize the VB Editor, and then open the Orders form in Form view. Test the code using the first record. Press **Tab** until you reach the ExpectedShipDate, and then press **Tab** one more time to verify the code does nothing because an expected ship date already exists. Then, delete the expected ship date and test the code again by pressing **Tab** until you are past the OrderedShipDate field to verify today's date plus two appears.

i. Switch to Design view. Select the form using the Selection type box at the top of the Property Sheet. Double-click the **Before Update event** on the Events tab. Click **Build** to open the VB Editor. Type the code from the *Sub Form_BeforeUpdate* section inside the procedure, as shown in Code Window 21.

```
Private Sub Form_BeforeUpdate(Cancel As Integer)
    'Validate freight amount. Must be between 0 and 199.
    If Me.Freight >= 0 And Me.Freight <= 199 Then
        'do nothing
    Else
        MsgBox "Freight must be between 0 and $199", vbOKOnly, _
            "Invalid freight amount"
        Cancel = True
    End If
End Sub
```

> **TROUBLESHOOTING:** Your procedure may be at the top of the code window or under the other procedures. The order is not important.

j. Test the code using the first record. Type **200** into the **Freight field**, and then click **Next Record** to advance to the next record. Verify the message *Freight must be between 0 and $199* appears. Press **Esc** to clear the data entry, and then close the form. Save the changes.

k. Open the Products report in Design view. Open the Property Sheet if necessary, and then click the **Event tab**. Double-click the **On Open event**.

l. Click **Build** to open the VB Editor. Type the code shown in Code Window 22 inside the procedure.

```
Private Sub Report_Open(Cancel As Integer)
    'Declare variables
    Dim intCategory As Integer
    Dim strRS As String


    'Revise the records source -- filter by category
    If MsgBox("Do you want to filter the report by category?", vbYesNo, _
            "Input required") = vbYes Then
        'Filter by Category
        intCategory = InputBox("Enter category (1-8)")

        'Set the record source = the filtered products table
        strRS = "SELECT Products.* FROM Products WHERE CategoryID =" & intCategory
        Me.RecordSource = strRS
    Else
        'Set the record source = the whole products table
        Me.RecordSource = "Products"
    End If

End Sub
```

CODE WINDOW 22 ▲

m. Save the code, and then minimize the VB Editor. Test the code by opening the report in Print Preview. Verify the messages appear and that there are no typographical errors. Click **Yes**, and then enter a value in the second message to verify that you can filter the report by one category. Close the report.

n. Save and close the database, and submit it based on your instructor's directions.

2 Employee Benefits

A local accounting firm provides employee benefit management services to its larger accounting customers. They have a database that contains sample employee data and forms. They want to use this data to make the forms more user friendly and also improve their efficiency. An employee report also exists. They would like to customize this report so they can print employees by state. This exercise follows the same set of skills as used in Hands-On Exercises 1 and 3 in the chapter. Refer to Figure 51 as you complete this exercise.

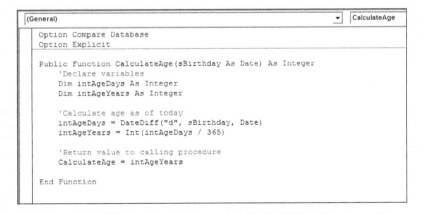

FIGURE 51 Public Function Calculates Age ➤

a. Open *v3p2benefits*. Save the database as **v3p2benefits_LastnameFirstname**, and then enable the content.

b. Click the **Database Tools tab**, and then click **Visual Basic** to open the VB Editor.

c. Click **Insert** on the menu bar, and then select **Module**. Use the code shown in Code Window 23 and type the entire Public Function CalculateAge into the Code window.

Customizing Access with VBA

```
Public Function CalculateAge(sBirthday As Date) As Integer
    'Declare variables
    Dim intAgeDays As Integer
    Dim intAgeYears As Integer

    'Calculate age as of today
    intAgeDays = DateDiff("d", sBirthday, Date)
    intAgeYears = Int(intAgeDays / 365)

    'Return value to calling procedure
    CalculateAge = intAgeYears

End Function
```

CODE WINDOW 23 ➤

The CalculateAge function contains the following components:

- The calling procedure must supply a date (birthdate)
- The function will return an integer (age)
- The DateDiff function is used to calculate days old
- Days old divided by 365 is the age of the employee in years
- The Int function is used to trim the partial years from the age

d. Save the code as **Module1**. Next, you will call the function from a procedure inside the Employee Data form.

e. Open the Employee Data form in Design view. Double-click the **birthdate box** to open the Property Sheet for this control.

f. Click the **Event tab**. Double-click the **On Dbl Click event**. Click **Build** to open the VB Editor. Type the following code inside the procedure:

MsgBox "This employee is " & CalculateAge(Me.birthdate) & " years old."

g. Save the code, and then minimize the VB Editor. Open the Employee Data form in Form view. Type your birth date into the **birthdate field** of the first record.

h. Click **zipcode**, and then double-click the **birthdate box** to test the function and calling procedure. Click **OK** when your age is displayed in a message box. Close the form, and then save the changes if prompted.

i. Open the Employees Report. The employees on the report reside in various states. You will add a procedure to the report that will enable the user to filter employees for a selected state.

j. Switch to Design view. Open the Property Sheet if necessary, and then double-click the **On Open event** on the Event tab. Click **Build** to open the VB Editor. Type the procedure shown in Code Window 24.

```
Private Sub Report_Open(Cancel As Integer)
    'Declare variables
    Dim strState As String
    Dim strRS As String

    'Revise the records source -- filter by state
    If MsgBox("Do you want to filter the report by state?", vbYesNo, _
            "Input required") = vbYes Then
        'Filter by Category
        strState = InputBox("Enter state (az, ca, co, etc.)")

        'Set the record source = the filtered products table
        strRS = "SELECT Employees.* FROM Employees WHERE State = '" & strState & "'"
        Me.RecordSource = strRS
    Else
        'Set the record source = the whole products table
        Me.RecordSource = "Employees"
    End If

End Sub
```

CODE WINDOW 24 ▲

k. Save the code, and then minimize the VB Editor. Test the code by opening the report in Print Preview. Click **Yes** at the first message to verify that you can filter the report by one state. Enter a state at the second message. Close the report, and then save the changes if prompted.

l. Close the database, and submit it based on your instructor's directions.

Customizing Access with VBA

A network of speakers who present on topics relating to college life is attempting to improve its Access database. The organization is new and currently has only a handful of speakers. The database has a table, one form, and one report. They need assistance with improving the efficiency of the form as well as making the report more versatile. Refer to Figure 52 as you complete this exercise.

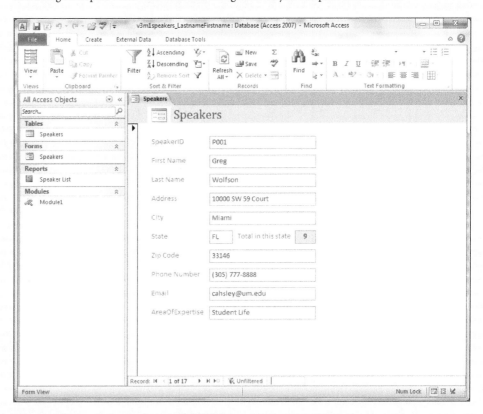

FIGURE 52 Form Showing Other Speakers from This State ➤

a. Open *v3m1speakers*. Save the database as **v3m1speakers_LastnameFirstname**, and then enable the content.

b. Open the Speakers form in Design view. Reduce the width of the State box, as shown in Figure 52. Place a new text box next to *State*. Resize and rename the label, as shown in Figure 52.

c. Type **txtSpeakersInState** as the Name property for the new text box. Change the TabStop property to **No**. Change the BackColor property to **Dark Blue, Text 2, Lighter 80%**.

d. Switch to Form view, and then tab through the fields of the first record to verify the form contains no errors; also verify the insertion point does not stop on the new text box.

e. Open the VB Editor. Insert a new module. Type the procedure into the Code window as shown in Code Window 25.

```
Public Sub FindSpeakersFromState()

    'Declare variables
    Dim db As DAO.Database
    Dim rst As DAO.Recordset
    Dim strStateOnForm As String
    Dim intCounter As Integer

    'Set the current database
    Set db = CurrentDb

    'Set the recordset
    Set rst = db.OpenRecordset("Speakers")

    'Set the state
    strStateOnForm = Forms![Speakers]![State]

    'Cycle through the records
    Do While Not rst.EOF
        If rst!State = strStateOnForm Then
            intCounter = intCounter + 1
        End If
    rst.MoveNext
    Loop
    Forms![Speakers]![txtSpeakersInState] = intCounter

    'Close the recordset
    rst.Close
    Set rst = Nothing
    Set db = Nothing

End Sub
```

CODE WINDOW 25 ➤

f. Save the code, and then minimize the VB Editor.
g. Open the Speakers form in Design view, and then add the following code to the On Enter event of the State box:
    Call FindSpeakersFromState
h. Minimize the VB Editor. Open the Speakers form in Form view. Tab to the State field and verify the new Total in this state field is showing the correct number. Save the form.

DISCOVER

i. Click **State** in the first record, and then click **First Name**. The total field reads 9. Advance to the next record; the total field still incorrectly reads 9. Add an apostrophe to the statement in step g to change it to a comment. Add the same statement to another event on the form in order to correct the problem.
j. Advance to the last record in the form's record source, and then advance once more to a new record. Error 94 occurs: *Invalid use of null*. To correct this problem, add the error handling code shown in Code Window 26.

```
Public Sub FindSpeakersFromState()
On Error GoTo Error_Routine

    'Declare variables
    Dim db As DAO.Database
    Dim rst As DAO.Recordset
    Dim strStateOnForm As String
    Dim intCounter As Integer

    'Set the current database
    Set db = CurrentDb

    'Set the recordset
    Set rst = db.OpenRecordset("Speakers")

    'Set the state
    strStateOnForm = Forms![Speakers]![State]

    'Cycle through the records
    Do While Not rst.EOF
        If rst!State = strStateOnForm Then
            intCounter = intCounter + 1
        End If
    rst.MoveNext
    Loop
    Forms![Speakers]![txtSpeakersInState] = intCounter

Exit_Routine:
    Exit Sub

Error_Routine:
    If Err.Number = 94 Then
        Forms![Speakers]![txtSpeakersInState] = ""
    Else
        MsgBox Err.Number & " " & Err.Description & vbCrLf & _
            "Contact your  technical support staff.", vbCritical, "An error has occurred."
    End If
    Resume Exit_Routine

End Sub
```

CODE WINDOW 26 ◣

k. Advance to the new record again to verify the error is gone. Close the form.

l. Save and close the database, and submit it based on your instructor's directions.

2 Charity Benefit Auction

You are a volunteer for a local charity that is holding a benefit auction. Donations are collected from friends and business partners and the donations are then auctioned off at the annual charity event. The event organizers would like to know the statistics of the donations as they are being collected. You create a form to provide that information. Refer to Figure 53 as you complete this exercise.

FIGURE 53 Statistics Form
Calls Recordset Procedure ➤

a. Open *v3m2charity*. Save the database as **v3m2charity_LastnameFirstname**, and then enable the content.

b. Open the Donations table to view the donations to date. Close the table.

c. Create a new form using the Form Design tool. Add a title (label), a rectangle, a button, and three text box controls, as shown in Figure 53. Set the Enabled property of the three text box controls on the Data tab to **No**. Set the Format property of the three text box controls to **Currency**. Change the Name of the button to **cmdRefresh**. Rename the text boxes as **txtLowDonation**, **txtHighDonation**, and **txtAverageDonation**.

d. Save the form as **Statistics**.

e. Open the VB Editor, create a new module, and then type the procedure shown in Code Window 27.

```
Public Sub CalculateLowHighAverage()
    'Declare variables
    Dim db As DAO.Database
    Dim rst As DAO.Recordset
    Dim curLowDonation As Currency
    Dim curHighDonation As Currency
    Dim curTotalDonation As Currency
    Dim lngCounter As Long
    Dim curAverageDonation As Currency

    'Set the current database
    Set db = CurrentDb

    'Set the recordset
    Set rst = db.OpenRecordset("Select Donations.* From Donations Where ItemValue Is Not Null")

    'Cycle through the records
    Do While Not rst.EOF
    If lngCounter = 0 Then
        'set the low donation
        curLowDonation = rst!ItemValue
    End If
        If rst!ItemValue < curLowDonation Then
            curLowDonation = rst!ItemValue
        End If
        If rst!ItemValue > curHighDonation Then
            curHighDonation = rst!ItemValue
        End If
        curTotalDonation = curTotalDonation + rst!ItemValue
        lngCounter = lngCounter + 1
    rst.MoveNext
    Loop

    'Update the fields on the statistics form
    Forms![Statistics]![txtLowDonation] = curLowDonation
    Forms![Statistics]![txtHighDonation] = curHighDonation
    Forms![Statistics]![txtAverageDonation] = curTotalDonation / lngCounter

    'Close the recordset
    rst.Close
    Set rst = Nothing
    Set db = Nothing
End Sub
```

CODE WINDOW 27 ▲

f. Save the code, and then minimize the VB Editor.

g. Open the Statistics form in Design view, and then add the following code to the On Click event of the Refresh button:

Call CalculateLowHighAverage

h. Save the form. Switch to Form view, and then click **Refresh** on the Statistics form. Compare your results to the values in Figure 53.

i. Return to the VB Editor, and then add the error handling code shown in Code Window 28.

```
Public Sub CalculateLowHighAverage()
On Error GoTo Error_Routine

    'Declare variables
    Dim db As DAO.Database
    Dim rst As DAO.Recordset
    Dim curLowDonation As Currency



    'Close the recordset
    rst.Close
    Set rst = Nothing
    Set db = Nothing

Exit_Routine:
    Exit Sub

Error_Routine:
    MsgBox Err.Number & " " & Err.Description & vbCrLf & _
            "Contact your technical support staff.", vbCritical, "An error has occurred."
    Resume Exit_Routine

End Sub
```

CODE WINDOW 28 ▲

DISCOVER

j. Save the code. Click **Refresh** on the Statistics form again to test the new code. Close the form if everything is working.

k. Open the Donations List report. Add a procedure that will enable a user to filter the report by category. The procedure should be triggered by the On Open event.

l. Save and close the database, and submit it based on your instructor's directions.

CAPSTONE EXERCISE

You work as a sales agent at the McManus Real Estate Agency. You need to create a function that will enable the agents to see the ranking of each property, compared to all of the other properties. You also add a procedure to a report that will enable you to view all properties above a certain value. You also add error handling to the function.

Database File Setup

Open a database, save it with a new name, and then enable the content to start this capstone exercise. You will then create a function, modify a form, and then call the function from the form. You will also add a procedure to an existing report.

a. Open *v3c1realestate* database.

b. Save the database as **v3c1realestate_LastnameFirstname**, and then enable the content.

c. Open the Properties table, and then examine the records.

d. Sort the table by ascending PropertyValue. Close the table without saving.

Create a Function

You need to create a function that will rank the properties by PropertyValue as compared to the other properties. The ranking will be displayed as each property is displayed in the Properties form.

a. Open the VB Editor, and then insert a new module.

b. Enter a new function, as shown in Code Window 29.

```
Public Function PropertyPriceRanking(sPropVal) As Integer
    'Declare variables
    Dim db As DAO.Database
    Dim rst As DAO.Recordset
    Dim intCounter As Integer

    'Set the current database
    Set db = CurrentDb

    'Set the recordset
    Set rst = db.OpenRecordset("Select Properties.* From Properties Where " & _
            "PropertyValue Is Not Null Order By PropertyValue")

    'Cycle through the records
    Do While Not rst.EOF
    intCounter = intCounter + 1
        If rst!PropertyValue = sPropVal Then
            Exit Do
        End If
    rst.MoveNext
    Loop

    'Return the value to the calling procedure
    PropertyPriceRanking = intCounter

    'Close the recordset
    rst.Close
    Set rst = Nothing
    Set db = Nothing

End Function
```

CODE WINDOW 29 ⋀

c. Save the code.

Add an Error Routine

You need to add an error routine that will display a helpful message if an error occurs.

a. Add the following code, as shown in Code Window 30.

```
Public Function PropertyPriceRanking(sPropVal) As Integer
On Error GoTo Error_Routine

    'Declare variables
    Dim db As DAO.Database
    Dim rst As DAO.Recordset
    Dim intCounter As Integer

    'Return the value to the calling procedure
    PropertyPriceRanking = intCounter

    'Close the recordset
    rst.Close
    Set rst = Nothing
    Set db = Nothing

Exit_Routine:
    Exit Function

Error_Routine:
    MsgBox Err.Number & " " & Err.Description & vbCrLf & _
            "Contact your technical support staff.", vbCritical, "An error has occurred."
    Resume Exit_Routine
End Function
```

CODE WINDOW 30 ▲

b. Save the code.

c. Minimize the VB Editor.

Modify the Properties Form

First, you will modify the Properties form, and then you will call the new function from the On Current event of the Properties form.

a. Open the Properties form in Design view.

b. Reduce the width of the PropertyValue box by one-half.

c. Add a new text box to the space to the right of the PropertyValue box.

d. Name the new text box **txtPropertyRank**. Name its label **Rank:**.

e. Change the BackColor property of the text box to **Text 2, Lighter 80%**.

f. Change the Enabled property to **No**.

g. Save the form.

Call the Function from the On Current Event of the Form

Now that the form modifications are complete, you will call the new function from the On Current event of the Properties form.

a. Open the Property Sheet and verify the form is selected.

b. Create an Event Procedure in the **On Current event** of the form.

c. Type the following line of code in the VB Editor:
**txtPropertyRank =
PropertyPriceRanking(PropertyValue)**

d. Save the procedure.

e. Minimize the VB Editor.

f. Switch to Form view.

g. Advance to the next record, and then verify the rank is being updated. Note the rank.

h. Open the Properties table, sort by PropertyValue, and then compare the table rank to the form's rank to verify the rank.

i. Verify the rank of several more properties. Close the table and the form.

Add a Filter Procedure to the Properties Report

Add a procedure to the On Open event of the Properties Report that will enable you to filter for properties greater than a certain value.

a. Open the Properties Report in Design view.

b. Add an Event Procedure to the On Open event of the report.

c. Type the procedure shown in Code Window 31 in the VB Editor.

```
Private Sub Report_Open(Cancel As Integer)
    'Declare variables
    Dim lngPropertyValueFloor As Long
    Dim strRS As String

    'Revise the records source -- show properties with value > X
    If MsgBox("Do you want to see only properties with value > X ?", vbYesNo, _
            "Input required") = vbYes Then
        'Filter by Category
        lngPropertyValueFloor = InputBox("Enter the minimum property value (ex. 550000)")

        'Set the record source = the filtered properties table
        strRS = "SELECT Properties.* FROM Properties WHERE PropertyValue > " & lngPropertyValueFloor
        Me.RecordSource = strRS
    Else
        'Set the record source = the whole products table
        Me.RecordSource = "SELECT Properties.* FROM Properties WHERE PropertyValue Is Not Null"
    End If

End Sub
```

CODE WINDOW 31 ⋀

d. Save the procedure.

e. Minimize the VB Editor.

f. Open the report in Print Preview.

g. Click **No** in response to the message box. Close the report.

h. Rerun the report, and then click **Yes** in response to the first message box.

i. Enter **1000000** in the next message box.

j. Verify the records displayed are for all properties over $1,000,000.

k. Close the report.

l. Save and close the database, and submit it based on your instructor's directions.

Create a Late Fee Procedure

GENERAL CASE

The *v3b1loans* file contains data from a local community bank. The database contains information about customers, loans, and loan payments. You will create a procedure that will calculate the late fees of loan payments after they are received. Create a form with a command button that will call the procedure and calculate the late fees. Open the *v3b1loans* file, and then save the database as **v3b1loans_LastnameFirstname**. In the new database, open the Payments table, and then review the data in the table. Open the VB Editor, and then create a procedure in a standard module that updates the LateFee field if the payment was received after the due date. The grace period is five days; after five days, assess a percent of payment fee based on the number of days late. For example, a payment eight days late would be charged an 8% late fee. Revise the Payments form and add a new procedure to the Update Late Fees button. Add a statement in the code that will refresh the form; add error handling to the button code. Close the database, and then exit Access. Submit the database based on your instructor's directions.

Create a Recordset Using ADO

RESEARCH CASE

All of the recordsets that you have created in this chapter were created using the DAO object library. In this exercise, you will create a recordset using the ADO object library. Open the *v3b2doctors* file, and then save the database as **v3b2doctors_LastnameFirstname**. In the new database, open the Doctors table, and then review the data. Open the VB Editor, click Tools on the menu bar, and then click References. Add a reference to the Microsoft ActiveX Data Objects 2.8 Library. Search Help and the Internet to find an example of how to create a recordset using ADO. Create a recordset that changes all records with zip code 33070 to 33099. Close the database, and then exit Access. Submit the database based on your instructor's directions.

Debug a Recordset Procedure

DISASTER RECOVERY

The Mountain Top Lodge would like you to calculate the total guests in each service category. You created a standard module and added a new procedure. The procedure is producing an error. Try to debug the error, run the procedure, and then verify the total in each party. To begin, open the *v3b3lodging* file, and then save the database as **v3b3lodging_LastnameFirstname**. Open the VB Editor, and then run the procedure. Debug the error, and then fix the procedure. Run the procedure again, and then verify the number of total guests in ServiceID 1.

GLOSSARY

ADO (ActiveX Data Objects) An object library designed for connecting to a wide range of external data sources.

After Update An event that is triggered after a record is saved.

And operator A logical operator that requires that two or more conditions be met to evaluate to True.

Argument A value that provides necessary information to a procedure or a function.

Before Update An event that is triggered before a record is saved.

Bound control A control that is connected to a data source in the host application.

Calling procedure A statement within a procedure that calls or executes a function.

Class module A module that stores public code definitions of a class, such as properties and methods.

Code window A text editor for writing and editing VBA procedures.

Collection A group of objects with similar characteristics and behaviors.

Comment A textual description that explains a section of programming code. In VBA, comment lines start with the prime character (') and appear in green in the Code window.

Concatenate The process of joining two or more text strings.

Condition An expression that determines if a situation is true.

Constant A programmer-defined name that stores values that remain the same (or constant) during run time.

ControlSource property An attribute that defines the cell to which a control is bound.

Counter variable A variable used to count the number of times a loop repeats.

DAO (Data Access Objects) An object library specifically created to work with Access databases.

Data type An indicator that specifies what type of data (such as text or number) can be stored in the variable or constant.

Data validation The process of checking data entered to ensure it meets certain requirements, such as a numeric value or a value within a specified range.

Decision structure A block of code that uses relational operators to make comparisons and then executes alternative statements based on the outcome.

Declaration A statement that creates a variable or constant and specifies its data type and name.

Design time The mode for designing, writing, and editing programming statements.

Do...Loop statement A repetition structure that repeats designated statements as long as a condition is true or until a condition is satisfied.

Edit A method that enables you to change the data in a recordset.

Enabled property An attribute of True or False that determines whether a control can receive focus and respond to the user.

Error trapping The process of intercepting and handling errors at run time.

Event An event is what happens when a user takes an action; an event can also trigger the execution of code.

For...Next statement A repetition structure that repeats statements a specific number of times.

Format function A function that formats the first argument (such as a number) into a particular appearance, such as a currency format or date format.

Function procedure A procedure that performs an action and returns a value.

If...Then statement A statement that performs a logical test and executes one or more statements if the test is True.

If...Then...Else statement A statement that performs a logical test and executes different statements based on whether the test is True or False.

Immediate window A window used to enter and run small segments of code.

Input box A dialog box that prompts the user to enter data.

InputBox function A function that displays a prompt dialog box to the user to enter a value.

Integral data type A data type that can store only whole numbers.

IsNumeric function A function that checks a string and returns True if the string can evaluate to a value or False if the string cannot evaluate to a value.

Iteration One execution of a loop statement.

Keyword Text or a symbol used for a specific purpose in a programming language.

Line-continuation character A space followed by an underscore that programmers manually insert to display one statement on two or more physical lines in the Code window.

Logical operator An operator that uses Boolean logic to perform a logical test.

Logical test A decision structure that uses a logical operator to evaluate a condition or relationship between two statements and returns a value of True or False.

Loop A set of statements that repeats for a repetition structure.

From the Glossary of *Exploring Getting Started with VBA for Microsoft® Office 2010,* First Edition, Robert T. Grauer, Keith Mulbery, Keith Mast, Mary Anne Poatsy. Copyright © 2012 by Pearson Education, Inc. Published by Pearson Prentice Hall. All rights reserved.

Message box A dialog box that displays a message or information and contains one or more options for the user to respond.

Method An action that can be taken by an object.

Module A container used to organize programming procedures within a project.

MoveNext A method used to advance through the records of a recordset.

MsgBox function A function that displays a message box onscreen and returns an integer to indicate which button the user clicked.

MsgBox statement A statement that displays a message box onscreen with optional buttons, icons, and title bar text.

Name property An object or control's attribute in which you reference that object in code.

Object An element, such as a worksheet cell, within a host application.

Object libraries Structures that contain the objects available in the applications that support VBA.

Object model A framework that organizes objects into a hierarchy.

Object-oriented programming language A language that uses methods to manipulate objects.

On Current The event that is triggered by a record being loaded into a form.

On Dirty An event that is triggered when a record is being edited.

On Enter The act of placing the insertion point in a text box.

On Error statement A statement that directs the code to skip to a particular line in the procedure when there is an error.

Operator One or more characters that performs a calculation.

Option Compare Database A statement used in a module to declare the default comparison method to use when string data is compared.

Option Explicit A statement used in a module to require that all variables be declared before they are used.

Or operator A logical operator that requires that only one condition be met to evaluate to True.

Order of precedence A rule that controls the sequence in which arithmetic operations are performed.

Posttest A test that executes the code within the loop one time and then performs the logical test to determine if the loop iterates again.

Pretest A test that performs the logical test first, and then executes the code within the loop if the test is true.

Private procedure A procedure available only to a specific object or module.

Procedure A named sequence of programming statements that perform a set of actions.

Programming structure The sequence in which the program statements execute at run time.

Project A collection of modules and objects in an Office file, such as an Excel workbook or an Access database.

Property An attribute of an object that defines a characteristic. For example, a VBA form has a Height property for which the user can specify the value of the height.

Property procedure A procedure that creates or manipulates a custom property.

Public procedure A procedure that is available to any object in the application.

Recordset A set of records in memory selected from a table or query.

Relational operator An operator that is a symbol or word that determines the relationship between two statements.

Repetition structure A structure that repeats the execution of a series of statements at run time.

Resume Exit_Routine statement A statement that directs the code to jump to the exit line.

RowSource property A property that specifies items through an Excel worksheet range that will appear in a list box or combo box at run time.

Run time The mode for executing a program.

Scope A designation that specifies which statements can access a variable or constant.

Select Case statement A statement that compares an expression and then executes the code for the matching case.

Sequence structure A structure that executes the statements in the sequence they are listed in the procedure.

Software development life cycle (SDLC) A structured process for planning, designing, testing, and implementing an application.

Standard module A module that stores procedures available to an object or by any event in the application.

Step value The number by which the counter is incremented or decremented during each iteration of the loop.

Sub procedure A procedure that performs an action but does not return a specific value.

Syntax error An error that occurs when code contains a misspelled or misused keyword, incorrect punctuation, or undefined elements.

TabIndex property A property that determines the order in which a control receives the focus.

TabStop property A property that has an attribute of True or False that determines whether a control receives focus when the Tab key is pressed.

TextAlign property A property that specifies the horizontal alignment of a caption appearing in a label.

Toolbox A palette that contains the standard controls that can be added to a form.

Unbound control A control that is not connected to a data source in the host application.

Update A method that enables you to save the changes in a recordset.

Val function A function that converts a text argument into a numeric value and returns that numeric value for display, use in calculations, or to store in a variable.

Variable A programmer-defined name that stores values that can change or vary during run time.

VBA debugger A tool that enables the programmer to momentarily suspend the execution of VBA code.

Visual Basic for Applications (VBA) A programming language that enhances the functionality of Microsoft Office applications.

Index

Page references followed by "f" indicate illustrated figures or photographs; followed by "t" indicates a table.